The Malay Nobat

The Lexington Series in Historical Ethnomusicology: Deep Soundings

Series Editors
David Hebert (Western Norway University of Applied Sciences)
Jonathan McCollum (Washington College, USA)

The Lexington Series in Historical Ethnomusicology: Deep Soundings is a series from Lexington Books envisioned to offer rigorous, cutting-edge research that probes music of the past and mechanisms of sociomusical change. We champion innovative approaches and diverse methodologies, ranging from archival and oral histories, to syntheses of organological and music-archeological findings, to computational studies of musical evolution across decades, as well as novel interpretations of non-western music philosophy. The series also features original works that synthesize the oeuvre of influential scholars whose publications are primarily in languages other than English. Books in this series offer theoretically robust presentations of unique discoveries, written in lucid prose appropriate for liberal arts colleges and universities, as well as professional researchers.

The Malay Nobat: A History of Power, Acculturation, and Sovereignty, by Raja Iskandar Bin Raja Halid
Ethnomusicology and Cultural Diplomacy, edited by David G. Hebert and Jonathan McCollum
Activism through Music during the Apartheid Era and Beyond: When Voices Meet, by Ambigay Yudkoff

The Malay Nobat

A History of Power, Acculturation, and Sovereignty

Raja Iskandar Bin Raja Halid

LEXINGTON BOOKS
Lanham • Boulder • New York • London

Published by Lexington Books
An imprint of The Rowman & Littlefield Publishing Group, Inc.
4501 Forbes Boulevard, Suite 200, Lanham, Maryland 20706
www.rowman.com

86-90 Paul Street, London EC2A 4NE

Copyright © 2022 by The Rowman & Littlefield Publishing Group, Inc.

All rights reserved. No part of this book may be reproduced in any form or by any electronic or mechanical means, including information storage and retrieval systems, without written permission from the publisher, except by a reviewer who may quote passages in a review.

British Library Cataloguing in Publication Information Available

Library of Congress Cataloging-in-Publication Data

Names: Iskandar Raja Halid, Raja author.
Title: The Malay nobat : a history of power, acculturation, and sovereignty / Raja Iskandar Bin Raja Halid.
Description: Lanham : Lexington Books, 2022. | Series: The Lexington series in historical ethnomusicology: deep soundings | Includes bibliographical references and index. | Summary: "The Malay Nobat: A History of Power, Acculturation, and Sovereignty explores the history and meaning of the nobat, its spread throughout the Muslim empire, and its emergence as a symbol of power and sovereignty, ultimately showing how existing nobat ensembles in Malaysia and Brunei are the last living legacy of the Mulism world"—Provided by publisher.
Identifiers: LCCN 2022011501 (print) | LCCN 2022011502 (ebook) | ISBN 9781666900880 (cloth) | ISBN 9781666900903 (paperback) | ISBN 9781666900897 (ebook)
Subjects: LCSH: Music—Southeast Asia—History and criticism. | Music—Political aspects—Southeast Asia—History. | Courts and courtiers—Southeast Asia—History. | Islam—Southeast Asia—History.
Classification: LCC ML330 .I75 2022 (print) | LCC ML330 (ebook) | DDC 780.959—dc23/eng/20220602
LC record available at https://lccn.loc.gov/2022011501
LC ebook record available at https://lccn.loc.gov/2022011502

For

Mak and *Abah*

Contents

List of Figures	ix
List of Abbreviations	xiii
Note on Spelling	xv
Preface	xvii
1 Introduction	1
2 Early Histories	11
3 The Malay Nobat	43
4 The Nobat in Early Malay Literature: A Lesson from Patani	87
5 The *Adat Aceh* and Seventeenth-Century European Encounter	123
6 From British Colonialism to Independence	151
7 Conclusion	181
Appendix	191
References	209
Glossary	221
Index	229
About the Author	241

Figures

2.1	Folio from a manuscript of al-Jazari's *Book of Knowledge of Ingenious Mechanical Devices*: the castle water clock	22
2.2	Folio from a manuscript of al-Jazari's *Book of Knowledge of Ingenious Mechanical Devices*: the water clock of the drummers	23
2.3	A leaf from al-Wasiti's *Maqamat al-Hariri*: soldiers sounding the *nafir* and *naqqara* during a religious celebration	28
2.4	Folio from the *Surname-i Vehbi* (*Book of Festival*): the *Mehter* in a procession	31
2.5	The *Naubat Khana* or drum house at the Red Fort, New Delhi, India	33
2.6	A sketch of the *naubat* ensemble during the reign of Mughal Emperor Shah Jahan in 1634, by Peter Mundy	33
2.7	The *naqqarakhana* of the Imam Reza Shrine, Mashad, Iran	35
2.8	Detail of a folio from the *Shahnama* of Shah Tahmasp: Qaran unhorses Barman	38
2.9	Detail of a folio from a copy of the *Shahnama* by Abu'l Qasim Firdausi (935–1020), commissioned by Shah Tahmasp: Faridun embraces Manuchihr	39
3.1	Fifteenth-century movements of the nobat based on the *Sejarah Melayu*	47
3.2	The nobat of Terengganu, circa 1917–18	50

3.3	The silver *Negara* of the Terengganu nobat	55
3.4	*Gendang Peningkah* of the Perak nobat	56
3.5	The silver *Gendang* nobat of Terengganu	56
3.6	The *Pipit* and *Caping* of the Kedah *Serunai*	57
3.7	The ivory and silver *Serunai* of the Terengganu nobat	58
3.8	*Nafiri* of the Perak nobat	59
3.9	Engravings on the Terengganu *Nafiri*	59
3.10	Old nobat instruments in the Riau Kandis Museum, Sumatera	60
3.11	The knobbed gong of the Kedah nobat	60
3.12	*Kopak-Kopak* of the Terengganu nobat	61
3.13	*Mahaguru* of the Kedah nobat	62
3.14	Percussion introductory sequence in the piece 'Jong Beraleh' of the Perak nobat	74
3.15	Introduction section from 'Lagu Iskandar Shah' of the Terengganu nobat	75
3.16	Excerpt of the 'guruh' section from 'Lagu Perang' of the Kedah nobat	76
3.17	Repetitive patterns in 'Arak-Arak Atandis' of the Perak nobat	77
3.18	8-beat *Gendang* patterns in 'Dang Gendang'	77
3.19	The Serunai Lagu of the Perak nobat	79
3.20	Excerpt from 'Lagu Iskandar Shah' of the Terengganu nobat	80
3.21	*Dai* of the piece 'Lagu Raja Burung' of the Kedah nobat	81
3.22	Remaining Malay nobat in Malaysia and Brunei	84
4.1	The Region of Patani and Peninsular Malaysia. The Northern states of Perlis, Kedah, Kelantan and Terengganu were vassal states of Siam and share certain cultural traits with Patani	88
5.1	Peter Mundy's sketch of Sultan Iskandar Muda's procession in 1637	142

5.2	An enlarged part of Peter Mundy's sketch of the musical ensemble	142
5.3	A sketch of a *naubat* instrument from *Ain-i Akbari*, by Abu'l Fazl	144
6.1	Plate from Winstedt and Wilkinson's (1934) article 'A History of Perak'	155
6.2	The plate from Skeat's book showing models of the Selangor state regalia	163
6.3	A memo from the Sultan of Terengganu's private secretary to the state secretary	166
6.4	A still from a film by British Pathé showing the nobat of Perak in 1952	168
6.5	A diagram of the layout of the Balairong Seri for the installation of first Yang Dipertuan Agong	171
6.6	A still from a British Pathé newsreel showing the nobat of Kedah playing at the Balai Besar in 1959	172
6.7	Tan Sri Dato' Dr. Haji Mubin Sheppard	174
6.8	One of the photographs of the Riau-Lingga nobat sent by John Miksik to Mubin Sheppard	176

Abbreviations

AA	*Adat Aceh*
ADO	Assistant District Officer
ANM	Arkib Negara Malaysia
ARM	*Adat Raja-Raja Melayu*
CO	Colonial Office
DO	District Officer
HHT	*Hikayat Hang Tuah*
HP	*Hikayat Patani*
HRP	*Hikayat Raja-Raja Pasai*
JMBRAS	*Journal of the Malayan Branch of the Royal Asiatic Society*
JSBRAS	*Journal of the Straits Branch of the Royal Asiatic Society*
MM	*Misa Melayu*
SM	*Sejarah Melayu*
UMNO	United Malay Nationalist Organization
VOC	*Vereenigde Oost-Indische Compagnie*
YAM	*Yang Amat Mulia*
YM	*Yang Mulia*

Note On Spelling

The spelling of most Malay names and places in this book is in current standard Malay. For example, 'Melaka' is used instead of the English 'Malacca', and 'Sumatera' instead of 'Sumatra'. Similarly, the newer spelling of 'Terengganu' is used rather than 'Trengganu'. However, certain places such as Penang and Singapore are maintained in their English spelling.

Preface

This book is about the Malay nobat and its history. It explores the development of this court ensemble with reference to important themes in Malay historiography which include pre- and Islamic influences, connections with South Asia and the Middle East, political rivalry and intrigues, interregional migration, ethnicity and foreign intervention. The *naubat, nauba* or *nuba* tradition across the Islamicate world in its different configurations (including the *tablkana* and *naqqarakhana* military/ceremonial band) has been documented and discussed by scholars since the early twentieth century. The tradition was also cited in debates concerning the origins of the Indian *shahnai* and *surnay*, often associated with accompanying *duhul* and *naqqara* drums. Yet its long and varied history throughout the course of Islamic expansionism has never been substantially covered. The difficulty of this task is understandable. The evolution of the Arabic *nauba* into different understandings resulted in a divergence of scholarly pursuits of different theoretical directions, with some focussing on the power-symbolism aspect of the Muslim court tradition and others the musical-performance structure of the nobat as a genre of Arab music. This difficulty is compounded by the issue of language, where one may need to access sources in Arabic, Persian, Turkish, Urdu and Malay.

Despite its importance, and although the nobat in the Malay world has been documented for more than a century, no comprehensive study on the subject has ever been published. It remains on the fringe of not only musical study but also Malay historiography in general. Largely in the form of short articles, chapters and passing references, earlier information about the Malay nobat came from British colonial administrators, facilitated by their close relationship with Malay rulers and access to official court ceremonies. From time-to-time, special attention was given to the nobat in newspaper reports covering the installation of sultans and the Yang di-Pertuan Agong.

Although scholars began to delve seriously into Malay traditional arts during the 1970s, the nobat received little attention. This neglect was mainly due to the problem of accessibility, since the instruments are part of the court regalia and considered sacred. It was not until the 1990s that the nobat caught the interest of ethnomusicologists and anthropologists, emphasising themes such as symbolism and power.

In 2006, I began researching on the nobat of Perak, one of the four nobat ensembles in the Malay Peninsula. I was fortunate to have been given access to the palace by the kind YM Raja Dato' Seri Mansur bin Raja Razman, the *Dato' Pengelola Bijaya Diraja* or Comptroller of the Perak Royal Household. He arranged a meeting with Encik Abdul Aziz, leader of the nobat ensemble who later brought me to the Iskandariah Palace and his *kampong* (village) in Central Perak. The focus of the research was the music; although, after considering the fact that I was not allowed to play or even touch the instruments, due to a strict set of *pantang larang*, or taboos, of the Malay nobat tradition, I managed to complete the task. Thanks to technology, I had the audio and video recordings and checked my transcriptions with Encik Aziz at his home. The research was completed in 2008 but was only published in 2018 by UMK Press.

The research paved the way for me to look further into the Malay nobat, this time looking more into its history. For centuries, there was a complex web of trade routes and religio-political affiliations across the Indian Ocean. This could have enabled the introduction of the nobat and its associated customs to the Malay world in the thirteenth century. Early Malay literature supported this idea and documented many of the customs and ceremonies involving the nobat. There was a need to look into these texts and revisit previous works and compare them with my ethnomusicological study on the nobat. This led me to my doctoral research at King's College London.

It was a cold winter morning in London. The Olympics was to be held in a few months' time. We arrived at our temporary flat in Leytonstone and the Olympic Stadium was visible from our bedroom window. It snowed a few days later and my children had a wonderful time building snowmen and lying on the sidewalk making snow angels. Now, a noisy family from Malaysia was playing in the snow on a London street in the middle of the night. However, the fun and excitement gradually melted once we realised the difficulty of finding an affordable two-bedroom flat and the complexity of the UK schooling system. The first few months in London were quite challenging, and my research had not even started! Thankfully, we gradually managed to overcome the obstacles (that came in different shapes and sizes) with the help of our new friends in London. It did not take long to appreciate what the city has to offer to a budding scholar—libraries, museums, galleries, archives, talks, seminars, concerts, scholars, study groups.

For my research, I employed a mixture of different methods, namely archival research, iconographical, organological and musical analysis, historiography and anthropology. Ethnographic work covered the states of Kedah, Perak and Selangor in Malaysia, where interviews were conducted with nobat musicians, court officials and members of royal families. Permission was given by the Kedah palace to film the nobat ensemble and interview some of its members. These audio and visual recordings, together with my collection of the Perak and Terengganu nobat were used to gain a general understanding of the instruments and music of contemporary nobat ensembles. This information was then used in comparison against the descriptions of the ensemble found in early Malay court literature and documentation during the period of British rule in the Malay Peninsula.

As in many historical studies covering a long period of time, some of the frustrations encountered were mainly due to the fragmentation and scarcity of available resources. This is more pronounced in the study of a subject which has been largely ignored, and writing a long diachronical history of the Malay nobat would have produced a thin narrative with large intermittent gaps. However, there are indigenous sources in the form of court chronicles or romances, produced over a number of centuries, which, despite their unreliability as historical records, still offer deep insights into the culture of premodern Malays. Most of these sources offer limited reference to the nobat, generally as literary devices to describe a particular joyous event or celebration. While a number of early indigenous works are cited in this study, I have chosen the *Hikayat Patani* and *Adat Aceh* as two of my three case studies. Unusually, these two court chronicles that also serve as manuals for court ceremonies, offer detailed instructions on the role and repertoire of the nobat.

The third case study covers the period of British colonization of the Malay Peninsula. Primary sources were mainly gathered from collections in the National Archives (London), Arkib Negara Malaysia (Kuala Lumpur) and Singapore National Library, including its online newspaper database. The whole study has been underpinned by primary and secondary sources from the enormous collections of the British Library, SOAS Library (University of London), Maughan Library (King's College London), the National Arts Library (Victoria and Albert Museum) and the National Archives. I am also indebted to the collections of musical instruments found in the Pitt Rivers Museum (Oxford), the Horniman Museum and Gardens (London), the Metropolitan Museum (New York) and the Aynalıkavak Palace (Istanbul).

My doctoral research at King's was funded by the Malaysian Ministry of Education and Universiti Malaysia Kelantan. I was privileged to be under the tutelage of Katherine Schofield, David Irving and Martin Stokes. Katherine meticulously guided me on the overall structure, while pointing to new areas of scholarship. David provided the links to the sources on Malay literature. Martin exposed me to some very complex theories and advised on using the case study approach. Before coming to London, I was already appointed Visiting Fellow at King's for the ERC Musical Transition research project Katherine was leading. Thank you, ERC, for funding and providing me the platform to present my papers in London.

To my parents, Rahamah Binti Hamam and Raja Halid Bin Raja Berima, to whom this work is also dedicated—I am forever indebted. Thanks to my wife, Dahlia, who has stood by me through all these gruelling years, my children, Adam and Tasnim, there are no words to describe their immense contribution and sacrifices. Thank you to the ERC team and my fellow students at King's, Jim Sykes, Richard Williams, Jenny McCallum, Adil Johan, David Lunn and Julia Byl for the insightful and wonderful discussions.

I am grateful to the *orang kalur* of Perak and Kedah for their help, friendship and willingness to share their knowledge. *Menjunjung kasih* to YAM Raja Nahzatul Shima ibni al-Marhum Sultan Idris Shah II (Raja Puan Muda of Perak), the late YAM Raja Shahruzzaman ibni al-Marhum Sultan Idris Shah II, the late YAM Tengku Dato' Setia Muhammad Yusof Shah ibni al-Marhum Sultan Alaeddin Sulaiman Shah (Tengku Aris Temenggong Selangor) and YM Raja Kobat Sallehuddin ibni al-Marhum Raja Muda Musa for welcoming me and the invaluable information shared.

Kota Bharu
August 2021

Chapter One

Introduction

The Malay nobat is the only court ensemble found in the Islamicate world that is still performed within its original context—to serve political rulers. It symbolises power and sovereignty, and no ruler who possesses a nobat is legitimately installed unless he is *dinobatkan* (drummed) to its sound. Guarded as part of court regalia, the nobat is revered for its perceived mystical powers and ability to consolidate and maintain social-political order (Andaya 2011). Like many musical traditions, the nobat institution is a product of a long process of encounters, shaped by interactions within and across imagined boundaries, and developed through the accommodation and acculturation of different cultures and beliefs. Who brought the nobat to the Malay world and why? How was the new musical culture adopted and indigenised? What crucial role did the nobat play in the development of Malay political and social systems? Did the nobat go through a critical transition as a result of Western colonization? By setting up a dialogue between indigenous and Western sources, this book situates the nobat in a wider, connected historical milieu (Subrahmanyam 2005) to find a common, multilateral historical thread contextualised within the Malay notion of sovereignty (Milner 1982; 2008) and communal identity (Stokes 1997).

A musical performance, both in its abstract and tangible forms, can be deeply symbolic in nature. In the Malay world, the musical sound, instrument and even musician can be perceived to possess mystical powers, signifying a certain degree of political might and potency. The number of players and the intensity of the sound produced is a manifestation of the will of those in power, in mimicking the thunderous sound of nature, to consolidate and maintain social order (Andaya 2011, 21–27). On battlefields, music was used for tactical purposes and encouraged soldiers, while instilling fear among enemies. Musical instruments become objects of reverence, anthropomorphised, guarded as symbols of power and agents of political change. There are also times when music acts as timekeeper, marking certain hours of the day reminding the faithful of his or her spiritual obligation. Thus, music may be understood by certain societies not only as a purely sensual experience (Brown 2006, 61–86) but also as a medium of sobriety and assertiveness. It communicates and constructs meanings that reflect a society's cultural subjectivities, while giving a sense of place and providing a context for social interaction and identification (Stokes 1997, 5).

The rise and expansion of Islam saw the movement of peoples across distant lands, in the desire to not only spread the *dīn* (religion) of Islam but also in search of worldly possessions. From the Near East to Southeast Asia, old empires were conquered and new kingdoms founded, which brought about a rapid increase in economic activities and the mixture of cultural traditions. Royal courts were established and urban centres became melting pots of ideas, and centres of learning and artistic growth. In the wake of these developments, there appeared a courtly tradition of ritual sound performance that later became part of the insignia of a ruler's status across the expanding Islamicate world. This percussion-based ceremonial/military musical ensemble—known as *tablkhana* (Abbasid, Fatimid), *naqqarakhana* (Afghan, Persian), *nauba* (Umayyad, Andalusian, North Africa), *naubat* (Mughal) or *nobat* (Malay)[1]—travelled across boundaries and went through processes of accommodation over time and space. It was patronised by some of the greatest Muslim empires and was played in palaces to install new rulers, announce the arrival of dignitaries and signal prayer times, and was used for tactical purposes and to instil courage among soldiers on battlefields. Via the ancient trade routes of the Indian Ocean, this ensemble finally found its way from the Middle East to the Malay courts in the thirteenth century CE.[2]

With the arrival of Islam in Southeast Asia, the Malays' previous Hindu-Buddhist concepts of kingship and court culture were modified and gradually merged with the new belief system (Milner 1981, 50–52). Today, the nobat continues to become a symbol of a ruler's status and sovereignty, and forms part of the articles of the state regalia. Its importance is elevated to a point that no Malay sultan who possesses one is officially installed unless he is ceremoniously drummed to the sound of the ensemble. This is further emphasised by the use of the Arabic word *tabl* (drum) to denote the installation (*pertabalan*) of the sultan itself. Despite its earlier, more public use, the nobat gradually became more secluded and, to a certain extent, mysterious. Today, it is one of the least exposed of Malay traditional art forms due to the rareness with which the music is played and the protocols involved in its performance.[3] Largely confined within palace walls, this royal orchestra performs only on certain occasions, such as the installation of the sultan and to mark the beginning of royal functions or ceremonies. Unlike any other traditional Malay music, nobat has a tradition that prohibits anyone other than the ruler, members of his family and the hereditary court musicians from playing or even touching the instruments. No performance is allowed without the consent or command of the Sultan.

The demise of independent Muslim sultanates across the colonial Indian Ocean world of the nineteenth and twentieth centuries saw the nobat no longer performing in the courts and its instruments ending up in museums. Nevertheless, a number of ensembles survived. Today, nobat and its numerous variations are still being performed in the Sufi shrines of India, such as the Sabir Kaliyari *dargah* in Haridwar, the mountains of Nepal, Central Asia, North Africa, Turkey and the courts of Malaysia and Brunei. The remaining nobat found in the Malay courts of Kedah, Perak, Selangor, Terengganu and Brunei are probably the last examples of a musical tradition that is still performed within its original context—to serve caliphs and sultans.

THE UNKNOWN NOBAT

Although the Malay nobat can be seen as a living legacy of the ancient Muslim world, its history and development has not previously been the subject of a major scholarly study. The history of Malay musical traditions in general has, to date, received little scholarly attention. Discussions of Malay and foreign musical interactions centre largely on the period of Western colonization, notably during British intervention and especially from the late nineteenth century onwards (e.g. Tan 1993, 81; Mohd Anis 1993, 35; among others). Although the Middle East and Indo-Islamic influence on Malay music is well documented by scholars (e.g. Wilkinson 1932, 84; Sheppard 1983, 21; Mohd Ghouse 1992, 145; Mohd Anis 1993, 6–7; Hillarian 2004, 111; Mohd Hassan 2005, 116–17; Andaya 2011, 24), the issue demands further exploration, with a study of the history and development of the Malay nobat as a particularly appropriate vehicle. In fact, the whole Middle Eastern, South and Southeast Asian nobat institution still remains in the periphery of ethnomusicological studies, as noted by Reis Flora:

> When one considers the early history of this ensemble and the various remnants of *naubat* traditions in West, Central and Southern Asian regions during the twentieth century, which extend from the mehter ensemble of Turkey to the Malay peninsula and the Riau archipelago of Indonesia, in this vast Asian area we appear to have a tradition of a relatively unknown, and relatively little researched, instrumental ensemble that very probably rivals and parallels the well known instrumental ensemble tradition of East Asia. (1995, 54)

Historical discourse on the Malay nobat is mostly based on premodern indigenous historiography but diverges into two different conclusions. The ensemble is said either to have originated directly from the Middle East (Affan Seljuq 1976, 141; Harun Mat Piah 1982, 6; Ku Zam Zam 1993, 2) or from/through South Asia (Wilkinson 1932, 84; Sheppard 1983, 21; Andaya 2011, 24). Some scholars point to the Muslim holy city of Mecca; this argument is refuted by anthropologist Ghulam-Sarwar Yousof, who argues that the idea of using Mecca as the origin of nobat by court chroniclers was just to elevate a sultan's Islamic status (Raja Iskandar 2018). This idea is shared by Laffan (2011) who stresses that 'the emphasis on Meccan validation more likely reflects regal concerns with genealogies of power and a long running fascination for that city as the eternal abode of the family of the Prophet' (5).

These statements on the history of the nobat mirror the arguments put forward by scholars for more than a century regarding the coming of Islam to Indonesia and the Malay world at large (see Drewes 1985, 7–19; Azyumardi Azra 2006, 1–25). The history of this court ensemble, in one way or another, thus becomes inextricably linked to the Islamization and establishment of Muslim sultanates in the *alam Melayu*. Thus, it is important that a historical study of the nobat follow the lines of these arguments, especially those espoused by scholars such as Snouck Hurgronje, J. Pijnappel, G. E. Marrison, S. N. al-Attas and S. Q. Fatimi, as discussed by Drewes and Azyumardi Azra. So far, no move has been made by music scholars in this direction.

The cultural impact of Islamization has also been debated (al-Attas 1969, 5–6; 1978, 171; Reid 1993, 151; Milner 1981, 51). One view suggests that Islam brought about a total change of ideas and practices, sidelining the earlier pre-Islamic cultural imprint. This view is very much prevalent in discussion of Malay political history, largely focussing on the Melaka Empire in the fifteenth century as a starting point. Milner (2008) however, warns of the danger of 'assuming a complete transformation' while proposing the idea of 'gradualism' and 'fusion' as a more accurate way of looking at the issue (45). While Islam had an obvious impact on Malay culture, little study has been done on the gradual changes that took place with regard to the nobat, a product of a long history of encounters and accommodation. The interactions of the Malays with foreign cultures and beliefs also brought about a syncretised notion of power known as *daulat*, which would later help to underlie the Malay idea of identity. The association between the royal ensemble and this important aspect of the Malay court milieu, especially in relation to the sustainability of the nobat, needs further scholarly attention. Who brought the nobat and why? What impact did these pre- and postcolonial encounters have on the ensemble? How has the nobat been used in the construction of Malay identity? Ethnomusicology, or more precisely historical ethnomusicology, with the potential to offer alternative explanations, has yet to sufficiently contribute to not only the history of nobat but also Malay culture in general.

The main purpose of this book is to present a historical account of the development of the Malay nobat. I shall attempt to explore this vis-à-vis the expansion of the Malay sultanates by looking into the nobat's organological development, courtly functions and role in the socioeconomic and political dynamics of these polities especially after the arrival of the Europeans in the sixteenth century. The idea here is to situate the nobat in a wider, connected historical context (Subrahmanyam 1997, 761–62) and to find a common, multilateral historical thread framed within the Malay notion of sovereignty and identity (Milner 1981, 49; 2008, 84–90). Milner proposes the term 'Malayness' instead of 'Malay', since he argues that to define a particular ethnic group of people with sub-ethnicities, who may not identify themselves as Malay, is problematic (ibid.). I will situate the nobat within this idea of 'Malayness' and also A. B. Shamsul's discussion on the more contemporary 'pillars of Malayness' (1996b). In relation to the nobat, this study will also shed some light on a number of important themes in Malay historiography which include pre- and post-Islamic influences, connections with South Asia and the Middle East, political rivalry and intrigues, interregional migration and the impact of Western colonization.

According to S. Q. Fatimi (1963, 92), the weakening and eventual *qiamah*- (end of time)-like catastrophic fall of the Baghdad caliphate in 1258 resulted in an awakening: a rise in Islamic awareness across Muslim lands. This aftershock led to an increase in missionary work by Sufi *tariqas* of the thirteenth and fourteenth centuries, mainly from or via India through long established trade networks across the East Indian Ocean (Johns 1961, 10–23; Milner 2008, 41; Laffan 2011, 5–19). Islam became the new rallying point of Indian traders and certain sultanates—through connections with Middle Eastern caliphates—in gaining a foothold in economically fledging Malay entrepots with a promise of economic prosperity, political influence and inclusion in the Muslim brotherhood (Van Leur 1955, 112). The nobat became a symbol of this agreement, in a region where the musical instrument had long been revered as a sign of authority and sovereignty (Wade 1998, 5; Bhatia 2001, 106). This happened in a highly connected and densely textured Indian Ocean Islamic world, where the interlocking political, economic and social network provided the impetus by which Malay arts and culture were shaped.

While acknowledging the change forged by Islam across the region, there are also the underlying elements of continuity with previous eras. The Indians' presence in the Malay world was well established from the past two millennia, and the land of the *kelings* (Indians) had long been viewed with admiration (Harrison 1957, 9–20). These very same traders and theologians who, centuries earlier, had brought the Malay elites Hinduism and Buddhism, now introduced a new belief system. I shall seek to illustrate that instead of displacing the long-standing Hindu-Buddhist culture, there was a smooth transition process due to the accommodating nature of the Sufi-based Islam introduced, resulting in an absence of resistance. Being an integral part of certain sects of Sufism, music played an important role in court culture and continued with its symbolic and spiritual functions intact. This amalgamation resulted in a uniquely 'Malay' version of the Middle East/South Asian nobat tradition as a continuation of any existing court musical ensemble. Thus, the Malay nobat is not simply an extension of Middle East/South Asian Islamic culture but also a product of indigenous agency, a conscious adaptation and fusion to reinforce preexisting culture without totally displacing it. This process would situate the nobat institution as a potent symbol of Malay identity.

The precolonial Malay world was a fragmented and fluid region with a multiplicity of polities, or *kerajaan* (Milner 1982, 112; 2008, 75). Although bonded by cultural, religious or even familial ties, rivalry among these sultanates was rife and often led to war. In order to gain recognition and forge closer ties with one another, the nobat was exchanged as a symbol of respect and friendship (Andaya 1979, 271). As part of royal regalia, it became an integral part of Malay courtly *adat* (customs) and was central to the resistance of colonial political and cultural influence. This was evident in the British colonial policy of non-interference in matters relating to Malay *adat* and religion, where aural representation of authority was as important as the visual or physical (Andaya 2011, 22). The process was reinforced by the Malay notion of divine royal power or *daulat*, which was fundamental to the establishment of a *kerajaan*. The nobat, seen as part of this essence of divine power, crossed into a different realm of existence; anthropomorphised and sacralised by Malay rulers. Its importance led to its numerous references in early court chronicles in relation to the details of Malay courtly *adat* and *istiadat* (ceremonies). Music thus creates order and organises society under the divinely ordained ruler bestowed with *daulat*. The close relation between *daulat* and nobat, and how this partnership continues amid the changing political and cultural dynamics of the Malays, is worthy of closer inspection. The underlying Malay notion of power—*daulat*—is crucial in the cultural unity and sustainability of the nobat within the *kerajaan* political system.

The colonial and postcolonial period of the nineteenth and twentieth centuries saw the weakening and eventual demise of a number of sultanates in the Indonesian part of the Malay world. On the Malay Peninsula, on the other hand, nine sultanates agreed to be part of the nation-state of Malaya while maintaining their (now limited) political power and sovereignty. This development eventually led to the creation of a unique rotational post called the Yang Dipertuan Agong (Supreme Ruler) in 1957 to enable each remaining sultan to become the head of the new state. The nobat was thus propelled into a new era. Its sights and sounds are no longer seen and heard only within the confines of palace walls but are now mass-mediated through technology, both print and electronic, reigniting the nobat's original role as 'the royal sound system'. This evolution will be discussed against the backdrop of the construction (and reconstruction) of Malay cultural identity through the rising tide of both nationalism and Islamization, where the nobat clings to the concept of *daulat*. I suggest that, despite the strict adherence to long indigenised tradition, the nobat went through a subtle but critical transitional process as a result of the courts' sustained encounter with the British, the rise in Malay nationalism and Islamic resurgence.

ORGANISATION OF THIS BOOK

I begin my history of the nobat with a background chapter (chapter 2) looking at the early history of the Islamicate military/ceremonial band across Eurasia and the Indian Ocean. It considers the conceptual and organological development of the ensemble and the different terms used to describe it using iconographical and literary evidence from mainly Arabic, Persian and Western sources. Chapter 3 provides a general overview of the contemporary Malay nobat, its instruments, musical repertoire and how the ensemble functions as an important part of the court *adat* (customs) and *istiadat* (ceremonies). I explore the underlying plural concepts and ideas that moulded Malay court culture and how the nobat is used as a symbol of power and sovereignty in relation to the concept of *daulat* (divine essence) and *tulah* (divine retribution). Given the grave importance of this underlying concept in the royal institution, a close servant-master relationship between the nobat and the ruler has developed which affects the overall music of the ensemble.

The nobat is often mentioned in classical Malay literature, which spans more than five centuries until the nineteenth century. Chapter 4 thus constructs the history and development of the nobat in the period of these literary texts by piecing together fragments of narratives found in Malay court chronicles before focussing on one particular work, the *Hikayat Patani*. It examines the political and social dynamics of a Malay sultanate between the sixteenth and seventeenth centuries and establishes how the nobat played a central role in the construction of identity as a result of the cross-fertilisation of ideas among interregional migrating Malays. This chapter also espouses the idea of Sufi influence, gradual cultural transformation and continuity in a fledging polity asserting itself as a regional power.

Chapter 5 considers another Malay court, Aceh, through the literary masterpiece the *Adat Aceh* and studies it in connection with early European encounters with the nobat in the seventeenth century. The chapter begins with an overview of the rise of Aceh as the new Malay centre after the fall of Melaka to the Portuguese in 1511. This is followed by a look into the detailed description of the nobat and its functions in the religious ceremonies of the Acehnese sultanate. The ceremonial sequence, pieces and instruments mentioned in the text are also analysed.

An examination of the impact of British rule in the Malay Peninsula follows in chapter 6. I will bring into discussion the depiction of the nobat by British colonial administrators from the nineteenth to the twentieth century through the publication of journals, books and film recordings. This chapter also discusses the ensemble's role in the formation of the independent nation-state of Malaya (1957) and the introduction of a new constitutional monarchy as its system of government. This chapter considers the challenges faced by Malay sultanates in the run-up to independence and the reinvention of court culture resulting in a disjuncture of the nobat's traditional practices. This conceptual break can be seen as a consequence of British colonial influence and the rise of modern Malay nationalism. The study concludes in chapter 7 with a summary of the findings and arguments presented and offer observations and suggestions for further research.

SUMMARY

The Malays' long interactions with Hindu-Buddhist and Islamic beliefs and practices shaped their syncretic traditional culture. The indigenization of foreign traditions continued with the coming of the Europeans which profoundly altered the lifestyles of Malay ruling elites and customs of royal institutions. These encounters and interplay created a society with a rich layer of influences, which can be seen in its traditional performing arts. The nobat, with its Islamic roots, went through transitions in the Malay world and evolved into what it is today. The royal ensemble had to negotiate local cultural, political and religious dynamics to stay relevant and guarantee its survival as an important symbol of a Malay sultan's power and sovereignty.

NOTES

1. The last three are all variant transliterations of the same Arabic word.
2. This estimation is based on the year of Sultan Malik al-Saleh's death, stated as 1297 on his tomb in North Sumatera. According to *Hikayat Raja-Raja Pasai*, Sultan

Malik converted to Islam and was the first ruler to be installed to the nobat brought by to Pasai from the Middle East through India.

3. The Kedah nobat was the most publicly performed ensemble due to its use to signal the daily Muslim prayers from the Balai nobat, a tower in the middle of Alor Setar town. However, as I learned during my recent interview with its players, certain prayer times are no longer signalled by the nobat due to logistical reasons.

Chapter Two

Early Histories

The Malay nobat is a living legacy of the Islamicate world.[1] It is the last of the long line of military/ceremonial court tradition that is still being performed within its original context in the Malay courts of Malaysia and Brunei. Its roots can be traced back to the *tablkhana* (drum house), *naqqarakhana* (kettledrum house) or *naubat* (plural of *nauba*, or 'periodic playing') military/ceremonial ensembles since the time of the Abbasid caliphate in the eighth century. The tradition has long been documented and discussed by scholars of Middle Eastern and South Asian traditions, with notable landmarks such as the pioneering work of H. G. Farmer and later A. K. Lambton, paving the way for future studies and discussions. However, studies of this global ensemble remain fragmented to date and at the periphery of larger musical or historical studies (e.g. Jairazbhoy 1970; Flora 1983; Dick 1984; Tingey 1994). Due to its long and complex history, a comprehensive history of the *tablkhana* or *naubat* Islamicate court tradition has yet to be fully undertaken, and a number of questions remain to be answered.

Many scholars are in agreement as to the pivotal role of music, and the performing arts in general, in the formation of political group identity (see, for example, Stokes 1997, 5; Attali 2003, 6; Turino 2008, 1–2; Hesmondhalgh 2013, 151). But, how and why did the *tablkhana*, *naqqarakhana* and *naubat* musical traditions become the means for a complex mix of ethnicities scattered within a vast and varied geographical region to represent themselves? Did the ensemble present the 'deepest feelings and qualities' (Turino 2008, 2) of twelfth/thirteenth-century Abbasid or sixteenth-century Mughal society? Despite variations across the region, in this chapter, I will suggest that there were successful elements of institutional continuity that functioned as powerful 'iconic signs' (ibid.) connecting various ethnicities within the larger Muslim *ummah* (brotherhood). The nobat ensemble's role in the long process of Muslim cultural (and subcultural) identity formation will be the focus of this chapter.

The early history of the nobat (Malay spelling) can be seen as a process of encounters, adaptation, mimicry and reinvention that spanned about a thousand years. There was also a clearly profound triangular relationship between sound, power and the sacred. What started as a religious quest in seventh-century Arabia, developed rapidly into a glorious period of Muslim enlightenment, fostered by powerful political centres, that saw great artistic and scientific achievements that, for centuries, remained unparalleled. The epic campaign of proselytization that began in the seventh century had an impact on both the conquered and conqueror. According to Islamic tradition, when Umar al-Khattab (579–644), the second caliph and one of the closest companions of Prophet Muhammad, visited Jerusalem to accept the city's surrender, he was furious to see his governor and generals in fine clothing. It was reported that he pelted them with stones and reprimanded them for mimicking the ways of the Persian royals and forgetting their humble roots (Numani 2004, 43). Noticing that the caliph was in ragged and patched robes while entering the city, there was a feeling of nervousness among the generals about the prying gaze of the city's culturally superior inhabitants. Despite their military might, there was still a conscious sense of inferiority among the early conquering Muslims; something that would change when the empire grew further in size and wealth.

Despite Umar's warnings, Muslim rulers succumbed to the trappings of royalty; the pomp and ceremonies, the sights and sounds of the *kuffar* (infidels) civilizations they initially abhorred. This introjection to the superior symbols of political power brought about the development and eventual establishment of the military/ceremonial ensemble into an institution that signified Muslim supremacy. The *tablkhana, naqqarakhana, naubat* tradition became part of the fluid process of identity formation, largely defined by the higher structure of a heterogeneous Islamic society—the caliphs, sultans, governors, Military commanders, emirs—what A. B. Shamsul (1996, 477) describes as the 'authority-defined' social reality. Detached, cleansed from its previous non-Islamic religious connotations, the ensemble and its accompanying traditions was Islamically legitimized, by incorporating it into religious rituals such as the daily call for prayer and the two *'Eid* celebrations. With this newly invented tradition (Hobsbawm and Ranger 1983, 1) an imagined sonic boundary was thus drawn not only between Muslim-controlled territories and the 'Other' but also among regional rulers within the sphere of Islamic influence. While ubiquitous as an Islamic tradition, its dispersed variety can also be viewed as a process of transplantation and localisation across a vast geopolitical domain.

The establishment of the nobat as a court institution can be viewed as not a result of a collective agency of the masses but largely of the needs and desire of the ruling elites. The ensemble developed in a period when societies were governed by absolute monarchs, military commanders or regional governors, the only ones who had the means and reasons to patronise it. The ruling class was also responsible for the advancement of the arts and sciences where musicians, poets, painters, philosophers and scientists were under court patronage. This resulted in the emergence of new musical styles and concepts (e.g. *nauba*), wonderful paintings and literature (e.g. *Shahnama* of Fidausi) and ingenious inventions (e.g. al-Jazari's water clocks). As we shall see, these surviving products provided invaluable insights into the history and development of the *tablkhana*, *naqqarakhana* and *naubat* ensemble.

The aim of this chapter is to provide the longer background to the history of the Malay nobat, considering its forebears' conceptual and material development across the Islamicate world during the most intensive period of Islam's expansion, beginning in the seventh century. It is, however, beyond the scope of this chapter to fully reconstruct the history of the earlier ensembles. I will instead attempt to expand existing discussions and fill certain gaps by looking into selected literary and iconographic sources that encapsulate the whole notion of the ensemble as surmised by al-Faruqi (1981, 234–35) and Wade (1998, 4–12), which include its uses as timekeeper, symbol of power (including ceremonial functions) and military unit. This historical setting, including some theoretical interventions, will hopefully provide a clearer understanding of the origins of the main focus of this book—the Malay nobat tradition.

MIMICRY AND POWER

The *jahilliah*[2] Arabs of the *hijaz* (Arab Peninsula) were at the periphery of the two most powerful and advanced civilizations of the time: the Roman Byzantine to the West and the Persians to the East. Although secluded in the shadows of these politically superior empires, the Arabs were not without their own rich cultural heritage, including music and poetry (see Shiloah 1995; Touma 1996). The spread of Islam brought about the cross-fertilization of cultures across different lands that created a dynamic cultural environment. This idea of mobility and movement of people would form an important pillar of Islamic historiography, as Flood (2009, 1) notes:

> The idea of mobility is . . . intrinsic to the history and prescriptions of Islam, a religion whose zero year is measured not from the birth of the Prophet but from the migration from Mecca to Medina. Moreover, the duty to make the pilgrimage to Mecca at least once in a lifetime imbues Islam with an institution that is

global in its extent and impact, not least on the circulation of artistic concepts and forms. Without entailing a deterritorialized concept of identity, the need to negotiate between the local and the translocal, the lived experience of the quotidian and the ideal of the *umma*, an imagined community with a global reach, has been a distinguishing feature of Islamic cultures from their inception.

Musicologists have traced the development of the major musical traditions of the Arab world from the Umayyad and early Abbasid periods (the seventh to ninth centuries) embedding this mobility in their very origins. Henry Farmer argues that by the end of the tenth century a number of Persian instruments, such as the *surnay* and *nakkara*, were fully incorporated into the Arab military ensemble (1987, 35).

The Sassanid Empire was the last pre-Islamic Persian Empire and one of the two main powers in Western Asia and Europe, alongside the Roman Empire. Founded by Ardashir I (180–242 CE), the empire encompassed what is known today as Iran, Afghanistan, Iraq, Syria, the Caucasus and parts of Central Asia, the Arabian Peninsula and Pakistan. For more than four hundred years, the Sassanid Empire's cultural influence reached as far as Western Europe, Africa, China and India. Seljuq (1976) suggests that this was where *naubat* music developed to symbolise royal status, and also as a method to announce important proclamations. This tradition of the Sassanians, together with its concept of kingship and elaborate court rituals, was later adopted by Muslim rulers of the region and subsequently spread throughout the Muslim world (Irwin 1997, chap. 1). Considering early Arab-Persian musical encounters, Hormoz Farhad (2004, 3) observes that

> the musical documents from the ensuing Islamic period abound in references to the music of the Sassanian era. An investigation of these works leaves little doubt that the music of the Sassanian period had been the germinating seed from which much of the music of the Islamic civilization grew.

The Arabs' conquest of Persia in 642 CE engulfed the empire within the framework of the vast Muslim Empire for the next six centuries. In Persia, the Arabs found culture considerably in advance of their own and not long after the conquest, Persian musicians were imported into every corner of the Muslim world. The fall of the Sassanid Empire to the Muslims also saw Zoroastrianism, previously the state religion, being slowly obliterated and replaced by Islam. Sassanian royal customs were, however, resisted by the early Muslim caliphs but were slowly adopted by later rulers, especially by those with strong Persian roots. In line with nineteenth- and twentieth-century colonial narratives, where the colonised subject, in a process of being 'reformed', would (either voluntarily or not) imitate the coloniser; on the other hand, the period of Muslim expansionism saw the strategy of what Homi Bhabha (2007, 121) calls 'mimicry' happened both ways. Apart from the desire for a reformed (in this case Islamised), recognisable Other, the Arabs themselves mimic their conquered subjects to create a recognisable 'I', an introjection as part of the formulation for suitable symbols befitting of the newfound power. This process, however, did not happen overnight but developed gradually after the rule of the early caliphs.

The death of Prophet Muhammad in 632 marked the beginning of the rule of what was known as the *al-Khulafa al-Rashidun*, or the 'righty-guided' caliphs—Abu Bakar (r. 632–634), Umar ibn al-Khattab (r. 634–644), Uthman ibn Affan (r. 644–656) and Ali ibn Abi Talib (r. 656–661). Although the Muslims gained considerable geographical influence, wealth and power, these early caliphs held true to the teachings of the Prophet and were not induced by worldly indulgences. Royal power was denounced for its ubiquitous wastefulness and selfish purposes that could turn them away from the remembrance of Allah. Caliph Umar al-Khattab once disapproved of his Syrian governor Muawiya ibn Abi Sufyan's clothing for emulating the Persian royals. According to historian Ibn Khaldun (1332–1406), this abhorrence of royal customs and symbols was shown when early Muslim rulers refrained from using the beating of drums and blowing of trumpets. However, they were later incorporated when they themselves became royalty and began to indulge in the luxury and splendour of the world—encouraged by their association with Persian and Byzantine subjects (Ibn Khaldun 1958, 215, vol. 1). This transition from 'caliphate to royal authority', according to Ibn Khaldun (ibid., 414–28, vol. 1), began during the Umayyad period.

After the assassination of the fourth 'rightly-guided' (*al-Khulafa al-Rashidun*) Caliph Ali ibn Abi Talib in 661, a new chapter in Islamic history began when Muawiya ibn Abi Sufyan was appointed caliph and established the Umayyad dynasty in Damascus. One of the legacies of the Umayyads was the transformation of the caliphate from a religious institution, as practiced by the *al-Rashidun*, into a dynastic one. In following pre-Islamic Arab practices, titles and lineage formed an important part in political legitimacy in this early Muslim polity; this led to the germination of *al-mulk*, or 'kingship', concept of leadership and the adoption of royal customs. Patronised by the Umayyad caliphs, music and the arts flourished. Farmer argues that it was during this period that kettledrums were incorporated into the earlier pre-Islamic military band, as they were seen as 'better accompaniments' to the *mizmar* (reedpipe) than the *duff* (tambourine) (Farmer 1987, 35). However, it was not until the rule of the Samanids (819–999) and later the Buyids (945–1055) that the title of *malik* (king) and *malik al-muluk* (king of kings) (Houtsma 1993, 204) and *shahanshah* were introduced as a conscious revival of old Persian traditions (Wink 1996, 21).

The ascendancy of the Abbasid dynasty (750–1258) saw the seat of the caliphate moved from Damascus to Baghdad, within former Persian territory. Islamic arts and culture continued to be developed, dominated and influenced by Persian artists and scholars in all fields. In continuing with the tradition of the Sassanids and Umayyads, musicians and poets were patronised by the Abbasid courts. It was during this period that the idea of the nauba and its plural form naubat began to evolve into different but related meanings; the term, which according to al-Faruqi (1985), could be used for performances at specific times, suite compositions and the ceremonial/military band.

DEVELOPMENT OF THE TIMEKEEPING ENSEMBLE

At the Abbasid court, musical performances were held in a formal indoor or outdoor *majlis* (gathering) attended by the caliph, high-ranking officials and wealthy individuals. This gathering would convene under the order of the caliph and last-minute arrangements were common (Sawa 1989, 117). Thus, male and female slave musicians of the court were always on standby, day and night. Some musicians, however, were given a day or two's notice before a *majlis* to give them time to prepare new compositions, especially during festivals. This order applied only to non-slave musicians who were not part of the royal household and were given accommodation at the palace during the performance period (ibid.).

Besides this 'abruptly' organised *majlis*, certain performances were held on specific days of the week, in which musicians and poets would take turns to perform. For example, a poet would perform on a Tuesday, followed by a musician on a Wednesday and so on. These 'turns' were described by Abu'l Faradj al-Isbahani (897–967) in his *Kitab al-Aghani* as *nauba* (Wright 1987, 1042). This was probably the earliest mention of the word as a non-technical but music-related term, and the practice was said to have been adopted by the Abbasid caliphs such as Harun al-Rashid (d. 809), followed by his successors al-Amin (d. 813), al-Ma'mun (d. 833) and al-Wathiq (d. 847).

During these court gatherings, a variety of songs were performed with selections differing from *majlis* to *majlis*. A singer would sing when his or her *nauba* (turn) came, followed by another singer until a cycle was complete. This succession of songs, according to Farmer (1967, 199), became an 'important class of composition' similar to the Western suite. However, Sawa (1989, 169–70) argues that, although there was a series of songs performed, this did not amount to a suite. This was because the pieces performed were often interrupted by intervals and were not formally organised as a cyclical form. This repetition of songs later became a more refined practice, as suggested in the *Kamal Adab al-Ghina* by al-Hasan al-Katib (late tenth or early twentieth century) and *Hawi 'l-Funun* of Ibn al-Tahhan (d. 1057), where singers were advised to perform songs of different mood and tempo to suit the mood of the audience (Wright 1987, 1042). The use of *nauba* to describe a musical suite became clearer when 'Abd al-Qadir ibn Ghaibi (d. 1435) described the four movements of *nauba* as *qaul, ghazal, tarana* and *furu dasht dasht* (Farmer 1929, 200).

The *nauba*, as a musical suite or form, was geographically divided into two distinct styles: that of the *Maghrib*, or the Western Arab world, consisting today of countries such Morocco, Algeria, Tunisia and Libya; and that of the *Mashriq*, or the Arab East, spanning from western Egypt to Iran. The *Maghrib* or north African *nauba* was also known as *al-musiqa al-andalusiyya* (the music of al-Andalus) as it was believed that the music was brought by Muslims and Jews from Spain between the tenth and seventeenth centuries (Davis 2004, 2). It has also been suggested that the seeds of the North African *nauba* were sown earlier by the celebrated ninth-century Persian musician Abu l-Hasan 'Ali Ibn Nafi' (789–857), known as Ziryab, who moved from Baghdad to Andalusia (ibid.). Although the *nauba* of al-Andalus exists to this day, Wright (1987, 1043) argues that there is no proof that it is an evolution of the earlier *nauba*, which, according to him, disappeared entirely by the middle of the sixteenth century.

The Abbasids adopted the Persian *surnay* in place of the *mizmar* and introduced different types of *naqqara* (kettledrums), horns and trumpets into their military band (Farmer 1987, 35). Its initial military purpose was slowly overtaken by ceremonial function, and was also used to signal the five prayer times at a caliph's residence. This ensemble was known as *tablkhana* or *naqqarakhana* and was reserved exclusively for the caliph. Similar to the earlier *nauba* or turns of musicians and poets performing at a *majlis*, the daily prayer signals by the *tablkhana* were also called *nauba*. By the tenth century, this ceremony/military band (*tablkhana*), its periodic playing (*nauba*) and the flying of banners and flags (*'alam*) became the *'alah* (outfit) or symbol of a caliph's power and authority (ibid.).

The Egyptian historian Ibn Taghri Birdi (1409–1470) in his *al-Nudjum al-Zahira* (*The Resplendent Stars*) wrote that, in the year 978, the Abbasid Caliph al-Ta'i (974–991) was the first to have the *tablkhana* played in front of his palace (Shiloah 1995, 71). According to Hilal al-Sabi in his *Rusum Dar al-Khilafah* (*The Rules and Regulations of the Abbasid Court*), traditionally, the beating of drums in the capital was only reserved for the caliph, but the privilege was later given to crown princes and army commanders. However, such beneficiaries were only allowed to signal times for three prayers—the early morning and two evening prayers—and while travelling or away from the presence of the caliph. Al-Sabi further narrated that the caliph al-Muti'lillah did not grant Mu'izz al-Dawlah the privilege to beat his drums at his residence in the city but later consented when Mu'izz built his residence away from the city on the condition that the drums not be beaten beyond the gate facing the desert and for only three prayers. When the Buyid ruler 'Adud al-Dawlah found about the custom, he too requested and was granted permission from Caliph al-Ta'i, the practice later becoming a Buyid tradition (al-Sabi 1977, 115). The ensemble and the number of times it was allowed to be played (three or five-fold *nauba*) became honours that were bestowed by the caliph upon deserving generals, ministers and governors. This custom was further practiced when the caliphate started to fragment and emirs or semi-independent rulers (who probably had their own private army) began to assume the privilege of owning the *tablkhana* and playing of the *nauba*. Later Muslim rulers, including the famous Central Asian conqueror Timur (1336–1405), and rulers of the Mughal Empire, continued with the tradition.

During the tenth and eleventh centuries, attempts were made to sustain a link between the old Sassanid traditions with Islamic kingship. This was done by the Buyids, or Buwaihids, who were originally from Dailam, in the Alborz Mountains, southwest of the Caspian Sea (Wink 1996, 21). Of Iranian origin, the Buyids controlled Shiraz, Ray and Baghdad before they were defeated by the Seljuks in 1055 CE. The rise to power and dominance of these bands of nomadic chiefs from Central Asia marked the beginning of Turkish rule in the Middle East that would last until the twentieth century. The Seljuks, however, being originally nomadic peoples, disassociated themselves from the Iranian tradition by introducing a ruling concept of the Sultanate rather than maintaining the Sassanian *Shahanshahs*. As 'protectors' of the Abbasid Caliphate, the Buyids (945–1055), Seljuks (1055–1184) and, later, the Khawarizmian (1184–1231), provided a conducive environment for the development of the *nauba* (Wade 1998, 7).

This developing connection of music and timekeeping in the twelve and thirteenth centuries can be best exemplified through the genius of one man—Shaykh Ra'is al-A'mal Badi' al-Zaman Abu al-'Izz ibn Isma'il ibn al-Razzaz al-Jazari, simply known as al-Jazari (d. 1206). This renowned engineer was born during the Abbasid period, also known as the golden age of Islam, when there was a systematic development of the arts and sciences. During the rule of Caliph al-Ma'mun (r. 813–833), for example, large amounts of resources were invested in cultural activities and scientific scholarship. Between the eighth and eleventh centuries, Greek texts were translated into Arabic, and knowledge drawn from Greek, Indian and Chinese intellectual traditions were fused with Islamic science and technology. In addition, contemporary cultural surroundings inspired many Muslim scholars and scientists to produce some of the most creative works.

Al-Jazari was born in al-Jazira, or Mesopotamia, a region that covers what is today northern Iraq, parts of southern Turkey and eastern Syria. From 1174 until his death in 1206, al-Jazari served the Artuklu Palace, the royal residence of the Mardin branch of the Artuqid dynasty, under sultans Nur al-Din Muhammad ibn Arslan (1174–1185), Qutb al-Din Sukman ibn Muhammad (1185–1200) and Nasir al-Din Mahmud ibn Muhammad (1200–1222). This Turkmen sultanate of eastern Anatolia was a vassal state of the Zengid dynasty, which was part of the Seljuk Empire based in Mosul, Iraq (Öngë 2007).

Al-Jazari is known today for his inventions, which he documented in a book called *al-Jami' bayn al-'ilm wa 'amal, al-nafi' fi sina'at al-hiyal* (*The Book of Knowledge of Ingenious Mechanical Devices*). This work was compiled in 1206 under the order of the Sultan Nasir al-Din Mahmud ibn Muhammad. One critically important aspect of the book was that not only did al-Jazari explain his inventions in writing but also illustrated them. Among his inventions were two water clocks, one called the 'castle clock' and the other 'water-clock of the drummers'. The 'castle clock' was a large astronomical clock measuring about 3.3 m high; besides timekeeping, it displayed the zodiac and the solar and lunar orbits. The invention was probably intended to be placed inside a palace, but al-Jazari did not specify and even proposed that it could be modified to suit different environments. He suggested that:

> Individual parts may be omitted or added according to the place for which it is constructed. For mosques and shrines it may be limited to what is necessary for telling the hours; for kings, what may be fitting, such as pictures and other things. (1974, 25)

One innovative feature of the device was the use of five mechanical musicians forming a *tablkhana* ensemble that automatically played when triggered by levers operated by a hidden camshaft attached to a water wheel. Al-Jazari's use of the *tablkhana* to mark the hours of the day showed the ensemble's actual function in daily Abbasid-Seljuk life in the late twelfth and early thirteenth centuries. The use of the ensemble, which al-Jazari called the *nauba*, was clearly an important part of Seljuq court customs and ceremonies. Undoubtedly, this invention had elements of entertainment or even absurdity, but his mention of its possible use in mosques and shrines showed its strong religious connotations; and for kings, it could also be as a symbol of power and wealth. Did the actual *nauba* ensemble play in mosques and shrines during the Abbasid-Seljuk period? The playing of the *naubat* at Sufi shrines can still be seen today in parts of South Asia; however, the ensemble's history and connection to Sufism is yet to be fully understood.

In one of the leaves from an Egyptian copy of al-Jazari's books illustrating the 'castle clock' (M.F.A. 14.533) and dated 1354, during the Mamluk period (1250–1517), mechanical musicians are seen playing two *nafir* (trumpets), a *naqqara* (kettledrum), a slung *tabl* (double-headed drum) and a pair of small cymbals (figure 2.1). Similar illustrations may be found in one of the earliest copies of al-Jazari's book, dated from the first half of the thirteenth century (Istanbul 3072). The Boston illustration, like many similar Arab miniature paintings produced in the thirteenth century, shows the influence of Byzantine and Syrian Christian art, notably in the use of the golden halo around the heads of important people. Could the use of the halo by al-Jazari indicate the musician's religious stature, or be merely for aesthetic purposes? The musicians are also painted dressed in colorful patterned clothes of red, blue and green, giving an impression of joy and merriment.

In the painting, the colors gold and brown were used for the musical instruments that aptly represent the brass *nafir* and cymbals, and the copper *naqqara* and *tabl*, which, according to al-Jazari, was the material to be used for the device. The drum lace that stretches the heads across the cylindrical body of the *tabl* was clearly drawn. One curious aspect of the ensemble is the missing *surnay*, which, according to Farmer (1987), was included in the Abbasid military ensemble. Why wasn't the *surnay* included by al-Jazari in his device if the instrument was actually played in a *tablkhana* or *nauba* ensemble during his time? Were there differences in the distribution of instruments between ensembles across different geographical areas within the Abbasid Empire? The *surnay* is also not part of the *tablkhana* military ensemble as depicted in an illustration of the *Maqamat al-Hariri*, produced during the same period in Baghdad (figure 2.3).

The *nafirs* in the illustration are depicted being played with the instruments slightly tilted upwards, to enable the sounds to travel further. The two drums are struck using what al-Jazari called *sawlajan*, or drumsticks with curved ends, while the cymbals are played horizontally. The only musician sitting is the *naqqara* player, who is also the only one wearing a turban and sports a moustache and beard. The beardless musicians could represent youths, and this portrayal is also commonly found in the other contemporary *maqamat* paintings (Guthrie 1995, Introduction). The *naqqara* player's central playing position and 'stately' appearance could indicate a person with authority, perhaps the leader of the ensemble. The *tablkhana* or *nauba* depicted in al-Jazari's drawing must have been fashioned after an ensemble of a Seljuk sultan or military commander, but it is, however, uncertain whether the size and combination of instruments were standard practice during his time and place of residence. In his instructions, al-Jazari explained that the mechanical musicians were programmed to play five times a day: at daybreak, noon, afternoon (*Asr*), evening (*Isya'*) and midnight, similar to the times of Muslim daily prayers. The five-fold *nauba* honour was usually reserved for the caliph or sultan, and this therefore suggests that the clock was intended to suggest rulership.

Another invention of al-Jazari was the water clock of the drummers which used seven mechanical musicians. In an illustration from his book (figure 2.2), two of the musicians are seen blowing the *nafir* (trumpets), two striking the slung *tabl* with drumsticks (*sawlajan*), two cymbalists and a seated musician playing a pair of *naqqara* (kettledrum). Regarding the functioning of the water clock, al-Jazari (1974, 42) explained that:

> every hour the sound of the cymbal is heard, since for this device the operation is the same in the night and in the day, nothing whatsoever being omitted (in the night). When an hour has passed the musicians (*nauba*) perform with a clamorous sound which is heard from afar.

It is interesting to note al-Jazari's use of the term *nauba* to describe the ensemble, which must have been in general use to refer to the ensemble by the late twelfth and early thirteenth century. Except for the *nafir*, all of the other instruments were double the size of the castle clock, but as in the previous painting, the *surnay* is not included. This time the *naqqara* is seen played as a pair and, as in the previous painting, the *naqqara* player (this time beardless) is seated in the middle. There is still a sense of merriment with the colorful costumes and the *sharbush* caps worn by four of the musicians. The caps came into use during the Mamluk era, suggesting the date the painting was copied (c. 1315) but the present whereabouts of it is unknown (Nicolle and McBride 2006, 35).

Al-Jazari's invention of the water clocks not only displayed engineering ingenuity but also his ability to connect daily Abbasid-Seljuk tradition with his modern creations. Although some of the surviving paintings were made more than a century after his death, they were still based on his detailed descriptions and instructions. These paintings show the possible size and combination of instruments for a thirteenth-century *nauba* ensemble played at a ruler's palace. These ensembles were most likely played indoors in a specially made enclosure due to the small size of the drums and playing positions. Military-type *nauba* are often depicted as having larger *naqqara* drums, which are mounted on camels, horses or mules. However, most importantly, al-Jazari's work shows the development of the *nauba* from the concept of 'turns' into a time-keeping ensemble; and what better way to immortalise that through an extraordinary technical invention.

Figure 2.1. Folio from a manuscript of al-Jazari's *Book of Knowledge of Mechanical Devices*: the castle water clock. Egypt, Mamluk period, 1354 (M.F.A. 14.533).
Source: © Museum of Fine Arts, Boston.

Figure 2.2. Folio from a manuscript of al-Jazari's *Book of Knowledge of Ingenious Mechanical Devices*: the water clock of the drummers. Probably Syria, AD 1315 (F1 942.10). *Source*: Calligrapher: Farruq ibn Abd al-Latif/Freer Gallery of Art, Smithsonian Institution, Washington, D.C.: Purchase—Charles Lang Freer Endowment, F1942.10.

VISUAL AND AURAL SYMBOL OF POWER

Ibn Khaldun (1958, 48, vol. 2) observes that among the things loved by Muslim rulers were the *'alah* (outfit) or *maratib* (insignia) of royalty. These terms referred to a military unit of cavalry or foot soldiers carrying banners and flags in combination with an ensemble of mounted drums and wind instruments. The outfit, apart from being involved in battles, was also considered a symbol of royal authority and its use by officers or commanders was permitted as a sign of prestige. During the Abbasid period, banners and flags were also used during the two 'Eid celebrations, *'Eid al-Fitr* and *'Eid al-Adha*. In battles, the number of flags, the manifold colors and lengths of the *'alah* were intended to cause fear among enemies, and would accompany rulers and military commanders in processions. According to Farmer (1987, 36), the linking of flags, standards and musical instruments, and their elaborate organization as a military outfit, were conceived during the Fatimid period (909–1171). It was during this caliphate that the ceremony/military band *tablkhana* reached its zenith in terms of prominence and size; and continued to serve as a symbol of prestige and royalty (Shiloah 1995, 71). Ibn Khaldun (1958, 51, vol. 2) states that the outfit of al-Aziz Nizar of the Ubaydid (Fatimid), when setting out to conquer Syria in 977, comprised 500 banners and 500 trumpets. This Fatimid tradition was later adopted by successive Ayyubid (1171–1341) and Mamluk (1250–1517) sultans in Cairo. It was reported by Ibn Taghri Birdi that, during this period, the *tablkhana*'s major functions included playing at the sultan's coronation, accompanying feasts and participating in battle, including against the Crusaders in Egypt (Farmer 1929, 206–8).

The Muslim military outfit can be traced back to traditions of the pre-Islamic Persian Empire as narrated by the Persian poet Abu'l Qasim Firdausi (940–1019 or 1025) in his long poem *Shahnama* (*Book of Kings*). Written between 977 and 1010 CE, the *Shahnama* is a story of both the mythical and historical past of the Persian Empire up to the conquest of Islam in the seventh century. Although written during Islamic rule, Firdausi absorbed a number of pre-Islamic Persian works into his epic. In one of the verses, King Mihrab, ruler of Kabul, summoned his outfit to receive the legendary warrior Zal at his palace:

> The chieftain is upon his way with Zal
> And elephants and troops escorting them'.
> He went with speed and told Mihrab, who joyed;
> His cheeks grew ruddy as the cercis-bloom.
> He sounded trumpets, mounted kettledrums,
> And furnished forth his army like the eye
> Of chanticleer. Huge elephants and minstrels

Made earth a Paradise from end to end.
What with the many flags of painted silk
Of divers colors, sound of pipes and harps,
The blast of trumpets and the din of gongs,
One would have said: 'It is a festival,
The Resurrection or the Last Great Day.
(Warner and Warner [trs.] 1905–1925, vol. 1,
ch. 105, verses 217–18)

In the *Shahnama*, Firdausi used the term *karrenay* (also known as *karna*) to describe the trumpets and *kus* for the mounted kettledrums. Like the *nafir*, *karrenay* is a long trumpet and was also used in royal processions and usually made of brass, gold, silver or other metals. *Kus* is a large mounted kettledrum, played in pairs and made of wood or metal. Both these instruments are mentioned a number of times in the *Shahnama* in scenes of royal processions or war. In the above verse, Firdausi also included other instruments such as pipes, harps and gongs, alongside colored silk flags as part of the royal outfit. Names were also given to the sounding of the drums for specific announcements or attributions to particular individuals, for example, *kus-e-dolat* (to be played during war victories), *kus-e-id* (to be played during *'Eid* festivals) and *kus-e-Afrasiyab* (*kus* attributed to Afrasiyab).

Similar terms were also used during the Mamluk and, later, Mughal periods. During Mamluk rule, the term *nauba* was already attributed not only to the act of sounding the ensemble but also the ensemble itself. This is seen in a report by Mamluk historian Shams al-Din al-Jazari (d. 1339), in his *Hawadith al-Zaman* (quoted in Li Guo, 1998, 101–2):

> Then on Sunday, Rajab 21 (May 4, 1298), news of the capture of Tall Hamdun (Til Hamdoun) and its citadel after a siege was announced by musical bands in Damascus. And on Sunday morning, Ramadan 12 (June 23, 1298), the news was announced a second time, on account of the citadel of Tall Hamdun, which was captured on Wednesday, Ramadan 7 (June 18, 1298). A midday prayer was called out on the (Damascus) Citadel by the Khaliliya Band (*nawbat al-Khaliliya*).

The *tablkhana* became an important symbol not only to the Mamluk sultan but also his army commanders. Officers of different ranks, called *Amirs of Tablkhana*, were entitled to own a *tablkhana* and played in front of their houses as a mark of their seniority or power (Ayalon 2005, 70). Capture of the drums by enemies in battle meant defeat. Muslim influence also spread towards the East when Qutb-ud-din Aibak, a former slave of Muhammad Ghori, became ruler after the death of his master and established the Delhi Sultanate in 1206. It was during this sultanate that the term *naubat* was first mentioned in South Asia and seemed to have replaced the earlier Hindu-Buddhist royal band the *panchamahasabda* (Sadie 1984, 748). However, no definitive study has been made on the history of the kettledrum in South Asia (Tingey 1994, 19). Alastair Dick argues that certain instruments mentioned in Sanskrit texts of the tenth to early thirteenth centuries were probably brought by the Arabs to India after the conquest of Sind in 712 CE (1984, 88). Debates were also rife with regard to the pre-Islamic shawm found in India (Jairazbhoy 1970; Flora 1983; Dick 1984). Flora (1983, 285) looks towards the *naubat* ensemble of West Asia in the first millennium and points to the *naubat* shawm as the precursor of the Hindustani *sahnai*, but Tingey (1994, 21) argues that 'in none of its pre-Islamic usages does the shawm manifest the characteristics shared by the *pancai baja* (which is similar to the *naubat*) and *naqqara khana*'.

Before the arrival of the *naqqara khana*, the ensemble of conch and drums were already prevalent in South Asia and were used for sacred and military purposes. According to Tingey, both are mentioned in many ancient Hindu texts such as the *Rigveda*, *Atharvaveda*, *Bhagavadgita* and *Jatakas* (ibid.). The *Rigveda* mentions the drum *dundubhi*, which was used in battle to instill courage among warriors. It was considered sacred and the capture of the *dundubhi* on the battlefield meant defeat (Shakuntala 1968, 5–11). The conch was part of the *panchamahasabda* (five great sounds) together with the horn, gong and drums, as mentioned in the Jatakas (Dick 1984, 82–83). In the *Mahabharata*, Krishna uses a conch called *panchajauya* on the battlefield (Krishnaswamy 1965, 87) and in the *Ramayana*, the *sankha-nada* (the sound of the conch) was used to rouse the soldiers (Sambamoorthy 1967, 5). The conch and drums ensemble was already in place before the arrival of the *naubat*, corresponding in instrumentation and function. This already functioning Indian musical tradition was later reinforced by the cultural practice of Muslim rulers. According to Tingey (1994, 22), prior to the establishment of the Delhi Sultanate, Turkish Afghan and Persian invaders had brought with them the *tablkhana* or *naqqarakhana* and its associated customs from Central and West Asia. Consequently, this new ruling elite had an impact on the artistic and cultural landscape of northern India, and under royal patronage diverse musical practices were fused which resulted in a unique South Asian tradition (Trivedi 2010, 42–44). The term *naubat* became widely used and, besides accompanying the ruler in processions or battles, the ensemble was also played in a specially built pavilion situated at the gateway of palaces or Muslim shrines. From these pavilions, called *naubat khana*, the ensemble announced the arrival or departure of the ruler and guests; and signalled prayer times and state ceremonies. This was in accordance with the tradition practiced by the Mamluks in Cairo, where the ensemble was played over the Bab Zuwayla, the southern Fatimid gate of the city (Lambton 1987, 928). Similarly, the Safavids in Isfahan, too, had the *naqqarakhana* played on a balcony over the Kaysariyya at the entrance of the city bazaar (ibid.).

One of the earliest visual depictions of the outfit can be found in a thirteenth century copy of the *Maqamat al-Hariri*. The *maqama* (assembly) was a new literary genre developed in the tenth century and became popular throughout the Arab-speaking world. One of the best-known works of the genre was by Abu Muhammad al-Qasim ibn Ali al-Hariri (1054–1122). It relates a story of the adventure of a roguish Abu Zayd from Saruj, a town in Syria, as told by al-Harith, a travelling merchant. Due to its popularity, hundreds of copies were made, and one unique aspect about this particular work was that some of the copies were accompanied with illustrations. These beautiful miniature paintings served as a window to the social life during the Abbasid caliphate, including the function of music (see Guthrie 1995).

Arguably the best preserved and beautifully illustrated of the hundreds of copies of *Maqamat al-Hariri* that survived is the thirteenth-century MS Arabe 5847 of the Bibliothèque nationale de France, Paris. This work was copied and illustrated by Yahya ibn Mahmud ibn Yahya ibn Abi al-Hasan ibn Kuwwarih al-Wasiti and completed in 1237. It contains ninety-nine illustrations in which one is found to depict the instruments of the Abbasid *tablkhana*, during the reign of caliph al-Mustansir (r. 1226–1242). The painting in *maqamat* 7 shows the *maratib* (insignia) or *'alah* (outfit), a symbol of royal authority of the Abbasids that involved the display of banners and flags, the beatings of drums and blowing of trumpets and horns (figure 2.3).

The mounted military band *tablkhana* in *maqamat* 7 was illustrated by al-Wasiti to depict a ceremony announcing the end of Ramadan and start of *'Eid al-Fitr* (the first day of the month of Syawal). This miniature painting accompanies the narration of the *maqamat* where Harith, who was at Barka'id, the main city of Diyar Rabi'ah (in present day Iraq), wishes to attend the morning *'Eid* prayer at the mosque in his new clothes. In Muslim tradition, the congregational prayer marks the beginning of *'Eid al-Fitr* festivities which is also a time when rulers make a public appearance. Hariri's mention of 'horsemen and footmen', 'feast' and 'adornment' must have inspired al-Wasiti to come up with the illustration of the thirteenth-century Abbasid *alah* (outfit). It could have been part of a long tradition where this outfit was used to signal the start of *'Eid* festivities, or probably accompany the caliph or nobles to the mosque for the customary *'Eid* prayer. Later, this tradition was practiced by Uzbek sultans in the early sixteenth century, where Sultan Abu'l-Fath Muhammad Syaibani Khan (1451–1510) was accompanied by musical instruments and standards on his way back after performing the *'Eid al-Fitr* prayer (Fadl Allah b. Ruzbihan 1962). In seventeenth-century Aceh, this was

Figure 2.3. A leaf from al-Wasiti's *Maqamat al-Hariri*: soldiers sounding the *nafir* and *naqqara* during a religious celebration. *Source*: Bibliothèque Nationale, Paris, MS arabe 5847, fol.19a.

an elaborate ceremony in which the sultan was accompanied by thousands of people (including a nobat ensemble) to the mosque (see chapter 5). This tradition of announcing the breaking of fast and the end of Ramadan is still practiced by nobat ensembles in Malaysia today.

In the miniature, there are three musicians and four horsemen, three of whom are holding the black Abbasid standards. Black was the color used by the Abbasid as a sign of mourning for the martyrs killed by the Hashimites during their revolt against the Umayyads, and also in following the Prophet's prophecy about the coming of the messiah who would be heralded by a man carrying a black banner. Al-Sabi (1977) reports that drummers were part of the caliph's household and a budget was also allocated for the carrying of banners during *'Eid* celebrations. It is clear from the illustration that, while the riders wear the same Arabic turban, they are of different ethnic origins. Slave soldiers, or *mamluks*, of Turkish origin formed a considerable part of the Abbasid army in the ninth century (Lindsay 2005, 71–74) and could have been included in the *maratib* (insignia) of the caliph or military commanders. Of all the four Arabs depicted, three are musicians and the other holds the long Abbasid banner. Two of the musicians appear to be playing the long trumpet *nafir* and another a pair of the kettledrum *naqqarat* or *tabl al-markab* (mounted drum). A dark blue wooden board (*daffa*) is used as a base for the pair of *naqqara* mounted on a mule, which was used due to the animal's stronger nature as compared to a thoroughbred horse (Guthrie 1995, 38). Seated on specially built elevated saddle, the *naqqara* player used a pair of sticks slightly curved at the ends, which would produce a deep and rounded tone.

Guthrie further observes that, despite the joyous occasion, the faces of the men were glum due to the effects of fasting and, in addition, during the month of Ramadan Muslims should be in the state of constant fear and hope (1995, 34). This is a contradiction because if the ceremony was done in the morning of *'Eid al-Fitr*, it was already Syawal and the men would have ceased to fast. The tense faces of the men were likely due to a number of reasons. Firstly, these men were part of a highly disciplined army unit playing a crucial part in an elaborate royal ceremony. They needed to be on high alert since any mistakes would probably disrupt the flow of the ceremony and embarrass their ruler or military commander. Secondly, the playing of the *tablkhana* or nobat, being a ceremonial/military ensemble, was not primarily meant for entertainment purposes, albeit being part of joyous occasions. Hence, the musicians and those around them may not necessarily enjoy what they were playing or listening.

The two *nafir* players seem to be preparing to blow the trumpets, which are probably made from silver or brass, although al-Wasiti used olive green and red to color them. The brown goblet-shaped body of the *naqqara* drums were clearly made from wood and covered at the top with white-colored cowhide or goatskin. From the illustration, it can be estimated that the sizes of both instruments are similar to the *nafiri* and *nengkara* of the Malay nobat. The only difference is that the *nengkara* is played using straight bamboo sticks rather than curved wooded ones, which are only used on the *gendang*. The instruments depicted in the *Maqamat* are also similar in size as in the al-Jazari illustration, which was produced in the same period.

According to Ibn Khaldun (1958), the flags and instruments of the *'alah*, or 'outfit', could be increased indefinitely and varied between dynasties. The outfit formed a special procession behind the ruler called the *saqah* (rear guard) and some rulers restricted its use to themselves (caliphs) while others allowed their officials to use it. While in Fez, Ibn Khaldun found out that the Sultan Abu Al-Hasan 'Ali ibn 'Othman (r. 1331–1348, 51, vol. 2) of the Marinid dynasty had an outfit comprised of one hundred drums and one hundred banners of colored silk interwoven with gold. The seven-man Abbasid outfit illustrated by al-Wasiti could have been that of a lower rank military commander or regional governor. The disintegration of the Abbasid caliphate saw the earlier *nauba* principle of turns, successions and musical suite assume a different connotation altogether. In much of West and South Asia, it assumed a plural form *naubat* and was later used interchangeably with *naqqarakhana* to denote the military/ceremonial band itself (Wade 1998, 5).

The outfit was also used during the appointment of Uthman I (1258–1326), founder of the Ottoman Empire, as a prince, sent to him by the Seljuk Sultan Ala ad-Din Kayqubad III in 1289. The outfit, which consisted of flags and the large *kusat* drums mounted on elephants, continued to be used by Uthman during his reign as Sultan (Farmer 1987, 37). During a military campaign, it was reported that Sultan Uthman was accompanied by 150 kettledrums mounted on camels and elephants (Chelebi in Farmer 1937). The drums were also used to announce the times of the *Fajr* (morning) and *Isya'* (night) prayers, a custom introduced by Sultan Muhammad II (1451–1481). It was during the rule of Sultan Murad IV (d. 1640) that the Persian *karnay* or long trumpet was introduced as part of military music (Farmer 1987). During the seventeenth century, the Ottoman military/ceremonial band developed into what was known as the *mehter*, which by now consisted of several 'loud' instruments such as the *zurna* (double-reed shawm), *boru* (single-wound trumpet), *davul* (two-headed bass drum), *nakkare* (kettledrum) and *zil* (cymbals). Its sight and sound represented Ottoman military power and a full *mehter* was once used to accompany an Ottoman envoy to the court of Vienna in 1665 (Monelle 2006, 118–19).

Figure 2.4. Folio from the *Surname-i Vehbi* (*Book of Festival*): the *Mehter* in a procession. *Source*: Collection of the Topkapi Museum Library.

Ewliya Chelebi (1611–1669) in his *Siyahat nama* wrote that Ottoman musicians had their own guilds believed to be guarded by a certain *pir* or patron saint and the *chaliji mihtar* or military musicians were the most important of all. Numbering about three hundred men, these musicians were placed in quarters at the Iron Gate near the Palace Gardens and the *mehter* would play a *nubat* of three parts (*fasl*) twice daily from their tower. Chelebi also provided a list of the instruments, which included (apart from the ones mentioned above by Monelle), *chaghana* (jingling johnnie), *daf* (round tambourine), *kus* (large kettledrum), *qudum* (medium-sized kettledrum) and *nafir* (long metal trumpet) (Farmer 1937).

Some of the instruments mentioned above can be seen in an eighteenth-century painting by artist Abdulcelil Levni (d. 1732). A court painter under Sultans Mustafa II (r. 1695–1703) and Ahmed III (r. 1703–1730), Levni was commissioned to paint the festival commemorating the circumcision of the four sons of Sultan Ahmed III and as a result the *Surname-i Vehbi* (Book of Festival) was produced. In one of the folios from the book, there is a pair of miniatures depicting a *mehter* procession during the festival (figure 2.4). The miniature on the left shows *kus* drums mounted in pairs on camels and eight *davul* drums on horseback being played using long drumsticks. Behind them are *zil* cymbals played horizontally, similar in fashion to the musicians depicted in al-Jazari's book (figures 2.1 and 2.2) and followed by six single-wound *nafir* or *karnay* (also known as *karna* or *karranay*) trumpets. The other miniature shows five pairs of *nakkare* or *naqqara* and eight *zurna* shawms played on horseback.

During the Safavid period in Iran (1501–1736), like other previous and contemporary Muslim polities, the *naqqarakhana* served as the insignia of the Shahs. Similar to the Mamluks and Mughals, the ensemble was played in a high citadel to mark prayer times and announce important events, including the coronation of a new ruler. This was witnessed by a number of seventeenth-century European travellers such as Jean Chardin, Jean de Thevenot, Jean-Baptiste Tavernier and Engelbert Kaempfer (Lambton 1987, 928). In India, the tradition was also practiced by the Mughals (1526–1858) where the *naubat* constituted an important part of regal status. The ensemble was placed and played in specially built house called *naqqarakhana* or *naubatkhana* situated at the entrance of palaces (see figure 2.5). The *naubat* became very much involved and was constantly present in palace ceremonies and festivals, and became the official timekeeper of the palace, marking the passing of the day and provided accompaniment for female dances in the harem. The birth of an heir, marriages and the coming of the New Year were celebrated with the sounds of the *naubat*.

Under the section on 'the ensigns of royalty' in his *Ain-i Akbari*, Mughal chronicler Abu'l Fazl recorded that during the reign of Akbar (1556–1605), the *naqqarakhana* ensemble consisted of the *kuwargah* or *damamah* drums that produced 'a deep sound', the *naqqara* kettledrums, *duhul,* gold, silver or brass *karana,* Persian and Indian *surna,* the Persian *nafir*, the brass *sing* and *sanj* cymbals. Special troops were assigned to the department and received monthly salaries (1873, vol. 1, 50–52).

The Mughal *naubat* became not only a display of power towards neighbouring states but also European visitors (Brown 2000,10). During the reign of Shah Jahan, English traveller Peter Mundy (1909–1936, 237) wrote about a royal procession he witnessed in 1632:

> Wee made an other moccame by reason the Ckaun did solempnize his Nourose aforesaid with all the Magnificence the way could affoard, as by shooteing off his shutternall or Cammell peeces (because they are fitted with on Cammells backs), in number 16, beating of Drumms, whereof hee hath with him 6 or 7 paire, to bee carried on Eliphants backs, of which one paire weigh 16 Maund Jehangueere, which is neere 1000 [lb.] weight English, sounding of his trumpetts, having by report when hee came Oreshawe (Orissa) drums of silver and trumpetts of gold, which now the King is possessed of, as also Jewells and 9 great Elliphants.

Early Histories

Figure 2.5. The *Naubat Khana* or drum house at the Red Fort, New Delhi, India. *Source*: Photograph by Raja Iskandar, November 2010.

The procession related by Mundy above involved the *naubat* ensemble which, by this time in Mughal India, had certainly grown in prestige, shown by the size of the kettledrums and gold trumpets. The ensemble continued to be part of the outfit of the ruler as clearly as described by Mundy (1909–1936, 239–40):

> When himself is on the way, There first goe certaine Elliphants before him about ¼ mile distance with flags, then the measurer of the way, the troopes of horses, and among them other Eliphants with drums on their backs, continually beatings a kinde of March; and now and then the Trumpetts sound. Then a great number of flaggs carried by Footemen

Figure 2.6. A sketch of the *naubat* ensemble during the reign of Mughal Emperor Shah Jahan by Peter Mundy (1909–1936) in 1634. *Source*: Hukluyt Sociey.

Mundy's illustration (figure 2.6) and description of the Mughal royal procession clearly show the size of the emperor's outfit and the *naubat* ensemble involved. The large and heavy *naqqara* (kettledrums) described earlier are seen mounted on two elephants followed by a pair of the *nafir* or *karna* (long metal trumpets). However, these instruments sketched by Mundy are rather small in number, considering they were part of the emperor's *naubat* (compared to Abul Fazl's list of Akbar's instruments mentioned earlier). The use of trumpets, drums and flags in a royal outfit was a continuation of the *'alah* tradition developed centuries earlier by the Umayyad and Abbasids but was now adapted to a new environment. In India, the availability of stronger animals such as elephants, for example, meant that kettledrums could be made bigger and heavier, which could alter the sound qualities of the instrument.

In the early nineteenth century, the *naubat* continued to be viewed with reverence and served as a symbol of military pride even in lands no longer under the control of the Mughal Empire. During British rule in East India, retiring 'native' officers of the British East India Company's army were given the privilege of using the *naubat* in the company's territories by British commanding officers. An extract from a military letter written by J. R. Lushington, from Fort St. George in Madras on 13 April 1831, stated that:

> to confer native officer Mahomed Ghous the long intended honor of using the nobat the mark of honor so gratifying to the feeling of a distinguished musulman, the privilege of using the nobat in the company's territories together with the honorary symbol of that privilege and its appropriate establishment and title. (British Library, IOR/F/4/1339/53189)

The letter above reflects the importance placed by Muslim soldiers of rank—although being under the command of the British—on having the privilege of the *naubat* upon retiring, in keeping with Muslim military tradition. This 'gratifying' symbol of power—albeit on a small scale—can be seen as a crucial geographical (the Mughals were still in control of parts of India) and historical link to the centuries of *musulman* rule over India. It restored pride and provided a sense of cultural security at a time of increasing foreign threat and diminishing Muslim power. The fall of the Mughal Empire decades later finally brought to an end to the patronage of the *naubat*, but the ensemble continued to be played in Muslim shrines and public ceremonies.

Throughout the nineteenth century, the *naqqarakhana* continued to have ceremonial roles at the courts of the Qajar dynasty (1785–1925) in Tehran. The institution was placed under one of the royal offices governing the affairs of musicians and dancers. There was gradual decline in the role of the *naqqarakhana*, which was viewed as an outdated tradition, and attempts were made to stop the practice all together (Lambton 1987, 929). Writing in early twentieth century, P. Molesworth Sykes (1909, 163) notices that the *naqqarakhana* was still in practice as a mark of royalty in major cities of Iran and was also used to perform at the shrine of Imam Reza in Mashad (see figure 2.7). When Reza Shah Pahlavi (1878–1944) deposed Ahmad Shah Qajar, the last Shah of the Qajar dynasty in 1925, the *naqqarakhana* was taken into his possession and served as a symbol of his sovereignty. About a decade later, as players of the *naqqarakhana* (who were largely hereditary) were dwindling in numbers and without government support, the tradition eventually ceased to exist (Lambton 1987, 929).

Figure 2.7. The *naqqarakhana* of the Imam Reza Shrine, Mashad, Iran. *Source*: Undated black and white photograph (ca. 1900), from: Sykes (1909, 163), figure D.

Chapter Two

THE MILITARY ENSEMBLE

Apart from being the outfit and insignia of royalty, the *tablkhana* maintained its original function on battlefields. It was a crucial element in war where banners, flags and instruments were used for tactical purposes, and to instil courage among soldiers. The Muslim *'alah* and its influence on European martial music has been discussed by Farmer (1912, 1949), who describes the ensemble as being a crucial part of military tactics. According to Farmer (1949, 248–49):

> The band was allotted a place of importance in barracks, camp and battle, side by side with the colors and other insignia of sultan or amir. In the hour of battle it was drawn up, with the colors, away from the actual battle throng where the musicians belabored the drums, blasted their trumpets, piped their shawms and clashed their cymbals unceasingly to urge the 'true believers' to deeds of daring and to 'fear and affray' the enemy. Secondly the band being the headquarters of the sultan, amir or other commander, was a rallying-point, for so long as the band was sounding it meant that the battle was proceeding to victory.

The capture of the instruments by the enemy signified defeat and its protection was of paramount importance in a battle. Furthermore, evident from visual sources of the ensemble, the musicians were not armed and to be in battle 'protected' mainly by instruments they were carrying must had taken a lot of courage. The tremendous aural effect of the drums, trumpets and cymbals was related in a number of contemporary accounts of Christian-Muslim wars. Pseudo-Turpin, in his *Historia de vita Caroli Magni*, narrated that during Charlemagne's (742–814) campaign to liberate Spain from the Muslims, the sounds of the Saracen army so disconcerted the Christians that they had to cover the eyes and ears of their horses (Farmer 1949, 243). According to one Crusader, Geoffrey de Vinsauf (Devizes and de Vinsauf 1848, 234–35), the ensemble that produced such horrible noise comprised of trumpets, clarions, horns, pipes, drums and cymbals, and he noted that the greater the clamour the braver the Muslim soldiers would become. The French chronicler Jean de Joinville (1225–1317), who was captured by the Mamluk army in Mansurah, Egypt, during the seventh crusade, wrote about the music ensemble he witnessed in 1250:

> These musicians had Saracen horns, drums and kettledrums, and made such a din at daybreak and at nightfall that while they could be heard clearly throughout the camp, those close by to them could not hear one another speak. The musicians would never be so bold as to sound their instruments during the day

other than on the orders of the commander of the *halqa*.³ Accordingly, when the sultan wished to issue an order, he summoned the commander of the *halqa* and let him know his orders. Then the commander had the sultan's instruments sounded and all the army would come to hear the sultan's command; the commander of the *halqa* would announce it and the entire army would carry it out. (Joinville and Villehardouin 2008, 216)

Jean de Joinville's account above shows the use of the ensemble not only to signal daily prayers but also to summon the army to discuss military tactics. The musicians were also given a special tent next to the sultan's, as his mobile symbol of authority—as a form of communication—on and off the battlefield. Back in the security of a sultan's fort or palace, the ensemble would normally be placed in barracks, towers or tents to signal prayer times and announce important events. The loud instruments were necessary to convey tactical information across a large army, to incite their courage and frighten the enemy. Being part of a unit of the army the musicians seemed to be under strict military discipline and were bound by certain rules and conduct, which were crucial in times of war. One interesting observation made by de Joinville is the number of times the ensemble was played to signal prayer times; which, for a sultan, could have been at least three times not twice.

The military function of the *tablkhana* as part of an outfit was narrated as well as illustrated in copies of the *Shahnama* produced during the Safavid period (1501–1736). One of the surviving copies of the *Shahnama*, commissioned by Shah Tahmasp (1514–1576) the Shah of Iran, is considered the most beautifully illustrated. In the miniature from the Tahmasp *Shahnama* (figure 2.8), which depicts the battle between the Iranians and Turanians, musicians are clearly seen as part of the military unit that include flags and emblems. The Iranian musicians are identified by the Safavid *taj*, the red caps protruding from their white turbans. The blue background indicates a night battle, and the unarmed *'alah* is seen guarded by soldiers in battle gear. The instruments of the ensemble include a pair of *kus* (kettledrum) mounted on a camel, a straight and an S-shaped *karna*, and a long *surnay*. The manner in which the *kus* is played shows the physical power needed to strike the drums (as compared to the smaller *naqqara* in figure 2.9) and one could imagine the high volume of the sound produced.

Numerous battle scenes are also narrated in the *Shahnama* with references to a number of instruments used, which included gongs and Indian bells. The scenes were also written in such a way to depict a loud and chaotic atmosphere, with blaring sounds of the ensemble, shouts of soldiers and the trampling of animals. In one battle scene Firdausi wrote:

Figure 2.8. Detail of a folio from the *Shahnama* of Shah Tahmasp: Qaran unhorses Barman. *Source*: The Sarikhani Collection, I.MS.4025.

Figure 2.9. Detail of a folio from a copy of the *Shahnama* by Abu'l Qasim Firdausi (935–1020) commissioned by Shah Tahmasp: Faridun embraces Manuchihr. *Source*: Collection of the Metropolitan Museum of Art, New York, USA.

Rose at his gate the din of kettledrums: His warriors armed.
Upon the elephants the trumpets blared, the world was like a sea of indigo,
and when they bound the drums Upon the elephants heaven kissed the earth.
Then said the king: 'Ye chiefs and warriors!
When both sides sound the drum he is no soldier that laggeth.
Let our hearts be full of vengeance, full as the bodies of our foes with javelins!
Thus spake he to the troops, then bade to sound the clarions, cymbals, and the Indian bells.
Arose the war-cry and the blare of trumpets, the din of cornet, pipe, and kettledrum,
Earth shook beneath the trampling of the steeds,
The shoutings of the soldiers reached the clouds.
(Warner and Warner [tr.] 1905–1925, vol. 2, ch. 140)

In another sixteenth-century Tahmasp *Shahnama*, a battle scene shows two warring sides blowing the *karna* and *surnay* while two types of drums, the pairs of *naqqara* and *kus*, are beaten (figure 2.9). The smaller *naqqara* is depicted positioned ahead of the bigger *kus* and the playing technique clearly illustrates the lower volume the instrument produced. Being symbols of royalty, these musicians are grouped together with flags and emblems, typical of a military outfit. However, unlike the previous painting (figure 2.8) they are not guarded by armed foot or mounted soldiers. Abu Fazl, in his *Akbarnama*, relates the effect of the deafening sound of the ensemble in a battle:

> every corner there were hot encounters. After much contest, victory, by the help of God, declared itself. On the other side of the river, Fatḥ K., on hearing of the news, had sent his son Muḥammad K. with a body of troops. He came on, beating his drums. On the other side, Khanjarī, Shādāb, Askaran and others beat their drums, and advanced. On hearing the noise of these outside drums, the enemy became demoralised, and by daily-increasing fortune the setting fire to the city by the Kashmīrīs made them still more broken. By the illumination thereof, the skilful marksmen shot down many. At the end of the night the enemy withdrew after a thousand. (Warner, and Warner [tr.] 1905–1925, vol. 3, ch. 188)

The texts of the *Shahnama* and *Akbarnama* are, of course, not the only textual or visual sources to illustrate the ensemble's use in battle. Numerous other Indo-Persian sources describe the use of the *naqqarakhana* or *naubat* battle scenes with various combinations of instruments. This literary tradition would be transferred to the Malay world in the thirteenth and fourteenth centuries, together with the introduction of Islam and its accompanying culture.

SUMMARY

The history of the Islamic military/ceremonial ensemble is a complex one. It is closely related to the often-turbulent nature of the expansion process of Islam and governance of the controlled territories. The process also resulted in the migration of peoples, cross-fertilization of ideas and cultures, creating a vast network of political, economic and religious links; these could be further examined as part of what Sanjay Subrahmanyam terms 'connected histories' (2005, 2). But what is particularly interesting is the self-induced process of 'reformation' and 'transformation' on the part of early Muslim rulers, as a realization of the great temporal rewards gained. They were aware that greatness had to be justly manifested through proper symbols and what better way than to mimic the existing models of great civilizations under their control. However, being a religious endeavour, any worldly excesses had—at least to the eyes of the conquered subjects—to be religiously justified; thus, the Islamization of many aspects of social life, including politics and culture. The Zoroastrian ritual practice to announce certain hours of the day was incorporated into the Islamic military/ceremonial music to announce daily Muslim prayers. Rulers used titles such as the 'Caliph of God' and 'Shadow of God on Earth', and any form of rebellion against the caliph was seen as a rebellion against God (Houtsma 1993, 884).

The idea of the *nauba* as turns or cycle of songs developed during the early Abbasid period when caliphs were active patrons of the arts. This concept evolved alongside the development of the *tablkhana* or *naqqarakhana* military band that later diverged into two different configurations, geographically separated into the *Maghrib* and *Mashriq*. The term was used in the *Maghrib* to refer to suite-like song cycles but was associated to the announcement of prayer times and important proclamations in the *Mashriq*. These periodical or occasional pronouncements (*nauba*) were honours reserved only for the caliph or military commanders and were played by a military/ceremonial ensemble called the *tablkhana* or *naqqarakhana*. Together with flags and banners, the *tablkhana* ensemble and the playing of the *nauba* became known as the *'alah*, or 'outfit', that symbolised royal authority. Lower ranking officials or military commanders needed the caliph's permission for them to have their own *tablkhana* and sounding of the *nauba*. This outfit would accompany the ruler in battles for tactical purposes and used for religious celebrations, especially during *'Eid al-Fitr* and *'Eid al-Adha*. An important visual and aural symbol of Muslim power was thus created, not through the fluid, natural process of the collective agency of subjects but largely top-down decision-making.

The fragmentation of the Abbasid Empire saw individual emirs and aspiring rulers beginning to assume the right to their own *tablkhana* and *nauba*. The size of the ensemble also grew to reflect the power of a certain ruler while special buildings were made to house them. It became an important institution for succeeding empires and it developed further as the Muslim influence spread towards South Asia and Europe. The ensemble evolved into the *mehter* under the Ottomans, *naqqarakhana* in Safavid Iran and *naubat* during the period of Mughal rule in India. Different instruments were added, borrowed from other regions and cultures to be accommodated, hybridised and localised, without losing the larger Muslim identity. The size of the band also fluctuated—expanded and contracted by the whims and fancies of rulers in relation to their economic or political power. The institution developed at the behest of those in power and remained associated with power throughout much of the Islamicate world to this day. One significant reason for its power was its very ability to be absorbed into different geographical and cultural contexts; and transformed to appropriate other culture's symbol of power without totally severing its Islamic roots. The ensemble produced sounds that served as what Thomas Turino (2008, 7) describes as 'iconic signs' capable of making imaginative connections, conjuring up menacing images of marauding armies for enemies or joyous scenes of religious parades for ordinary subjects. It was what R. Murray Schafer (1994, 10) would call the 'soundmark' of the Muslims, a mobile sound system of authority similar to the sirens of outriders accompanying a president or prime minister's motorcade of today. Borrowing from Judith Butler's (1988, 519–20) discussion on gender identity, this early nobat and its 'soundmark' can be seen as a 'constructed identity' and 'instituted through a stylised repetition of acts', in iterating Muslim distinctiveness.

It is fortunate that this process was recorded and preserved—albeit as fragmentary evidence—through court-sanctioned texts and illustrations, and supported by European sources. The vast Islamicate economic and political network developed throughout the centuries saw the process of 'transformation' and identity formation continued across to the Malay world. In the following chapters, we shall see the transplantation of the ensemble into the Malay courts and how it later came to symbolise Malay royal authority and *daulat* (divine essence).

NOTES

1. This chapter is derived in part from an article published in *Double Reeds along the Great Silk Road* (2019 Logos Verlag Berlin).
2. The term refers to the pre-Islamic period of ignorance and backwardness in Islamic historiography.
3. The *halqa* was a military unit during the Ayyubid and Mamluk period, for a detailed discussion, see Ayalon (2005).

Chapter Three

The Malay Nobat

The nobat is a drum and wind ensemble played in the Malay courts of Sumatera,[1] Peninsular Malaysia and Brunei since the arrival of Islam in the region in the thirteenth century.[2] It is a Malay version of the Islamicate courtly tradition detailed in chapter 2, known as *tablkhana* (Abbasid, Fatimid), *naqqarakhana* (Afghan, Persian), *nauba* (Umayyad, Andalusian, North Africa) and *naubat* (Mughal). In the Malay world, for centuries it constituted an important part of the court regalia and served as a symbol of a Malay ruler's power and sovereignty. A Malay sultan who possessed one would not be legitimately installed unless he was 'drummed' to the sound of the nobat. The term *nobat*, as well as *tabal,* was also used to indicate the installation process itself; for example, in the *Sejarah Melayu*, it was narrated that the Raja of Kedah, in order to gain recognition and legitimacy from Melaka, asked for a nobat and was subsequently *dinobatkan* (installed) there (SM 229:14).

In traditional Malay society, the nobat signified the aural and visual display of authority and the demarcation of political boundaries. It was revered as a conduit of a sultan's *daulat* or divine essence and utilised as a means for social control.[3] In the nineteenth century Riau-Lingga Sultanate, it was obligatory for a person to prostrate and sit as if facing a sultan when hearing the sound of the *nafiri* (Syed Alwi [1960] 1986; A. Samad Ahmad 1985, 45). It was believed that any display of disrespect to the regalia of a Malay ruler was considered an act of *derhaka* (rebellion or disobedience) which may incur divine curse or *tulah*.

Similar to other traditional Malay performing arts, the Malay nobat institution consists of numerous different layers of cultural and spiritual influences. The Malay royal institution, with its Islamic roots and ubiquitous Hindu-Buddhist influence still maintains a certain primordial element to it. Behind the façade of religious order and regal splendour lies a deeply entrenched, almost universal animist belief system that some scholars refer to as Old Indonesian beliefs (Mohd Taib Osman 1989, 152). This is manifested in the visible and audible, and also physical and metaphysical aspect of the court ensemble. Malay indigenous arts were traditionally performed as part of ritualistic processes in connection with healing, guardian ancestor spirits, agricultural fertility, bountiful ocean catch or overall prosperity (Ghulam-Sarwar Yousof 2004, 64). The nobat as a ritual performance can be seen in part as a continuation of this ancient practice.

The Sultan's installation ceremony, in which the nobat plays a crucial role, is steeped in Hindu-Buddhist and animistic beliefs. In Perak, the Sultan has to sit motionless while the piece 'Nobat Tabal' is played. In Siamese Buddhism, the ability to sit perfectly for hours is considered a sign of the commencing divinity of a king. It is believed that the longer the Sultan sits motionless while the nobat plays, the greater the *daulat* (divine essence) and length of the Sultan's reign. In this ceremony the duration of the piece is measured by the number of *man*, or 'rhythmic sequences', in the piece 'Nobat Tabal' and usually a Sultan sits still between four and nine *man* during the ceremony (see Raja Iskandar 2018).

The Sultan sits on the east side of the *Balairong Seri* or audience hall, with the nobat orchestra situated on the west side. According to Waterson (1990), in traditional Southeast Asian rituals, east is considered 'the direction of life, the rising sun, deities, and life-affirming rituals' (105). The color of the rising sun is reflected in the color yellow used in Malay societies to symbolize royalty. In Malay royal traditions, there is also the tradition of using the numbers four, eight, sixteen and thirty-two, derived from Hindu astrology (Winstedt 1951, 33). This is shown in the numbers of high-ranking chiefs in the state of Perak and also the sets of pillars in an old Perak palace. During official ceremonies at the palace, sixteen palace bearers are lined up in the Balairong Seri and sixteen bowls are used to hold the lustration water for the bathing ceremony.

The demise of a number of Malay sultanates in the nineteenth and twentieth centuries resulted in the inevitable attenuation of the nobat institution. Instruments were lost or kept in museums, transferred to other sultanates or continued to be occasionally played by remaining members of the dethroned royal families (see Kartomi 1997). At present the nobat is still found in four states in Peninsular Malaysia—Kedah, Perak, Selangor and Terengganu, and one in the Kingdom of Brunei, a sovereign country bordering the state of Sarawak in East Malaysia. In Malaysia, apart from installing rulers in these four states, the nobat is also used to install the *Yang Dipertuan Agong* (the Supreme Ruler) otherwise referred to as the King of Malaysia, a unique position rotated every five years among nine ruling sultans. For this particular purpose, sultans without their own nobat are installed using the nobat of Kedah, considered the oldest, at the Istana Negara (National Palace) in Kuala Lumpur. The first Yang Dipertuan Agong, Tuanku Abdul Rahman, ruler of the state of Negri Sembilan was installed using the Kedah nobat in 1957. Despite some changes to its repertoire, instruments and performance practice, these remaining nobat are probably the last examples of this Islamic court tradition that are still performed within their original context—to serve kings.

BRIEF HISTORY

Expanding Muslim influence through military conquest, trade and pilgrimage brought the *naqqarakhana* and *nauba* tradition eastward towards South and Southeast Asia. The ensemble continued to evolve while retaining certain elements of the original Islamicate military/ceremonial band and the *nauba* performance practice (see Sawa 1989, 115; Shiloah 1995, 97). As in South Asia, the Malay nobat ensemble reinforced any similar prevailing Hindu-Buddhist ideas and synthesised them with Islamic ones. This syncretic nobat upholds its original symbolic function and combination of instruments, namely the *nengkara* (kettledrum), *nafiri* (long trumpet) and *serunai* (shawm), while adding indigenous ones such as *gendang* (double-headed drum) and *gong* (bossed circular metal disc).

According to the *Sejarah Melayu* (Malay Annals),[4] the nobat institution was firmly established and incorporated into the customs and ceremonies of the Melaka sultanate by the fifteenth century. The text further narrates that prior to its existence in Melaka, the nobat was first used by the Queen of Bentan and later brought to Temasek (now Singapore) by her son-in-law Sri Tri Buana, who established a kingdom there. The *Hikayat Raja-Raja Pasai* (*Chronicle of the Pasai Kings*) (Jones 1997)[5] narrates that the nobat was brought to Pasai by a certain Sheikh Ismail from Mecca and was used in the installation of Sultan Malek al-Saleh as Pasai's first Muslim ruler. Yet, considering Southeast Asia's long trade and economic relations with South Asia, it has been suggested that Pasai's nobat could possibly have come from or via India (Wilkinson 1932, 84; Andaya 2011, 24). It was a marriage alliance between Melaka's first ruler Parameswara and a princess from Pasai that resulted in the introduction of the nobat to Melaka (Sheppard 1983, 19; Azyumardi Azra 2006, 57).

The rise of Melaka as a regional power made it a crucible of Malay culture and identity. The nobat not only played a crucial role in the installation of rulers and other court ceremonies, it was also used to bestow honour and prestige upon lesser polities as a symbol of Melakan suzerainty over them.

The nobat was a political tool and the expansion of the Melaka Empire and the subsequent spread of the nobat to other Malay kingdoms (see figure 3.1) was narrated in the *Sejarah Melayu*:

Maka Seri Bija Diraja dititahkan baginda diam di Pahang, dianugerahi gendang nobat dengan selengkapnya, melainkan nagara juga yang tiada, dan dianugerahi payung iram-iram berapit oleh jasanya menangkap Maharaja Dewa Sura itu. (SM 92:33)

Then Seri Bija Diraja was ordered by his majesty to live in Pahang, bestowed with the full installation drums, except for the nagara, and presented with a pair of umbrellas in recognition of his success in capturing Maharaja Dewa Sura.

Arakian maka Raja Menawar, anak Sultan Alau'din pun besarlah, maka oleh Sultan Alau'd-Din anakanda baginda itu dirajakan di Kampar, dinobatkan dahulu di Melaka. (SM 173:24)

Then Raja Menawar, son of Sultan Alau'din came of age, Sultan Alau'din then asked his son to be installed as king in Kampar, drummed first in Melaka.

Maka Raja Beruas pun dipersalinkan baginda dan dinobatkan sekali, digelar Tun Aria Bija Diraja. Maka Manjong pun diserahkan kepadanya, maka Tun Aria Bija Diraja pun bermohonlah kepada Sultan Mahmud kembali ke Beruas. (SM 190:12)

Then the king of Beruas was given robes of honor and drummed, styled as Tun Aria Bija Diraja. Manjong was thus given to him, Tun Aria Bija Diraja then requested Sultan Mahmud to be excused to return to Beruas.

Maka Cau Seri Bangsa pun berbuatlah negerilah di sana. Setelah sudah, maka negeri itu dinamai baginda Pak Tani, mengikut nama payang itu, maka disebut orang datang sekarang Petani. Maka Cau Seri Bangsa pun menyuruhkan menterinya Okun Pola namanya, mengadap ke Melaka, memohon nobat pada Sultan Mahmud Syah. (SM 228:21)

Then Cau Seri Bangsa established a state there. Once completed, it was called Pak Tani, after the fisherman's name, and it is known by people today as Petani. Then Cau Seri Bangsa sent his minister Okun Pola to pay obeisance to Melaka, to ask for a nobat from Sultan Mahmud Syah.

Maka oleh Sultan Mahmud Syah, Raja Kedah dianugerahi pesalinan, dan dinobatkan sekali. Maka Raja Kedah pun kembalilah ke Kedah; setelah sampai ke Kedah maka baginda pun nobatlah di Kedah. (SM 229:39)

Then Sultan Mahmud Syah gave the robes of honor to the Raja of Kedah and drummed. The Raja of Kedah then returned to Kedah; where he was thus drummed there.

Kedah, however, has its own versions of the history of its nobat. According to the *Al Tarikh Salasilah Negeri Kedah* (1927), nobat was first used in Kedah by its first king, Maharaja Derbar Raja, who was said to have come from Iran (Ku Zam Zam 1994, 3). Another Kedah text, *Peraturan-Peraturan Isti'adat Diraja Kedah* (*Guidelines of the Kedah Royal Ceremonies*) (Hanapi Mohd Ariff 1984, 7), states that a Kedah prince, Tengku Mohammed Jewa, was so impressed by the *naubat* he saw in India that he suggested to his brother Sultan Ataillah Mohammed Shah (1426–1474) that a similar ensemble be played to signify the honour and status of the Kedah court.

Figure 3.1. Fifteenth-century movements of the nobat based on the *Sejarah Melayu*. Source: Made by author.

The fall of Melaka to the Portuguese in 1511 led to the establishment of two Malay sultanates, Johor and Perak. Retreating from the Portuguese, Sultan Mahmud Shah (r. 1488-1511), Melaka's last sultan moved south to Johor, Bentan and, finally, to Kampar, Sumatera, where he died in 1528. His sons Sultan Alauddin Riayat Shah and Sultan Muzaffar Shah were made rulers of Johor and Perak respectively. Both sultanates considered themselves successors of the Melaka Empire and following the customs of Melaka, had their own nobat. The Johor sultanate grew to become the Johor-Riau or Johor-Riau-Lingga Empire, which by the early eighteenth century was the most powerful kingdom in the Malay world. Although officially a Malay sultanate, the Bugis from Celebes had considerable influence and the kingdom was thus demarcated into Malay and Bugis spheres of influence. The Malays, represented by the sultan would rule from Lingga while the Bugis were based on the Riau islands of Bintan and Penyengat under Yang Dipertuan Muda ('regent', also called Yamtuan Muda) (Matheson 1989, 156). Although the sultan was considered higher in status than the Yang Dipertuan Muda, both rulers had their own nobat. In continuing the practice of Melaka, the nobat was played when receiving guests and letters, including in the nineteenth century the Dutch resident (*Besluit* no. 8, January 1897; Abdul Samad Ahmad 1985, 90). It was during the reign of Sultan Abdul Rahman Muadzam Shah II (r. 1883–1911) that the sultanate was reconciled under one sultan in 1899, and thus a single nobat.

The Anglo-Dutch treaty of 1824 resulted in the partition of the Johor Empire into British-controlled Johor on the Malay Peninsula and the Dutch-administered Riau-Lingga. The nobat continued to be played and customs relating to the ensemble were documented in a nineteenth-century text called *Kitab Thamaratul Matlub Fi Anuaril Qulub*, published as *Kerajaan Johor-Riau* in 1985 (Abdul Samad Ahmad 1985). While reinforcing Johor's claim to Melaka's legacy, this book also details the role of the nobat in many aspects of court ceremonies, including a list of its pieces and instruments. Close relations were maintained with other Malay kingdoms, such as Perak and Inderagiri, and nobat pieces from these sultanates were added into the Riau-Lingga's repertoire. Despite the enforced political separation, Riau also maintained connections with Johor on the Malay Peninsula and this was manifested when the Riau nobat was played at the Johor court during the lying-in-state ceremony after the death of Sultan Abu Bakar in 1895. The *Singapore Free Press* and *Merchantile Advertisement* reported that:

> At the end of the big hall was the Malay band of the Rajah of Rhio, which he had brought with him for the occasion, special funeral music being played. The band consists of five performers, there being two large drums and a smaller one, a kind of kettle drum; one long horn, about a yard in length, and a much

shorter one, some 15 inches in length, a sort of oboe or flageolet, which plays the melody. (9 September 1895, 3)

The same newspaper also reported that before the funeral:

> the sound of the weird funeral music of the Malay oboe and the Moslem drum played in quaint syncopated rhythm, issuing from the throne room where the body was lying in state, attracted a large number of visitors to the eastern front of the Istana [palace]. (Ibid.)

The 'two large drums' mentioned in the report probably referred to the pair of big silver *gendang ibu* (mother drum) and *gendang anak* (child drum), specially made by the Dutch as a gift to Tengku Embong Fatimah, mother of Sultan Abdul Rahman. It is however interesting to note that the nobat was played during the lying-in-state ceremony at the throne room but did not accompany the cortege to the cemetery. It was instead accompanied by the Johore Band, which played Mendelssohn's 'Marche Funèbre' and Beethoven's 'Funeral March'. The band was conducted by bandmaster M. Galistan, who was largely responsible for its establishment, under the instruction of the late sultan himself (*Singapore Free Press*, 9 September 1895; *Straits Times*, 8 April 1930).

Five centuries after Melaka's demise, the Johor-Riau nobat tradition finally ended when Sultan Abdul Rahman, under Dutch pressure, abdicated in 1911 and moved to Singapore together with his nobat instruments.[6] In 1917, the Lingga nobat was acquired by the Terengganu court, which for more than a century had forged a close relationship with Lingga (figure 3.2). Prior to this, the Lingga nobat had been borrowed on a number of occasions by the Terengganu court, to be performed during marriage ceremonies and other important occasions (Sheppard 1989; Jelani Harun 2008, 3). It was played during the installation of both Sultan Muhammad ibn Almarhum Sultan Zainal Abidin III (r. 1918–1920), who was married to a daughter of Sultan Abdul Rahman; and his younger brother Sultan Sulaiman Badrul Alam Shah (r. 1920–1942). During the reign of Sultan Sulaiman, the nobat was officially incorporated into Terengganu court customs with the publication in 1928 of *Adat Istiadat Negeri Terengganu* (Customs and Ceremonies of the Terengganu State), which was based on the customs of Melaka, Pahang and Johor-Riau-Lingga (Jelani Harun 2008, 7). Court records also show that relationships with Lingga still persisted in relation to the nobat with a certain Tabak Bin Sulung, a nobat player from Riau, applying by letter for a post at the Terengganu court (*ibid.*). The new regalia of the Terengganu court was even requested by the Selangor palace (through the British resident) to be played at the installation of Sultan Hisamuddin Alam Shah (r. 1938–1942, 1945–1960) (Arkib Negara

1957/0339361). One of the Lingga nobat's original instruments, the *nafiri*, surfaced in Singapore in 1966. It was under the care of Tengku Embong Fatimah,[7] Sultan Abdul Rahman's niece in Singapore (*Straits Times* 1966) and was finally handed over to the Terengganu palace in 1990.

North of the peninsula itself, Patani (now the southernmost part of Thailand) rose to become a major port city by the early seventeenth century. Like a number of other Malay sultanates, Patani documented its history and court customs in a text known as the *Hikayat Patani* (*The Story of Patani*) (Teeuw and Wyatt 1970; Siti Hawa 1992) (to be discussed in chapter 4). Unlike any other known Malay court literature, this court chronicle and manual allocated an entire section to the nobat, documenting the ensemble's instrumentation, repertoire and playing instruction. The number and great value of the instruments documented as part of the royal inventory even outweighs present-day ensembles and underlines the wealth and influence enjoyed at the height of Patani's existence as a regional power. The text also provides a long list of repertoire, together with detailed mnemonic syllables of pieces and techniques for playing the *nafiri*. Towards the end of the eighteenth century, Patani's power began to decline and it was subjugated by the Siamese in 1785. Although its power base shifted to Kelantan, Patani's nobat tradition was lost and replaced with a court ensemble called the *gendang besar* (big drum), which served the same function. The fate of the gold and silver Patani nobat mentioned in the *Hikayat Patani* remains unknown.

Figure 3.2. The nobat of Terengganu, circa 1917–1918. *Source*: Photograph, Arkib Negara Malaysia, ANM 2001/0025628.

Across the Straits of Melaka, Aceh began to assert itself as a powerful Malay sultanate in the sixteenth century. After annexing Pasai and its neighboring polities in 1524, Aceh began to replace Melaka as the centre of the Malay world. The nobat continued to be played in the Acehnese sultanate and its use in court ceremonies was documented in a seventeenth century text called the *Adat Aceh* (Customs of Aceh) (to be discussed in chapter 5). The Aceh sultanate held elaborate ceremonies and celebrations, which involved the playing of the nobat in street processions, which were seen as an important visual and aural representation of the ruler's authority and presence. During the reign of Sultan Iskandar Muda (r. 1606–1636), considered Aceh's greatest ruler, the nobat was played in a weekly procession that was reportedly accompanied by about 200 elephants and 4,500 men (Best 1934). Towards the end of the seventeenth century, Aceh's power began to decline but it remained an important supplier of pepper in the region. The sultanate became a center of a power struggle between the British and the Dutch, which led to a number of treaties that eventually gave the Dutch full control over Sumatera in 1871. Aceh saw this as a threat to its sovereignty and in 1873 war between Aceh and the Dutch began, known as the Aceh War. After three decades Sultan Muhammad Daudsyah (r. 1874–1903), Aceh's last ruler, finally surrendered ending five centuries of the Acehnese sultanate. As in Patani, the fate of the Acehnese nobat remains unknown.

Perak, like Johor, continued with the court tradition of Melaka. The nobat continued to be an important part of court ceremonies but it is difficult to ascertain whether the original Melaka nobat was brought to Perak in 1528. However, Sultan Muzaffar Shah as a Malay ruler of the Melaka household surely did not go to Perak without one, as suggested by Winstead and Wilkinson (1934, 11):

> The eldest son of the last ruler of Melaka, greatest of Peninsula empires, did not come to Perak without followers and without tradition. The Perak court still cherishes armlets, a chain, a sword, a seal and a creese, reputed heirlooms from its first Sultan, which must be worn at installation by every one of his successors while, to the music of drums headed miraculously with the skins of tiny lice and of clarionets fashioned miraculously from the narrow stems of nettles, they sit preserving that immobility which to their Buddhist ancestors of Palembang was a mark of the commencing divinity of a king.

According to an indigenous Perak source collected by W. E. Maxwell (1882, 91–92), which he named 'Legend of the White Semang', the Perak sultanate began with the installation of a Johor prince who brought along 'the insignia of royalty, namely, the royal drums (*gandang nobat*), the pipes (*nafiri*), the flutes (*sarunei* and *bangsi*), the betel-box (*puan naga taru*), the sword (*chora mandakini*), the [smaller] sword (*perbujang*), the scepter (*kayu gamit*), the jewel (*kamala*), the '*surat chiri*', the seal of state (*chap halilintar*) and the umbrella (*ubar-ubar*). Although this version of the history of Perak was never officially recognised, it showed not only the close relations between Perak and Johor, but also the importance of the regalia in the establishment of a Malay sultanate.

The significant role of the Perak nobat in the eighteenth century was highlighted in the *Misa Melayu* (Ahmad Fauzi 1992),[8] written by Raja Chulan (d. 1787). A number of ceremonies were mentioned in which the nobat was involved including royal burial and mourning (53:24, 59:6, 114:15, 192:26), marriage celebration (47:23) and installation (187:27, 192:27). A complete list of the nobat repertoire was also documented in the *Misa Melayu* including a short history of how the pieces came about (194:11). However, the most important information derived from *Misa Melayu* is the origin of the nobat of Selangor.

In 1745, a young Bugis prince by the name of Raja Lumu was proclaimed ruler of Selangor, a state under the control of the Johor-Riau Empire. He began to assert his power and rebel against his cousin Daeng Kemboja, the Yamtuan Muda, or 'regent', of the empire. However, it was not until 1766 that Raja Lumu was ready to declare his independence from Johor-Riau. A year earlier, Sultan Mahmud Shah (r. 1765–1773) was installed as the new sultan of Perak who began to show a more favorable attitude towards the Bugis in Selangor. Raja Lumu saw this as an opportunity for him to finally seek his independence. As a ruler in a Malay world (although he was a Bugis), he needed the necessary symbols of kingship such as a title, seal and his own nobat to fully claim sovereignty. To achieve this, an alliance was needed with Selangor's northern neighbor Perak, long considered the rightful heir to the Melaka and Palembang Malay sultanates (Andaya 1979, 265–72).

Amid opposition from the Dutch and his own Raja Muda (regent) and Raja Bendahara (prime minister), Sultan Mahmud received Raja Lumu and a meeting ensued in Pasir Pulai, Perak. A contract was signed between both states, pledging a 'lasting peace' and a promise of mutual assistance in the advent of third-party attacks. The treaty was sealed with the installation of Raja Lumu and a gift of the nobat as narrated by *Misa Melayu*:

> *Adapun, setelah sudah putus mesyuarat yang demikian itu, maka diperbuatlah gendang nobat dengan selengkapnya; telah itu, maka ditabalkan baginda Raja Selangor itu dengan seperti adatnya. Maka digelar Sultan Salihud-din serta dikurniai baginda cap istimaya. Setelah sudah Raja Selangor menerima kurnia nobat baginda itu, antara beberapa lamanya, maka ia pun hendak bermohon pulang ke Selangor.* (Misa: 187:27–32)

After an agreement was reached in the meeting, then a complete nobat drum was made; thereafter, his highness the Raja Selangor was installed according to the proper customs. Then he was styled as Sultan Salihud-din and given a special seal. Bestowed with the nobat, after a period of time, he then asked for leave to return to Selangor.

The nobat continued to be performed in Selangor and was used during the installation of Sultan Muhammad (r. 1826–1857). However, during his reign, the state regalia were destroyed on the advice of a certain Sheikh Abdul Ghani, a religious scholar from Sumatera (Wan Mohd Amin 1966, 89). The regalia were not replaced by Sultan Abdul Samad (r. 1857–1896) and the institution simply ceased to function. However, there were differing opinions whether the nobat was also destroyed and this will be discussed further in chapter 6.

Nearly half a century later, the nobat institution of Selangor was restored with the help of Sultan Idris Shah I (r. 1887–1916) who sent a set and the *orang kalur* to perform at the installation of Sultan Alaeddin Sulaiman (r. 1898–1938) in October 1903. The nobat was later used to install subsequent sultans of Selangor and was last used during the *istiadat pertabalan* of Sultan Sharafuddin Idris Shah in 2003 at Istana Alam Shah in Kelang. Since its arrival, the Selangor nobat has always been played by the same *orang kalur* family from Perak and maintained the same repertoire and instruments. Even players from the present Perak ensemble are sometimes requested to play in Selangor.

INSTRUMENTS

The Malay nobat is a percussion-dominated ensemble comprising membranophones, aerophones and idiophones. Instruments vary slightly between ensembles, in terms of materials used to make them, size, design and combination. For example, *gongs* are only used by the Kedah and Brunei nobat, while the *kopak-kopak* (small, handheld pair of cymbals) is only used in Terengganu. The *gong* is mentioned in the *Hikayat Raja-Raja Pasai* as being part of the Pasai nobat ensemble as early as the thirteenth century and was used in the Perak ensemble at least until the late eighteenth century, as described in the *Misa Melayu*. It is therefore clear that the *gong*—long being an indigenous Southeast Asian instrument—was incorporated into this foreign ensemble and became an important part of it. Further physical evidence of the use of the gong can be found in the old Riau-Lingga nobat set exhibited in the Riau Kandis Museum in Indonesia. The Brunei nobat, meanwhile, is the only ensemble without the *nafiri* (P. M. Sharifuddin and Abdul Latif Haji

Ibrahim 1977). While drums of the other ensembles are made of wood, drums of the Terengganu nobat are made of silver carved with intricate designs, said to be built by craftsmen from Batavia under the orders of the Dutch Resident of Riau (Sheppard 1989).

All of the instrument types in the present Malay nobat ensembles are present in many early Malay texts from the fourteenth century onwards. Some instruments are individually named as being part of a court ensemble while in other instances a more general term is used. For example, the *Sejarah Melayu* describes the *gendang*, *serunai*, *nafiri* and *nagara* as being part of the *alat kerajaan* or state regalia of fifteenth-century Melaka, while the *Hikayat Raja-Raja Pasai* uses the term *genderang tabal*, or 'installation drums', which could mean just the combination of *gendang* and *nagara* or the whole nobat ensemble. Instruments of the *alat kerajaan* or nobat are also mentioned together with other local instruments. It is possible that nobat instruments could have been used interchangeably with other instruments on auspicious occasions and eventually leading to some of them being absorbed into the court ensemble.

Instruments of the present-day Malay nobat ensembles are as follows.

Nengkara

The *nengkara* (Perak and Selangor), *nahara* (Kedah), *negara* (Terengganu) and *nakara* (Brunei), or 'kettledrum', can be said to be the most important instrument in a nobat ensemble. Similar names for this instrument are found throughout the Islamicate world such as *naghghareh* (Iran), *nakkare* (Turkey) and *naqqara* (India), which may be attached to another word *khana* or *khaneh* (house) to produce the term *naqqara-khana* (drum house) for the dedicated place in a fort where the nobat ensemble was stationed. The *nengkara* is a single-headed kettledrum that varies in size from one ensemble to another. The *nengkara* of the Perak and Selangor nobat are about 46 cm in height and 41 cm in diameter and are a few cm smaller than the negara of Terengganu, also known as *sendang saku*. The Kedah *nahara* measures 31 cm in diameter and is 26 cm in height. This goblet-shaped drum is struck using a pair of thin bamboo sticks about 51.5 cm in length with its body slightly tilted so that the drumhead faces toward the player. However, this is not the case with the Brunei nobat where the *nakara* is placed flat on a raised pedestal. Deer or goatskin is used to make its drumhead, which is attached to the wooden body using laces made of rattan. The *negara* of the Brunei and Terengganu nobat is made of silver and the latter uses tuning pegs similar to the European timpani (figure 3.3).

Figure 3.3. The silver *Negara* of the Terengganu nobat. *Source*: Photograph by Raja Iskandar, March 2011.

Gendang

There is a pair of two-headed cylindrical barrel drums in every nobat ensemble today. The pairs in the Terengganu, Kedah and Brunei nobat are (or are almost) identical in size while in Perak and Selangor there are slight variations. In Brunei these drums are called *gendang labik* while in Terengganu and Kedah the drums are differentiated by the name *gendang ibu* (mother drum) and *gendang anak* (child drum), similar to the pairs found in *makyong* and *wayang kulit* ensembles. The Kedah *gendang ibu* and *gendang anak* are about 52 cm in length, 38 and 41 cm in diameter at the small and large drumheads, respectively. In Perak and Selangor, the *gendang nobat* is known as *gendang melalu* or *nyenyalu* to denote the bigger of the two *gendang* used in those ensembles while the smaller ones are called *gendang kecil* or *gendang peningkah* (see figure 3.4). *Gendang melalu* is between 55 cm in length, 28 and 32 cm in diameter at the small and large drumheads respectively and *gendang kecil* is about 3 to 4 cm smaller.

As with the *nengkara*, the body of the drums is usually made of *jerun* or *nangka* wood. The two heads are made of deer, cowhide or goatskin and attached to the body using Y-shaped strings laced to the rim of the heads. Using encircling cowhide loops, the laces can be adjusted to tighten or loosen the heads to alter the pitch and timbre of the instrument. The *gendang* is played by striking the right (larger) drumhead using a curved wooden stick about 36 cm in length, and the palm of the hand on the left (smaller) drumhead. In Terengganu however, both *gendang* are made of silver and are tuned using Western-type tuning pegs on both ends of the drum face. As mentioned earlier, these silver drums (figure 3.5) were originally from Riau made to replace the old wooden ones, which are now kept at the Riau Kandis Museum

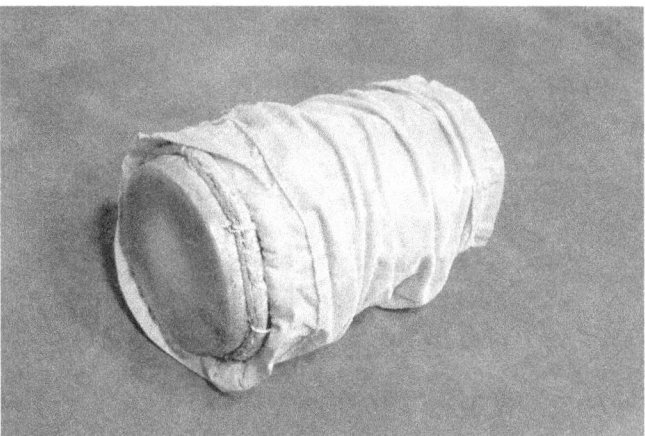

Figure 3.4. *Gendang Peningkah* of the Perak nobat. *Source*: Photograph by Raja Iskandar, December 2006.

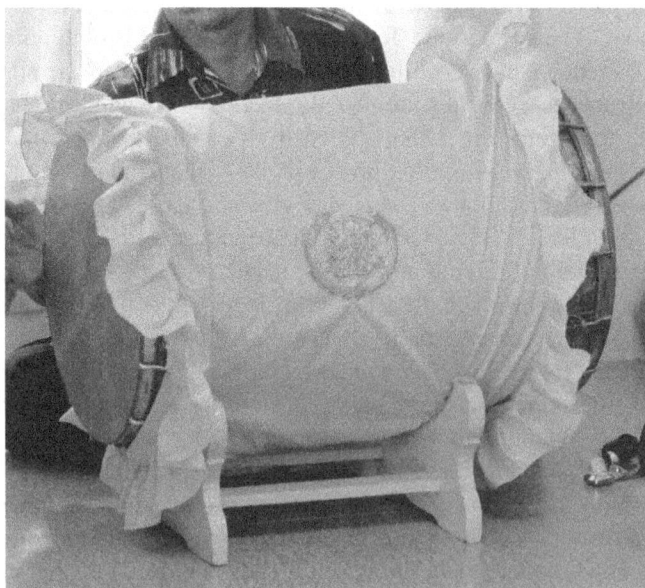

Figure 3.5. The silver *Gendang* nobat of Terengganu. *Source*: Photograph by Raja Iskandar, March 2011.

Serunai

The *serunai* is a quadruple-reed shawm with seven or eight holes, also known as *surnay* (Iran), *zurna* (Turkey) and *shahnai* (India). It is made of a bored conical hardwood, usually *kayu nangka* (jackfruit wood) or *merbau* (*Intsia Bijuga*), while ivory is used in Terengganu (see figure 3.7). The main body of the *serunai* is called *batang* (literally long straight object) or *baluh*. The tubular body expands slightly towards the end and is attached to a bell-shaped *ceropong*, made of moulded silver or brass usually ornamented with *pucuk rebung* (bamboo shoots) decorative motifs. The *kepala serunai* (literally, 'head of serunai') is attached on the other end of the instrument and is comprised of *pipit* (reed), *caping* (a small silver lip disc with a hole in centre) and *mali* (a conical silver tube that holds the reed) (Matusky 1993, 29). The *pipit* is made of four small, triangular-shaped dried palm leaves tied to the *mali,* which is placed below the circular *caping* or lip disc (see figure 3.6). The whole *serunai* comprising the *kepala serunai, baluh* and *ceropong* is between 42 to 43.5 cm in length.

In Perak the top six holes of the *serunai* are called *lubang petik* (literally, 'plucking hole') and the one at the bottom is called *lubang jerit* (literally, 'screaming hole'). The instrument is played by inserting the whole *pipit* into the player's mouth until the lips rest against the *caping*. Sound is then produced using a technique known as circular breathing, which is a combination

Figure 3.6. The *Pipit* and *Caping* of the Kedah *Serunai. Source:* Photograph by Raja Iskandar, August 2013.

of two blowing methods, played alternately to create a continuous, unbroken sound. One method requires air being blown from the diaphragm, with the other method from the mouth using muscles of the cheek. While this is being performed, air is concurrently inhaled through the nose to refill the lungs. These two methods are alternated smoothly in order to ensure the continuity of the *serunai* melody.

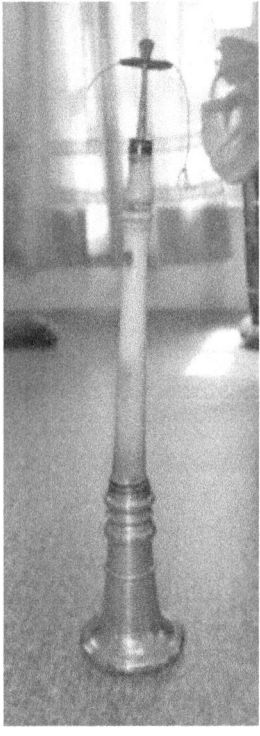

Figure 3.7. The ivory and silver *Serunai* of the Terengganu nobat. *Source*: Photograph by Raja Iskandar, March 2011.

Nafiri

The word *nafiri* comes from the Arabic *nafr*, which means a 'group' or 'troop', usually military. In standard Arabic the term *naffīr āmm* is used to refer to the general call to arms. The word *naffīr* later came to be associated with the long trumpet due to its use for military purposes. The *nafiri* of the Malay nobat is a long conical trumpet measuring between 80 to 83 cm in length. Its mouthpiece or circular opening is about 3 cm in diameter, and unlike modern trumpets it is part of the main tubular body of the *nafiri* and not separated. The body expands slightly downwards towards a detachable flower-like bell ornamented with *pucuk rebung* motifs, measuring between 14

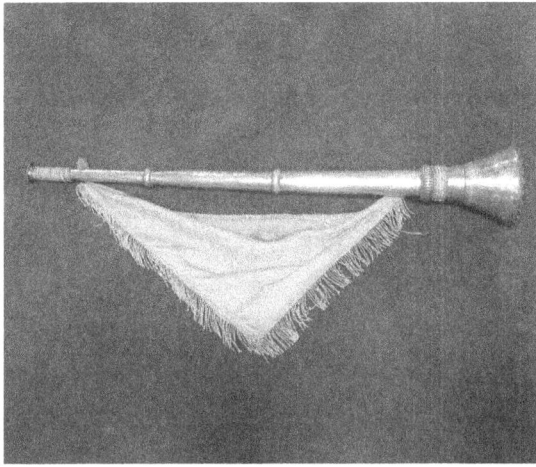

Figure 3.8. *Nafiri* of the Perak nobat. *Source*: Photograph by Raja Iskandar, December 2006.

to 19.5 cm in diameter. Made of molded silver, the *nafiri* has no finger holes and is used to play only one or two notes.

The *nafiri* is played by placing the closed lips into the circular opening of the mouthpiece until they are covered by the rim. Sound is then produced when air is blown through the opening that vibrates and resonates the mouthpiece, and as with the Western trumpet, pitch can be altered by adjusting the embouchure.

Figure 3.9. Engravings on the Terengganu *Nafiri*. *Source*: Photograph by Raja Iskandar, March 2011.

Gong

Gong is only used in the Kedah and Brunei nobat. There is however literary and other evidence that the instrument was earlier used by the Perak and other ensembles in the Malay world as well (see figure 3.10). Numerous references are found to the gong being played together with other instruments of the nobat (e.g. *Misa Melayu* 59:6). The *gong* used by the Kedah nobat is made of bronze and measures 48.5 cm in diameter while its boss is 14 cm (see figure 3.11).

Figure 3.10. Old nobat instruments in the Riau Kandis Museum, Sumatera. *Source*: Photograph by Arkib Negara Malaysia, ANM 2001/0020679.

Figure 3.11. The knobbed gong of the Kedah nobat. *Source*: Photograph by Raja Iskandar, August 2013.

Kopak-Kopak

Kopak-kopak (figure 3.12) is only used by the Terengganu nobat today, but according to players of the Kedah nobat, this instrument was also part of Kedah's original ensemble. It is a pair of small handheld cymbals about 20 cm in diameter, made of copper and attached to a string. *Kopak-kopak* is probably a later addition to the standard ensemble since there was no mention of the instrument in early Malay literature as part of *alat kerajaan*, or 'state regalia'. It is, however, mentioned alongside other instruments, including the instruments of the nobat played during auspicious occasions.

Figure 3.12. *Kopak-Kopak* of the Terengganu nobat.
Source: Photograph by Raja Iskandar, March 2011.

Mahaguru

Mahaguru (Great Teacher), or *Tongkat Semambu* (*Semambu* Stick), is a long stick about 173 cm in length carved from the *semambu* or Melaka cane and wrapped in yellow cloth (figure 3.13). Although not a musical instrument, the *mahaguru* is an important part of the Kedah nobat ensemble and is held by the leader of the group during a performance. Its inclusion could be attributed to the magical properties of the Melaka cane, which is believed to be the protector of the nobat. Instruments of the five Malay nobat ensembles are listed in table 3.1.

Table 3.1. Instruments of the Malay Nobat

Kedah	Perak	Selangor	Terengganu	Brunei
Nahara	Nengkara	Nengkara	Nekara	Negara
Nafiri	Nafiri	Nafiri	Nafiri	Serunai
Serunai	Serunai	Serunai	Serunai	A pair of Gendang
Gendang Ibu	Gendang Nobat or Melalu	Gendang Nobat or Melalu	A pair of Gendang Nobat	Labik
Gendang Anak				A pair of Gongs
Gong				
Mahaguru	Gendang Kecil or Peningkah	Gendang Kecil or Peningkah	A pair of Kopak-Kopak	

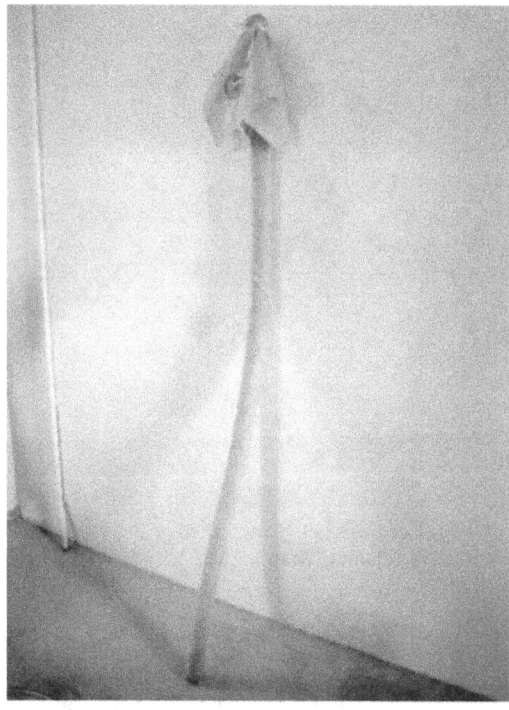

Figure 3.13. *Mahaguru* of the Kedah nobat. *Source*: Photograph by Raja Iskandar, August 2013.

SOUND PRODUCTION AND TRADITIONAL BELIEFS

The music of the *tablakhana*, *naqqarakhana* and *naubat* traditions in the Middle East and South Asia was loud and dramatic. It was produced by a large ensemble playing big drums and the sound was used in wars to incite courage among soldiers and demoralise the enemy. It was played to signal prayer times, announce important events and mark political boundaries. The Malay nobat carries this centuries-old Islamicate tradition to this day and the music is still considered a sound that signals something. Like the conch shells of ancient India, horns of Europe and the *beduk* drums of the Malay village mosque, the main function of the nobat is to signal events—royal events. However, the sound of the nobat is much less intense due to the small number of instruments. The music and overall sound of the nobat is not shaped by the different shades of emotions normally attributed to music-making, hence the highly monotonous nature of its form, intensity, melody and dynamics.

For centuries, the nobat has been governed and shaped by layers of underlying traditional Malay beliefs in relation to the royal institution. These include the primary concepts of *daulat* (divine essence) and *tulah* (divine retribution). All the instruments of the nobat and its music are considered *berdaulat* or bestowed with *daulat*. The nobat musicians, as subjects of the sultan, are subservient to the ruler, his family and the palace. Any transgression or disobedience leads to divine retribution and this subservience is reflected in the music. The aesthetics of the nobat lies in the structure of the pieces, largely guided by the rhythms and carefully executed according to tradition. No changes or improvisation are allowed, ensuring the nobat's music meets the ceremony's requirements, contributing to an overall successful ceremony.

The sounds of the nobat are also believed to be determined by how well the instruments are 'maintained' and 'respected', governed by certain *pantang larang* (taboos) (Raja Iskandar 2018). Instruments are wrapped in yellow cloth, placed in a special room and must not be stepped over. Rituals are regularly performed by the state shaman and leader of the nobat ensemble to ensure the instruments are 'alive' and produce the desired sound. This is associated with the inherent Malay belief in the unseen and indwelling spirits in the instruments called *saka* or djinn. The greatness of a sultan is not only manifested through the grandeur of the palace and ceremonies, but also the sound of the nobat. Many view the *daulat* of the sultan based on the 'eerines' and 'grandness' of the sounds produced by the nobat ensemble. However, in recent years some of the rituals have been altered or discarded due to the process of Islamization.

FUNCTIONS

Istiadat Pertabalan (Installation Ceremony)

The *raja berdaulat*, as a God-sanctioned sovereign ruler and the royal institution, needs to be justly manifested through elaborate ceremonies called *istiadat*. These ceremonies cover almost every aspect of a royal's life, from the cradle to the grave. Every transition in a series of a sovereign's life passage from birth, puberty, marriage, fatherhood, elevation to royal status, birthday celebration and death are marked by a certain *istiadat*, or 'ritual'. However, the sultan may not be present in all of these ceremonies and the nobat may be played with or without his presence. While most of the ceremonies are public in nature, some only involve close family members and invited guests. The nobat ensembles of different states may vary in the *istiadat* they are involved in but share a particularly important one: the *istiadat pertabalan*, or 'installation ceremony'.

The *istiadat pertabalan* can be seen as the most important ceremony in a Malay court since it officially legitimises the rule of a Sultan. *Tabal* comes from the Arabic word *tabl*, which means to 'beat a drum, drumbeat or drum' (Madina 1997, 395) and is the etymological basis of a number of drum names from the Middle East to South Asia (e.g. *tabla*). In the *Kamus Dewan* (Teuku Iskandar 1986, 1157), *tabal* is described as 'a gathering (or ceremony) to officially celebrate the crowning of a Raja'. The essential importance of the drums in the *istiadat* resulted in the term *tabal* ultimately being used to denote the whole installation ceremony. One of the earliest descriptions of an *istiadat pertabalan* where the nobat was used can be found in the *Hikayat Raja-Raja Pasai*:

> *Maka Sultan pun memakai selengkap pakaian kerajaan nugeraha dari Mekah, karna akan ditabalkan. Maka segala hulubalang pun sekaliannya bersaf-saf mengadap nobat Ibrahim Khalil, bentara pun berdiri berjabat salih, dan segala pegawai pun masing-masing membawa jabatannya. Maka genderang tabal pun dipalu oranglah dan segala bunyi-bunyian pun berbunyilah. (Pasai 32:3)*

> Then the Sultan wore the complete state attire, a gift from Mecca, for he is to be drummed (installed). Then all the nobles sat in rows facing the nobat 'Ibrahim Khalil' [and] the herald stood up holding the sword and all the officers carrying their own. Then the installation drum was beaten and all the instruments sounded.

This text mentions the 'complete set of state attire' worn by the Sultan, which was a gift (*nugeraha*) from Mecca. This shows the importance of special sanctioned attire being worn by a would-be ruler to set him apart from the others. The ceremony has to be attended by nobles (*hulubalang*) and officials (*pegawai*) sitting in rows (*bersaf-saf*) according to their ranks while facing (*mengadap*) the nobat 'Ibrahim Khalil'. This moment was followed by the firing of cannons and chants of '*daulat*' honouring the newly installed sultan. The playing of the nobat and firing of cannons at such occasions are still practiced in Malay courts today.

The precise sitting positions of dignitaries in facing the nobat in an *adat pertabalan* continued to be emphasised in fifteenth century Melaka, as narrated by the *Sejarah Melayu*:

Adapun jika mengadap nobat, barang orang besar-besar dari kiri gendang; barang orang kecil dari kanan gendang. (SM 73:72)

If facing the nobat, those of higher rank (sit) on the left side of the drum; those of lesser rank on the right side of the drum.

This only applies today when the nobat is placed facing directly towards the sultan, who is seated on the east side of the *balairong* or throne room.

Today, the remaining Malay sultanates have their own unique ways of conducting the *Istiadat Pertabalan* while maintaining the central elements of the ceremony including the special attire of the sultan, sitting positions of dignitaries, the chanting of '*daulat tuanku*' and, of course, the sounding of the nobat. In the Perak court, considered the last semblance of the Melaka sultanate, the *Istiadat Pertabalan* evolved into an elaborate process that involves four further ceremonies, *Tabal Kerajaan*, *Tabal Adat*, *Tabal Pusaka* and visits to the graves of previous Sultans (Tung 1999).

Another interesting aspect of the installation ceremony of Perak is the *Tabal Pusaka*. A day after *Tabal Adat*, *Tabal Pusaka*, formerly known as *Tabal Jin* (Installation of the Jinn) is held at the Balairong Seri and Panca Persada situated in the grounds of the Iskandariah Palace. Although other Malay courts of the Peninsular may have 'offering' rituals for guardian *djinns* or spirits, the ceremony was made an official one in Perak. The ritual remains an important part of the Sultan's installation process, even though the title was changed from *Tabal Jin* to *Tabal Pusaka*.[9] The ceremony is witnessed by a handful of invited guests, especially close royal relatives and state dignitaries.[10]

Istiadat Menjunjung Duli (Installation of Heirs and Chiefs Ceremony)

Possibly the most important ceremony after the installation of the sultan is the *Istiadat Menjunjung Duli*. This ceremony is conducted to appoint and install future successors to the throne (*waris negeri*) and noblemen (*orang-orang besar*). They are given royal titles in order of precedence and selected based on pedigree and merit. Traditionally this ceremony was also held as an event where chiefs declare their loyalty and allegiance to the sultan. In Perak, *istiadat menjunjung duli* is done biennially involving the act of kneeling on the floor and moving forward three times by the *waris negeri* and *orang-orang besar*. The ceremony is mentioned in the eighteenth-century Perak manuscript *Misa Melayu*:

> *Raja Muda naik ke balai lalu masuk menjunjung duli. Kemudian maka segala anak raja-raja dan orang besar-besar pun semuanya dipanggil naik lalu masuk berganti-ganti menjunjung duli baginda; demikianlah adatnya raja Melayu di dalam negeri Perak. Adapun setelah itu, beraraklah Sultan Iskandar Inayat Syah di atas takhta kerajaan.* (Misa 54:21)
>
> The Crown Prince enters the hall to pledge allegiance. Later all the princes and chiefs were called to enter in turns to pledge allegiance to the His Highness; that is the custom of Malay rulers in Perak. Then, Sultan Iskandar Inayat Syah was taken in a procession on his throne.

The ceremony also displays strong Hindu influences. Before the start of the official ceremony, the recipients would be asked to gather outside of the palace gate. They would be 'annointed' by the Toh Seri Nara Diraja, or the 'Court Herald'. The princes and chiefs would then be individually called to stand near the steps of the gate and a banana leaf is place over their heads. The *ciri* or proclamation written in Sanskrit is then read aloud by the Toh Seri Nara Diraja while standing on a stool. The recipients are then sprinkled with rice and scented water, a form of blessing practiced in Hinduism, before being taken to room to change.

Istiadat Kemangkatan, Pemakaman dan Berkabung (Passing, Burial and Mourning Ceremony)

The passing of a sultan is signalled by a gun salute. The sultan's body is bathed by the State Mufti and is then taken to the Balai Seri or Audience Room to be placed in a coffin wrapped in yellow. The body will lie in state until the new Sultan is announced, and the coffin is taken out of the palace for the *Istiadat Pemakaman*. There will be a mourning period or *Istiadat Berkabung* for one hundred days. During this period the drums of the nobat are wrapped in white cloths. During the reign of Sultan Iskandar Shah of Perak (1752–1765), the nobat was played during his procession to visit the grave of his father Sultan Muzaffar Shah (1728–1752) as recorded in the *Misa Melayu*:

> *Adapun setelah sudah tambak dan nisan itu pun, diaraklah dengan sepertinya dengan gendang negara nafiri serunai dan payung panji-panji dan beberapa pula derma sepanjang jalan itu.* (Misa Melayu 59:6)
>
> And after the grave has been covered and the tombstone erected, [the sultan] was then carried with the accompaniment of *gendang, negara, nafiri, serunai* and state umbrellas while offering charity along the way.

Besides the sultan, the nobat was also played to accompany the burial of close relatives and consorts. The burial ceremony of Tunku Abdullah Thani, son of the Sultan of Kedah in 1917 was an elaborate event which involved the playing of the nobat (*Straits Times*, 2 August 1917, 6). In the 1950s there were objections by members of the Malaysian Islamic Party (PAS) on the playing of the nobat during burials (Tunku Abdul Rahman 1983, 3) but the practice continued. As recent as 2003, the Kedah nobat was played during the burial ceremony of Tuanku Bahiyah, the Sultanah of Kedah who served as the fifth Raja Permaisuri Agong (1970–1975).

Istiadat Nikah Kahwin (Marriage Ceremony)

Apart from solemn ceremonies the nobat has been traditionally played to mark joyous occasions such as royal weddings. *Misa Melayu* describes how its instruments were played in celebration of the marriage of the Raja Muda, Raja Iskandar to Raja Budak Rasul in 1752:

> *Maka daripada siangnya itu diaraklah anak raja yang perempuan itu tujuh kali berkeliling kota dengan segala bunyi-bunyian gong, gendang, serunai, nafiri, negara dan segala bunyi-bunyian yang lain-lain pun berbunyilah semuanya.* (*Misa Melayu* 47:23)

> And from early in the day the princess was paraded seven times around the city with all the sounds of gong, gendang, serunai, nafiri, negara and together with all the other sounds.

Centuries later the sound of the nobat was again heard during the marriage of a Perak princess, Raja Zubaida Binti Sultan Sir 'Abdu'l Jalil with Sultan Sir Alaudin Sulaiman Shah of Selangor in May 1910, as reported in the *Straits Times* (1 June 1910). The most recent royal marriage was that of the Raja Muda of Perak, Raja Nazrin Shah in 2007, which saw the ensemble playing during the *bersanding* ceremony, where Sultans from other states and dignitaries do the *menepung tawar* (sprinkling of scented water and rice) on the royal couple. In Perak the *Istiadat Nikah Kahwin* can be divided into five main *istiadat*, which are *Istiadat Meminang* (Engagement Ceremony), *Istiadat Akad Nikah* (Solemnization Ceremony), *Istiadat Berlimau* (Bridegroom Bathing Ceremony), *Istiadat Bersanding* (Ceremonial Sitting Ceremony) and *Istiadat Bersiram Sampat* (Couple Bathing Ceremony). The nobat is involved in all of these ceremonies.

Other ceremonies involving the nobat (which varies between sultanates) include:

1. *Istiadat Keputeraan* (Birth Ceremony),
2. *Istiadat Memulih Perkakas-Perkakas Kerajaan* ('Revival' of the State Regalia Ceremony)
3. *Istiadat Bersiram Hamil* (Pregnancy Bath Ceremony)
4. *Istiadat Bersanding Hamil* (Pregnancy Seating Ceremony)
5. *Istiadat Bertaruh Sirih* (Placing of the Betel Chew Ceremony)—performed to *meminang* or engage a midwife.
6. *Istiadat Berkhatam Qur'an* (Completion of the Qur'an Ceremony). For a prince, this is followed by the *Istiadat Berkhatan* (Circumcision Ceremony).
7. *Istiadat Bertindik* (Ear Piercing Ceremony). In Perak, this ceremony is preceded by a number of *istiadat*. Similar to *Istiadat Berkhatan*, lustration water from seven tributaries is taken in preparation for the *Istiadat Berlimau* (Bathing Ceremony) and *Istiadat Bersiram Bertindik* (Ear Piercing Bathing Ceremony) where nobat is played during both journeys.

The numerous Malay royal *istiadat*, are a combination of traditional Malay practices, influenced by animistic, Hindu-Buddhist and Islamic influences. They are a continuation of the Srivijaya customs prior to the establishment of the Melaka sultanate where the Malay royal customs were developed and perfected in the fifteenth century. The royal '*sembah*' for example, where a person's palms are pressed together with fingers pointing upwards and placed on the forehead when saluting a sultan, is derived from the Anjali Mudra hand gesture practiced in Hinduism. It is still practiced as a form of greetings and salutation in Southeast Asia. Muslim-influenced ceremonies can be seen in the *Istiadat Berkhatam Qur'an and Istiadat Berkhatan* which are rites of passage for every practicing Muslim. However, some *istiadat* may have elements of both Islam and Hinduism, such as the marriage ceremony.

Religious and Healing Rituals

The nobat was also performed in the past to signal the five daily Muslim prayer times or *salah*. Although the voice of a *muezzin* or *bilal* was traditionally used to call prayer from the time of the Prophet Muhammad, the nobat began to be used in the courts of the Abbassid caliphs. This practice continued in the Malay courts and was recorded in several early Malay texts. The *Hikayat Patani* narrates how the nobat was used during the *Subuh* (early morning) and *Jumaat* (Friday) prayers in the court of Patani during the sixteenth century (see chapter 4). This is still practiced today in Kedah where the nobat plays before the *Subuh* (early morning), *Maghrib* (evening) and Friday prayers. In certain parts of India, the naubat is performed in Sufi shrines and mosques to call for prayer.

Currently, other than daily prayers, the nobat is also used to indicate other Muslim religious events, like the coming of Ramadan and Muslim celebrations of *'Eid al-Fitr* and *'Eid al-Adha*. In Terengganu, the nobat is played to signal the *iftar* or breaking of fast during the holy month of Ramadan and the evenings of the two *'Eid*. The Perak nobat is played on the evenings of the twenty-eighth, twenty-ninth and thirtieth of Syaaban, to signal the coming of Ramadan and is followed by performances on certain evenings of Ramadan, prior to Syawal, in which *'Eid al-Fitr* falls on the first. The same is done for *'Eid al-Adha*, only this time it is only for three days prior to the celebration, which are on the seventh, eighth and ninth of Zulhijjah. In the early mornings of both *'Eid al-Fitri* and *'Eid al-Adha*, nobat will also be played outside of the sultan's room to 'wake' him up and also signal the morning bath. On both days, the ensemble will also travel a short distance to the Ubudiah Mosque to signal the Sultan's arrival for the *'Eid* prayers and his departure.

The nobat is also used for healing purposes, either for the sultan or commoners. In Perak, the rituals are normally done by the Raja Cik Muda Pawang Diraja (Court Shaman) or Toh Setia Guna, leader of the ensemble. Normally, incense is burned and water (which has been blessed by the shaman) is poured into the *nafiri* from one opening to the other into a container. The water is then used to wash a patient's face or is drunk. In the old days, when a Sultan was sick, the nobat was played beside his bed and the blessed *nafiri* water is given for him to drink in order to bring back his *semangat* or strength. This was based on the traditional belief in the *daulat* or power of the instruments as part of the court regalia. In Kedah, despite the sultan's order, food offerings are still being made by certain members of the Malay society at the Balai Nobat in order to obtain fulfilment of certain wishes or heal the sick.

The Repertoire

The repertoire of the remaining nobat is well documented. However not all of it is still being played on a regular basis and throughout the centuries some pieces have been newly added, others changed, while still more have probably been lost. For example, the eighteenth-century *Misa Melayu* states that there were originally eight *lagu* (pieces) in the Perak repertoire and another eight new ones were added later. The *lagu* 'Nobat Isyak', which was part of the Perak repertoire listed in *Misa Melayu*, was changed to 'Nobat Raja' in *Adat Lembaga Orang-Orang Melayu Di Dalam Negeri Perak Darul Ridzuan* published in 1935. Apart from *Misa Melayu*, the other known literature that documents the nobat repertoire is *Hikayat Patani,* which includes instructions on how to play the repertoire (see chapter 4). The earliest known nobat lagu was probably 'Ibrahim Khalil',[11] as mentioned in the *Hikayat Raja-Raja Pasai,* which was part of the Johor-Riau repertoire and has become part of the Terengganu repertoire today while in Selangor it is known as 'Ibrahim Khalilullah'.

Other old *lagu* that are still played today include 'Nobat Iskandar' (*Syair Seratus Siti* and *Syair Siti Zubaidah*), 'Nobat Perang' (*Hikayat Patani*) and 'Nobat Iskandar Zulkarnain'[12] (*Hikayat Hang Tuah*). Pieces that are no longer found in any of the present ensembles include 'Gendang Adi Mula' (*Sejarah Melayu* and *Hikayat Patani*) and 'Nobat Ibrahim' (*Syair Seratus Siti*), as well as most of those listed in the *Hikayat Patani*. There are also a number pieces with similar titles found in the nobat ensembles such as 'Lagu Arak-Arak' (Arak-Arakan) and 'Lagu Perang' (or 'Nobat Perang').

Songs of the nobat were also referred to as '*man*' from the word '*mantra*' (Linehan 1951, 67; Ku Zam Zam 1993, 182). However, this term was not found in early Malay literature and denotes a different meaning in the Perak and Selangor nobat (see Raja Iskandar 2018). Below is the full list of the present repertoire of the Malay nobat (table 3.2).

Table 3.2. Repertoire of the Malay Nobat

Kedah	Perak	Selangor	Terengganu	Brunei
1. Raja Burong	1. Gendang Berangkat (Lagu Iskandar in Selangor)		1. Lagu Iskandar Shah	1. Gendang Perang
2. Lagu Seratan				2. Raja Lalu
3. Lagu Belayar			2. Lagu Ibrahim Khalil	3. Arak-Arakan
4. Lagu Bayat	2. Arak Antelas			4. Alih-Alihan Tengah
5. Lagu Bayok	3. Kubang Si Kumali		3. Lagu Seri Istana (Semang)	5. Alih-Alihan Ujung
6. Lagu Sapindin	4. Rama-Rama Terbang Tinggi			
7. Lagu Malawala	5. Arak-Arakan Panjang		4. Lagu Anak Kuda Ragam/ Raja Beradu	
8. Saduruna				
9. Mambang Berkayuh	6. Arak-Arakan Pendek		5. Lagu Seri Istana	
10. Mambang China	7. Dang Gidang			
11. Bujang Ilir	8. Puteri Mandi Mayang (Puteri Lenggang Mayang in Selangor)		6. Lagu Petang Khamis	
12. Tempoyak			7. Lagu Palu-Palu Melayu	
13. Gendang Anak	9. Jong Beralih		8. Lagu Lapan	
14. Lumat	10. Lenggang Encik Kobat (Ibrahim Khalilullah in Selangor)		9. Lagu Petang Jumaat	
15. Dewa Raja/ Hayat				
16. Arak-Arak			10. Lagu Palu-Palu Nyiri	
17. Berlimau	11. Gendang Perang			
18. Palu (Penghulu)	12. Anak Raja Basuh Kaki		11. Lagu Petang Khamis Perak	
19. Lagu Perang	13. Nobat Tabal		12. Lagu Arak-Arak	
20. Raja Berangkat	14. Nobat Khamis			
21. Raja Bertabal	15. Nobat Subuh		13. Lagu Perang	
	16. Nobat Raja (Isya)			

Based on the titles of the nobat pieces from different states, it is clear that most of them are played to accompany certain specific occasions. For example, 'Nobat Tabal' ('Installation Nobat') is played during the installation of a Sultan as the title implies, 'Raja Berangkat' ('The Raja Leaves') accompanies the ruler when he arrives or leaves and 'Nobat Subuh' ('Early Morning Nobat') is played in early morning. The titles also carry certain indigenous cultural, spiritual and religious connotations. 'Puteri Mandi Mayang' ('The Princess Bathes') and 'Anak Raja Basuh Kaki' ('The Prince Washes His Feet') are played during the bathing ceremony of the Sultan and consort during the installation or marriage ceremonies. The bathing ceremony is a form of 'purification' and is derived from Hindu, particularly Brahmin traditions and can also be seen in the Thai royal tradition. 'Mambang China' ('Chinese Spirit') and 'Mambang Berkayuh' ('Paddling Spirit') indicate the traditional Malay belief in the supernatural or guardian spirits that reside in certain places such as trees, rivers and rocks. Islamic influence is clearly seen in the pieces titled 'Ibrahim Khalilullah' ('Ibrahim the Friend of Allah') and 'Iskandar Shah' ('King Alexander'), two important figures in the Islamic faith and 'Nobat Isyak', signaling the night prayer time. For centuries these underlying beliefs form the layers in which the Malays shape their culture, especially within the royal institution. These pieces went through a process of adaptation, syncretization and indigenization, reflected through the syncretic use of traditional Malay and Arabic words in the song titles. Based on a number of early Malay literature, some of the nobat pieces existed as early as the fourteenth century and a list of the Perak repertoire was recorded in the eighteenth century. However, how the songs were composed, developed or adopted is not known.

THE MUSICIANS

Musicians of the Kedah, Perak and Selangor nobat are called *orang kalur* or *orang kalo* and it is a hereditary status (see Raja Iskandar 2018). Linehan (1951, 66) suggests that the term 'kalur' probably came from the Malay word *susur galur*, which means 'going back to the origins', or 'pedigree', and *orang kalur* was thus translated as 'men who have to do with genealogies'. This idea is supported by Sheppard (1983, 19) who argues that the *orang kalur* were also keepers of the royal family records. The Perak and Selangor musicians come from the same *orang kalur* family mainly based in central Perak. This tradition goes back at least to 1766 when Raja Lumu, the first Sultan of Selangor was awarded a nobat by Sultan Mahmud Shah of Perak (r. 1765–1773) (Andaya 1979, 271). However, the family's connection to the

Kedah *orang kalur* remains a mystery and it can only be assumed here that they are probably related due to the Sultan of Melaka's gift of the nobat in the fifteenth century, as narrated in the *Sejarah Melayu*. Similar to the *orang kalur*, the Indragiri nobat of Sumatera was once played by an ethnic group called Suku Mamak who were loyal subjects of the sultan, skilled craftsmen and shamans (Kartomi 1997, 6–7).

The Terengganu and Brunei musicians however do not strictly adhere to the hereditary rule; in the case of Terengganu, several the musicians are instead from the royal family itself. A list of Terengganu nobat players found in a letter dated 1939 in the court records shows four of the seven members carry the title 'Tengku' or 'Engku', which indicates royal descent. One of the players on the list, Tengku Muda, was the grandfather of Tengku Ibrahim, who at present plays the nafiri for the Terengganu nobat.

The idea of hereditary royal musicians is rooted in Hindu tradition. The Perak *orang kalur* believe they are descendants of the *orang muntah lembu* or literally 'people of the bull's vomit'. This is derived from the story in the *Sejarah Melayu* about the miraculous appearance of a herald named Bat from a bull's vomit. In Hinduism, a white bull known as Nandi is considered sacred and a servant of Lord Siva. Here, the bull's vomit symbolises the sacred nature of the *orang kalur* who were given the authority to install the Sultan, as keepers of royal genealogy and *adat istiadat* (customs and ceremonies).

MUSIC OF THE NOBAT

The music of the nobat has been described as 'discordantt, clamorous and full of noise' (Mundy 1919, 123), 'weird' (*Singapore Free Press* 1895, 3) and '*gegak-gempita*' (boisterous) (*Tuhfat al-Nafis* 194:7). These descriptions were reflective of the function of the ensemble within the context of court ceremonies throughout the centuries. Like its South Asian and Middle Eastern predecessors, the nobat continued to be performed, either indoors or outdoors, for royal proclamations and religious celebrations; thus, its sound needed to be heard a considerable distance. Consequently, the intensity of the sound produced was as important as the selection of pieces to be played during a ceremony. It is not surprising, especially to a Western ear that this constantly high aural intensity, produced with a combination of deep sounding drums, clashing of cymbals and the continuously piercing sound of the *serunai* may seem 'weird' and simply amount to 'noise'. However, this 'discordant' music actually has a considerably high level of organization and complexity that is worth examining.

My study of the music of the nobat here is based on a number of pieces recorded from the Perak, Terengganu and Kedah repertoire between 2006 and 2013. My analysis also draws on the previous work of Meilu Ho (1992) and Matusky (2004) on the Kedah nobat, and my own earlier work on the Perak nobat (2018). Since the Selangor nobat is identical in repertoire and instruments to its Perak counterpart, its music will not be considered in this section. It is not the main purpose of this book to fully document and analyse the music of all existing ensembles; only a small selection of key pieces from the recordings will be analysed. For a full transcription of a nobat piece from the Perak nobat, refer to the appendix.

Rhythm

The Malay nobat is a percussion-dominated ensemble, hence the general use of the term *gendang tabal* (installation drum) or *gendang nobat* (nobat drum) to denote the whole ensemble. In Kedah and Terengganu, a *lagu* or *ragam* (song or piece) is largely determined by both the melody and rhythmic patterns while in Perak it is only the rhythm that is important. This concept is clearly stated in the *Adat Lembaga Orang-Orang Melayu Di Dalam Negeri Perak Darul Ridzuan*:

> *bunyian yang lain itu hanyalah alatan bagi mengelokkan suara nobat.* (Raja Bendahara 1935, 39)
>
> the other instruments are there just as tools to beautify the sound of the nobat.

The 'other instruments' stated above refers to the *serunai* and *nafiri*, and in the case of other ensembles could include the *gong* and *kopak-kopak*. The use of 'nobat' in this context refers to the three main drums of a nobat ensemble: the *nengkara* and a pair of *gendang*. However, according to the Perak players, there is a specific *gendang nobat* which is the bigger of the two-barrel drums also known as *gendang melalu*. In Kedah and Terengganu these drums are called *gendang ibu* (mother drum) and *gendang anak* (child drum), although both are similar in size.

The rhythms of the drums build upon repeating patterns or figures. In the case of the Perak and Selangor nobat, a *lagu* may have a pattern that ranges from a short 6-beat to a long 136-beat phrase. The large rhythmic groupings are typical of traditional Southeast Asian music, which are generally binary or can be divided into smaller beat units of usually 4 or 8 beats. Rhythmic patterns of the Kedah nobat are largely comprised of 16 beats that are separated into smaller phrases (Matusky 2004, 239–45). In addition, the cyclical rhythms of the Malay nobat are also found to have a mixture of regular and irregular metres.

In Kedah, the basic rhythm of a piece is played by the two *gendang*, while in Perak it is the *nengkara* that identifies a piece. The Perak *nengkara* is played in unison with *gendang nobat* (also called *gendang melalu*), while the *gendang peningkah* plays interlocking rhythms to complete the whole rhythm section. In Terengganu and Kedah, the pair of *gendang* generally plays in unison while interlocking with the *nahara* or *negara*. The unison playing of the *gendang* strengthens the rhythmic patterns of a *lagu* while providing different timbres.

Nobat pieces are sectional, consisting of an introduction and repeated rhythmic sections. A piece starts with an introduction, signalled either by the long single notes of the *nafiri* (Perak, Selangor and Terengganu), *serunai* (Kedah) and followed by the *nengkara* that determines the tempo of the piece. In Perak the *serunai* plays the melody to beautify the piece until the *nafiri* or *nengkara* signals the end of a section or the *lagu*. As shown in figure 3.14, the *nengkara* starts right after the *nafiri* is played, followed in sequence by the *gendang nobat* and *gendang peningkah*. This is the standard sequence for most of the pieces in the Perak repertoire. *Gendang nobat* follows the pattern earlier since it plays in unison with *nengkara* and it is much simpler compared with *gendang peningkah* that has to wait until the right moment to *menyelang* or play intermittently. In the transcription below, the mnemonic 'tik' is represented by 't' and 'tam' by the capital 'T'; these are played by the left and right hand respectively on all three drums. The two *gendang* players use a drumstick to play the right-hand part.

The *nafiri* is also used in Terengganu to signal the start of a piece. However, as shown in figure 3.15, the three blows of the *nafiri* in 'Lagu Iskandar Shah' is preceded by a short pattern played by *gendang ibu* which is only ap-

Figure 3.14. Percussion introductory sequence in the piece 'Jong Beraleh' of the Perak nobat. *Source*: Excerpt from Raja Iskandar, 2018.

plicable to this piece. Unlike the Kedah nobat, the Terengganu *nafiri* is played without any accompaniment, and is followed with a section known as *guruh* (thunder). As the name implies, this part is played in unison with a crescendo and accelerando that creates a thunderous effect. This part of the piece is mentioned in the nineteenth-century *Kitab Thamaratul* (A. Samad Ahmad 1985, 45) that documented customs of the Johor-Riau nobat:

> *Apabila lepas tiga kali berbunyi nafiri itu, maka lalulah berbunyi guruhnya.*
>
> After the *nafiri* is sounded three times, then the thunder is heard.

Figure 3.15. Introduction section from 'Lagu Iskandar Shah' of the Terengganu nobat. *Source*: Transcribed by Raja Iskandar.

A similar instruction is found in *Hikayat Patani*, and the *guruh* technique is also played in Kedah, characterised by the syncopation of the two drums, also described in Malay as *terlingkah* or *tingkah* ('disagree' or 'alternate') (Meilu 1991, 115). In certain parts of the *guruh* section, the *gendang* can be seen mirroring each other where the right hand of the *gendang ibu* (played with a stick [S]) is simultaneously played by the left hand of the *gendang anak* (played with the hand [H]). (See figure 3.16.)

According to Henry Spiller (2004, 13), one of the characteristics ubiquitous to Southeast Asian music is the use of *ostinato* in instrumental accompaniment and this is clearly evident in the rhythmic patterns played by the drums of the nobat. The *nengkara* and *gendang* either play in unison or have a pattern each to repeat (in Perak it is the *gendang peningkah* that plays a different pattern) and this repeating combination forms the *lagu* or *ragam*. The repetition of the patterns not only provides a solid foundation for the accompaniment of the *serunai* but also identifies the piece.

In the piece 'Arak-Arak Atandis' from the Perak repertoire (figure 3.17) all the three percussion instruments play in unison and repeat the same rhythmic patterns in a cyclic manner. The only difference is the use of 'tik' and 'tam'

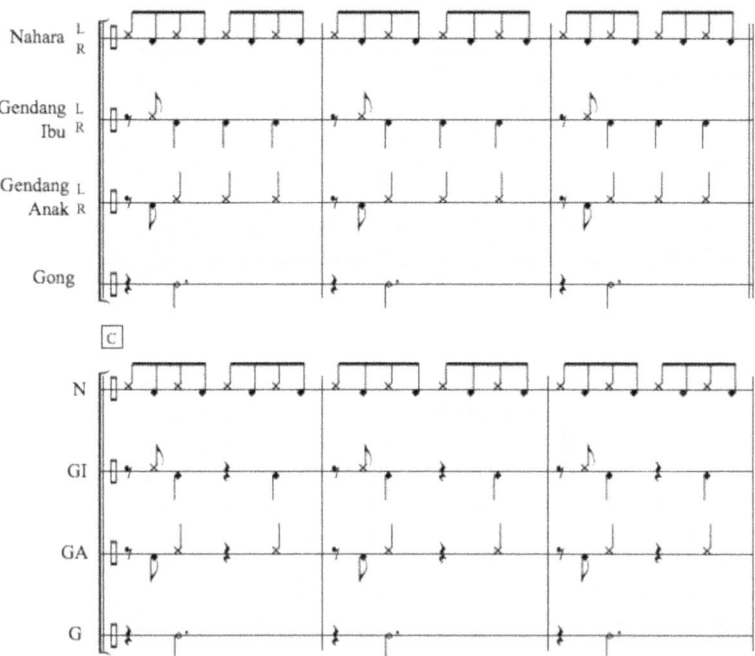

Figure 3.16. Excerpt of the 'guruh' section from 'Lagu Perang' of the Kedah nobat. *Source*: Transcribed by Raja Iskandar.

in striking the instrument (notice on the fourth beat of the second bar, the *gendang peningkah* plays using 'tam' while both the *nengkara* and *gendang* nobat use 'tik').

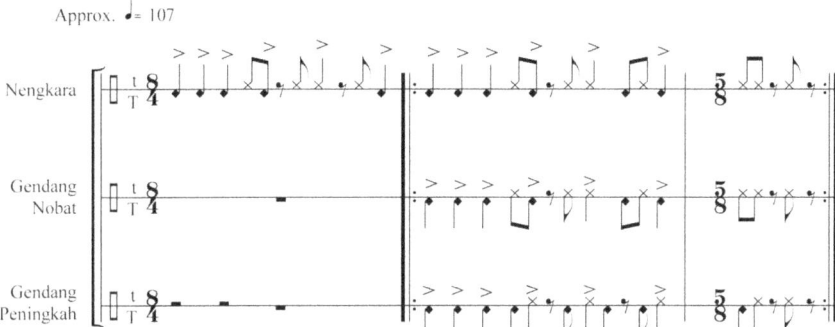

Figure 3.17. Repetitive patterns in 'Arak-Arak Atandis' of the Perak nobat. *Source*: Excerpt from Raja Iskandar 2018, 175.

Interlocking Parts

In my analysis of the music of the Perak nobat (Raja Iskandar 2018), apart from ostinatos mentioned earlier, there are interlocking rhythmic patterns that reinforce a certain *lagu*. This can be seen in the piece 'Dang Gendang' (figure 3.18), where the *gendang peningkah* plays a different pattern while the *nengkara* and *gendang* nobat play in unison. Interlocking patterns and ostinatos are characteristics of Southeast Asian traditional music and are found in the

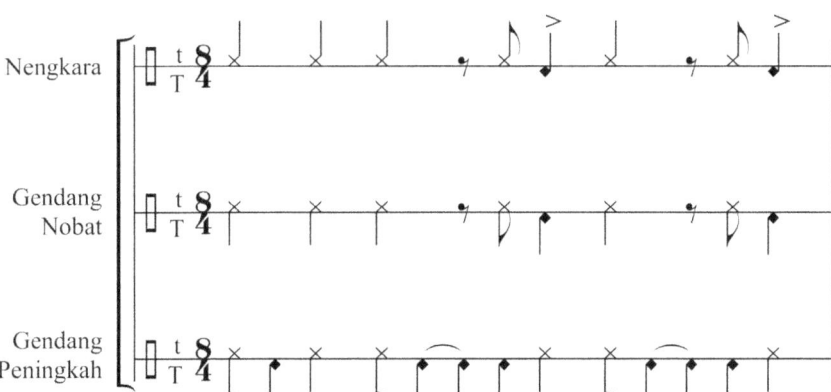

Figure 3.18. 8-beat *Gendang* patterns in 'Dang Gendang'. *Source*: Excerpt from Raja Iskandar 2018, 130.

music of *angklung* and *gamelan* of Indonesia, the Malay *wayang kulit* and in the bamboo and ensembles in the Philippines and Borneo (Matusky 2004, 50). This is part of the indigenization of the nobat apart from the inclusion of traditional beliefs into the performance of the ensemble.

Tempo and Dynamics

On average, nobat pieces are moderate in tempo. This establishes a mood of stateliness and majesty, befitting the status and power of a sultan. In Perak, there is no changing of tempi in the pieces, except when the *nengkara* tries to readjust the speed with the two *gendang*, or to end a piece. In Kedah and Terengganu, however, the changing of tempo in a piece is an important aspect of performance. The sections in a Kedah piece are marked by changes in tempo, which are signalled by different strokes of the drums and there can be up to four different tempi in a piece. The same applies in Terengganu where the rhythm accelerates in a section called *guruh* played at the beginning of a piece (see figure 3.15).

There are instances of dynamic changes as well, and, like changes in tempo, these are mainly applied to mark changes in sections. In Perak, there are slight crescendos towards the ending part, normally played by the *nengkara* to signal the end of the piece. Crescendos are also applied in the *guruh* section of a Terengganu piece to mark the opening of the piece. On average, the music of the three nobat ensembles is moderately loud with pieces played at almost the same level of intensity with minimal dynamic change and restricted timbral qualities. Although there are sectional divisions that structure the pieces, there are not many contrasting variations. With almost the same level of volume and timbre (in the case of Perak, the same melody), it is hardly surprising if the pieces ultimately provoke the same kind of emotional response among listeners. To an untrained ear, this regularity would add to the difficulty in differentiating the pieces.

Melody

Melody is played by the *serunai* in all of the nobat *lagu*. Although the *nafiri* can also be considered a melodic instrument, its function is limited only to playing static single notes, signalling the beginning and ending of a section or piece. Due to the manner in which the instrument is constructed and played, the *serunai* produces a loud and piercing sound that penetrates through the ensemble. In Perak, the function of the *serunai* is to only beautify rather than identify a piece and each *lagu* uses similar melodic contours and phrases, with limited variation or improvisation. The melody played by the Perak *serunai* is not meant to be individually discernable, which is contrary to the Western concept of melody as the abstract 'idea' that should be remembered in a piece of music. This treatment of melody is similar to the music of *wayang kulit Siam* in which identical melodic phrases played on the *serunai* are repeated in other different pieces in the repertoire.

Two types of melodic phrases (also called *lagu*) are played by the *serunai* in the Perak nobat, known as *senangin* (threadfin fish) and *merawan* (type of hardwood tree), which are indicated by the letters 's' and 'm' in figure 3.19. These phrases are played interchangeably in a particular piece or a medley of pieces until a signal is given on the *nengkara* to stop. The phrase *senangin*

Figure 3.19. The Serunai Lagu of the Perak nobat. *Source:* Excerpt from Raja Iskandar 2018.

has been described as *merayu* (pleading or begging) and is played using melodic ornaments and stepwise melodic contours that accelerate with semi- or whole-tone trills and embellishments. *Merawan* on the other hand is a phrase made up of long sustained and slow notes played *turun naik* (down and up) using semi- and whole-tone vibratos (Raja Iskandar 2018). It is interesting to note that the fast-moving and embellished notes are associated with a fish and the slower, long, 'up-down' phrases associated with a tree.

In contrast, in the Kedah and Terengganu nobat traditions both melody and rhythmic patterns are used to identity pieces. An analysis of the recordings of the three nobat indicates that the melody played by the *serunai* is generally a mixture of fast and highly embellished lines laced with ornaments such as trills, turns and acciaccatura; only in the case of the Perak nobat are long sustained notes commonly employed. In Perak, melody played by the *serunai* is not bounded by the rhythmic metres of the drums but is freer and fluid, resulting in a more linear feel to the music. In contrast, melodic lines are more pronounced in the Terengganu nobat and are rhythmically well synchronised with the drums. As shown in figure 3.20, the rhythm of the Terengganu *serunai* is firmly grounded and on certain beats precisely follows the drums indicating a carefully coordinated, pre-planned composition. There is no fixed tuning system for the *serunai*, so the pitch indicated in the transcription may vary slightly.

Figure 3.20. Excerpt from 'Lagu Iskandar Shah' of the Terengganu nobat. *Source:* Transcribed by Raja Iskandar.

Transmission

The repertoire and playing technique of the Malay nobat are passed down orally from generation to generation. In Perak learning usually starts at home where a student learns the basic rhythms of the sixteen pieces by tapping the mnemonic 'tik' and 'tam' using his forefingers on a table. This corresponds to the left- and right -hand movements of the drum player and is practiced before actual instruments are used. *Nengkara* parts are learned first as the instrument carries the main rhythm and determines the tempo of a piece. This is followed by the more complicated *peningkah* drum, which plays interlocking rhythm with the other two drums. Students are also taken to practice sessions and performances, and even perform before they are officially employed as nobat players. This normally happens in a small circle of the *orang kalur* family to ensure that musical knowledge is kept within the same family.

The only ensemble that notates its repertoire is the nobat of Kedah. Similar to the instructions found in *Hikayat Patani*, the Kedah nobat uses the mnemonic system symbolized by Jawi or Arabic alphabets called *dai*[13] in which the mnemonics 'dam', 'tang' and 'tik' are used (see figure 3.21). However, not every member of the ensemble is well versed in the notation and musical knowledge is still largely passed down orally.

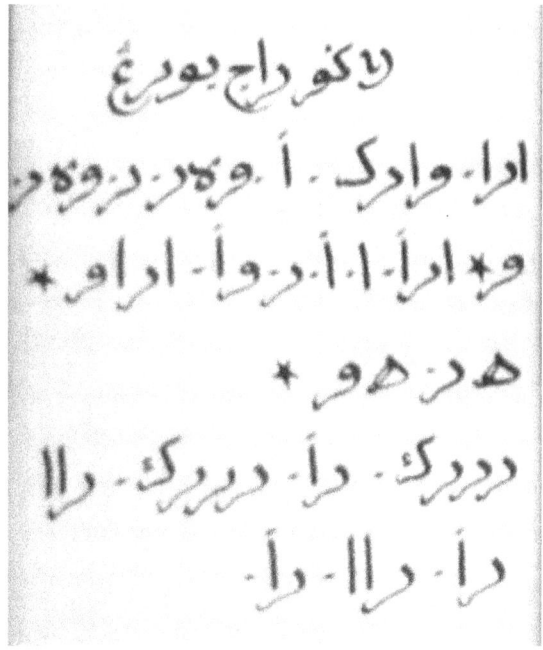

Figure 3.21. *Dai* of the piece 'Lagu Raja Burung' of the Kedah nobat. This hand-written notation is framed and hung on the wall of the Balai nobat in Alor Setar. *Source*: Raja Iskandar, 2013.

SUMMARY

The growing trade across the Indian Ocean in the thirteenth century not only brought Islam to the Malay world but also introduced the nobat. The court ensemble of today retains the basic concepts of its Middle Eastern and South Asian predecessors but was slowly indigenised over time. Besides serving as a symbol of a ruler's power and sovereignty, the nobat maintains its role as timekeeper and continues to signal prayer times and herald the beginning of festivities. Preexisting traditional and Hindu-Buddhist beliefs were slowly accommodated by the newly introduced faith and developed into what was known as the Malay *adat* (customs) and *istiadat* (ceremonies). One of the results of this fusion is the particular Malay conception of *daulat* (divine essence or ruling power) that forms the foundation in which the Malay sultanates were built; and where the nobat institution played a central role.

The nobat spread throughout the Malay world as a symbol of political alliance and religious legitimacy. Its instruments were part of the treasured court regalia and revered as not only a representation of power but also a source of maintaining and disseminating it. Consequently, the nobat became a tool for political domination and submission. Bestowed upon vassal states and individuals, the nobat was also sought after by aspiring kingdoms in order to establish their political boundaries and sovereignty. By the fifteenth century, the ensemble was firmly established as part of Malay royal customs and ceremonies, and immortalised in court literature as an essence of Malay culture and identity. Growing rivalry among Malay sultanates and European intervention in the region resulted in the dispersion and eventual demise of a number of ensembles. By the early twentieth century, only five nobat ensembles were left in the Malay world that are still being used to install rulers and announce religious events.

Although instruments of the nobat evolved throughout the centuries, the important ones remain to this day. The *nengkara, gendang, nafiri* and *serunai*, instruments documented in a number of early Malay texts, still form the basic nobat orchestra. These instruments continue to be part of court regalia and can only be played or touched by members of the royal family or musicians of the court. In Kedah, Perak and Selangor, these musicians are hereditary and known as the *orang kalur*; in the Terengganu nobat, players tend to be related to the royal family. While notation is used in Kedah, musical knowledge is still passed down orally from one family member to another and is largely influenced by traditional beliefs and taboos.

The nobat is a percussion-dominated ensemble whose music is polyphonic in nature. Melody is played by the *serunai* and backed by the *nengkara* and a pair of *gendang*, while the *nafiri* signals the start or end of a section. In certain ensembles, the *gong* and *kopak-kopak* provide a constant rhythmic pulse for the music. Although in certain ensembles the *serunai* leads and has a selection of different melodies or phrases; *ragam* (pieces) of the nobat are generally differentiated by the rhythms played by the drums. This is led by the *nengkara*, which not only plays the basic rhythmic pattern but also determines the tempo of a piece. The music is then organised using the ostinato and interlocking parts continuously repeated to help strengthen and identify a piece. In Perak and Selangor, the *serunai* is functionally relegated to beautification and does not identify pieces. Similar melodic phrases, also called *lagu*, are played by the *serunai* in all the pieces known as *merawan* and *senangin*.

While the repertoire and instrumentation changed through time, the nobat largely remains intact with regard to its court functions and religio-political significance. A comparison with early court literature suggests that certain pieces, performance practices and playing techniques continue to this day. Unlike other forms of music, the nobat repertoire was not dictated by the aesthetic needs of the audience, and unless ordered by the sultan, music of the nobat has had no reason for change. The application of a rigid set of traditions and beliefs ensured that radical change did not occur and the nobat institution is well preserved. In Malay society, this art form is still viewed with reverence, not due to the beauty of its melody or complexity of its rhythms, but the overall sound that it produces and its sovereign connotations. To the Malays, the unique layers of sounds are clearly associated with the authority of a Sultan, a manifestation of his divine right to rule, and a representation of Malay pride and identity.

For centuries, the nobat combined the harshness of its military past with courtly elegance that developed in tandem with growing economic and political power in the Malay world. Similar in function to conch shells and horns or the *beduk* (long, single-face log drum) of the Malay *surau* (small mosque), the nobat is sounded to communicate and signal events, both royal and religious. The music of the nobat can be viewed as 'signalling sounds'. As such, nobat music is not governed by the evocation of different shades of emotion often associated with the art of music making. In nobat repertoire, a piece entitled 'Nobat Subuh' ('Early Morning') may not necessarily conjure up the mood of a cold, misty morning but may instead be played at the same speed and intensity as a war piece. With the exception of a few pieces, the only literal attachment of nobat music generally lies in the time and place it is performed. 'Nobat Subuh' was named not due to the serenity of its music but its function of announcing the time of morning prayer or of the morning waking of the sultan. Thus, the high level of invariance in its timbre, dynamics and intensity underscores the true function and nature of the nobat.

Figure 3.22. Remaining Malay nobat in Malaysia and Brunei. *Source*: Made by author.

The music of the nobat can also be seen as a reflection of the subservient nature of the musicians towards the royal institution, governed by the concept of *daulat* (divine ruling power). A *raja berdaulat* as a divinely sanctioned ruler requires total obedience of his subjects and the sound and instruments of the nobat, as symbols of a sultan's *daulat*, require the same level of respect. The nobat musicians, as the archetypical Malay subject, were burdened with the responsibility of maintaining the power and relevency of these symbols. This required their utmost loyalty and strict adherence to *adat* (customs) and *pantang larang* (taboos). Any form of transgression may constitute an act of *derhaka* (disobedience) towards the sultan, which will incur *tulah* or divine wrath. This fear in turn deters them from exploring beyond the existing musical boundaries established by their forefathers—hence the static nature of the nobat institution. This has been going on for centuries and unless ordered or approved by the sultan, it is likely that the nobat shall remain the same for generations to come.

NOTES

1. The nobat was also known in certain parts of on the east coast of Sumatera as *tabuh larangan*, or the 'forbidden drum'. It is found in a number of Malay sultanates under the influence of Aceh and Melaka such as Langkat, Serdang, Siak and Kampar.
2. The nobat is a living tradition and since this is both a diachronic and synchronic work, I will be using past and present tenses to indicate the ensemble's present and past uses.
3. Based on accounts in early indigenous texts, prior to the twentieth century, the nobat or its instruments were also used in street celebrations and for entertainment purposes.

4. For this research I use A. Samad Ahmad ([ed.]1979), *Sulalatus Salatin* (*Sejarah Melayu*), Kuala Lumpur: Dewan Bahasa dan Pustaka, digitised under the Malay Concordance Project accessible at http://mcp.anu.edu.au.

5. References are based on the digitied version of the text through the Malay Concordance Project.

6. According to Sheppard (1989), there were two sets, a silver and a wooden one. The silver nobat was made by the Dutch and was played during the installation of Sultan Abdul Rahman in 1885. The old wooden nobat was left behind in a store in Penyengat.

7. Not to be confused with her grandmother, Sultan Abdul Rahman's mother who bore the same name.

8. For references, this chapter uses the digitized version of Misa Melayu from the Malay Concordance Project.

9. The change in name appeared during the installation of Sultan Azlan Shah in 1985.

10. For a comprehensive and detailed royal customs and ceremonies of the Perak court refer to Adib Vincent Tung, *Adat Pusaka Raja-Raja dan Orang Besar-Besar Negeri Perak Darul Ridzuan* (Ipoh: Compass Life Sdn. Bhd, 1999)

11. The name 'Ibrahim Khalil' also appeared in *Adat Aceh* and was thought to be a name for an installation drum. Whether it was the name of a drum or a piece, its importance in the installation process was undeniable and, in the Johor-Riau Sultanate, the piece 'Ibrahim Khalil' was solely assigned for the ceremony.

12. Iskandar Zulkarnain was another important figure in Malay royal history and Malay rulers claimed to be his descendants.

13. The *dai* are indicators for the *gendang* but there are occasional signals for the *nafiri* and gong. However there is no markings to indicate the tempo of a piece, see Meilu Ho (1992, 59–67).

Chapter Four

The Nobat in Early Malay Literature
A Lesson from Patani

The arrival of Islam to the Malay world saw the introduction of a new writing system.[1] The Arabic alphabet used in the teaching and learning of the new religion was soon adapted by the Malays in writing their own language. This was known as the Jawi alphabet, a term used by the Arabs in referring to the entirety of Southeast Asia and its people. Arabic inscriptions dating as early as the fourteenth century found in various places throughout Southeast Asia are evidence of early Islamic influence in the region (e.g. *Batu Bersurat Terengganu*, or the *Terengganu Stone*, which was written in 1303). The contribution of the Jawi script to the language and intellectual development of the Malays was immense. Although the Malays did not leave behind great monuments such as those found in Cambodia and Java, they nevertheless formed their own cultural tradition, as a foundation of their civilization, through literature. For centuries, Malay became a medium of communication not only between literatures of Southeast Asia but also opened the literary door to foreign works from the Middle East, Persia and South Asia (Braginsky 2004, 2).

Literature was soon utilised by Malay rulers to further elevate their status and consolidate their powers over their largely illiterate subjects. Influenced by Indo-Persian literary traditions—often imbued with myths and legends—these texts tend to downplay the factual and the circumstantial events of linear history, serving instead the purpose of glorification, edification and entertainment for the ruling elites who commissioned many of them. Mythology-based narratives in traditional Malay literature are according to Shome (2002, 15) 'euhemeristic that is they explain myths on a historical basis and adapt them for their leadership role-model'. Stories of miraculous births and exploits, and images of profound piety, are often necessary elements for the setting of moral precedence, especially in court chronicles. However, this existence of what Braginsky calls the 'second reality' does not diminish their importance as a rich source of information for scholars and provide invaluable insights into the cultural, social and political history of the Malays, including the role of music.

Perhaps the most important work for this book is the *Hikayat Patani* (hereafter HP), or Story of Patani, written down between the seventeenth and the eighteenth centuries, but describing earlier events. Categorised as a *sastera sejarah* (historical literature), HP is a court chronicle that not only narrates the genealogy of the royal house but also attempts to establish the Patani sultanate as a proud, sovereign Malay polity with its own distinct identity. It is also the only work of Malay literature that details the musical instruments of the regalia in the royal inventory, a complete repertoire of pieces (but see *Misa Melayu* and *Adat Aceh*) and instructions on how to perform them. In short, it can be argued that HP is the only available classical Malay work on music.

This unique aspect of the HP has not gone unnoticed by scholars. In trying to decipher the musical instructions found in the HP, A. Teeuw and D. K. Wyatt (1970) sought the opinions of ethnomusicologist Judith Becker and cultural historian Mubin Sheppard. An expert in Southeast Asian music, Becker concludes that the 'meaningless sequences of letters' (as described by Teeuw and Wyatt [1970, 288]), are drum mnemonics that were memorised and spoken by drummers before actually playing them. While suggesting that some of the mnemonics may refer to different playing techniques of the drums,

Figure 4.1. The Region of Patani and Peninsular Malaysia. The northern states of Perlis, Kedah, Kelantan and Terengganu were vassal states of Siam and share certain cultural traits with Patani. *Source*: Made by author.

she is, however, unsure as to the rhythmic indications. Mubin Sheppard, a renowned historian with an interest in Malay performing arts, saw some similarities between the playing of the Patani and Terengganu nobat. He also used references from the HP in his writings on the Malay nobat and the *asyik* court dance (Sheppard 1972; 1983). More recent work relating to the Patani nobat has been done by historian Barbara Andaya. Beginning with a discussion of sounds as symbols of authority in premodern Malay society (2011), Andaya takes a closer look at the HP and analyses the roles of cannons and drums in the creation of Patani identity (2012). Drawing upon indigenous and European sources, she argues that sacred court objects and animals, which include royal drums, cannons and elephants, were visual and aural representations of Patani-ness. While this promotion of a sense of cultural unity and identity is embedded in the text, the HP narrative can nonetheless be taken as a representative of the wider Malay world. Patani, like all the sultanates, had its distinct characteristics and sense of locality, but it is still a close part of the larger *dunia Melayu*.

This chapter discusses the *hikayat* in relation to the history and development of the nobat, to discern the ensemble's function and role in the political culture and manoeuvrings of a Malay polity between the sixteenth and seventeenth centuries. The last section of the manuscript, which deals specifically with the nobat, will be analysed and compared with existing ensembles. Despite its foreign origins, the nobat was well integrated into Malay court culture by this time and already central to the idea of what A. C. Milner terms '*kerajaan*' and 'Malay-ness' (9). Milner argues against the use of Western models in studying premodern Malay political culture, in particular, J. M. Gullick's (1958, 1) functionalism approach which views Malay government as a 'working system of social control and leadership'. The Raja, according to Gullick, was only the titular figure of authority but real power lay with the district chiefs.[2] This conclusion is seen as a 'distortion' by Milner, who suggests that, in the precolonial period, the Raja was not 'the "key institution" but *the only institution*' (113; emphasis mine). Apart from keeping Malay societies intact, the ruler was seen as the only means for social and spiritual development, and his subjects were the measure of his *nama* (name). In Milner's view, the Malays 'considered themselves to be living not in states or under governments, but in a *kerajaan*, in the "condition of having a raja"' (114). For Malays, being subjects of a Raja gives them a sense of belonging, a consciousness of a cultural cohesion and the essence of being 'Malay'.

For a *kerajaan* to be established, a Raja needs to be installed and, as established in the previous chapter, a ruler's ascension to the throne is not legitimate until he is drummed to carefully executed *ragam* (pieces) of the nobat. As court regalia and symbol of sovereignty, the nobat's use (or misuse) had the power to affect the lives of individuals and societies, political alliances, stable relations and the initiation and outcome of confrontations. The nobat institution became not only the nucleus of Malay political culture but also a signifier of communal identity. I would also like to draw a comparison to Benedict Anderson's (1990, 23) suggestion of the 'accumulation, concentrating and preserving of Power' within the traditional Javanese understanding[3] with the Malay concept of *daulat*, or 'divine ruling power', which is vital to the continued existence of the court ensemble and the kerajaan. The nobat's importance is reflected in the HP's documentation of its instruments, pieces and instructions on how to perform them, akin to preserving a magic *mantra*, or formula, to be used for the installation of future kings if need be. The connection of kingship and the use of nobat music in court ceremonies is the result of a long process, a continuation of pre-Islamic cultures and adaptation of new ones. In addition to the HP, I will also employ fragmentary evidence from both indigenous and foreign sources that will hopefully offer a clearer glimpse not only of Patani's cultural past but also of the wider Malay world.[4]

THE MALAY SULTANATE OF PATANI (SIXTEENTH–SEVENTEENTH CENTURIES)

The fall of Melaka in 1511 saw the emergence of a number of Malay sultanates in the Malay Peninsula, Borneo and Sumatera amongst which Aceh, Perak, Johor, Brunei and Patani were well known. The focus of this chapter is the Malay sultanate of Patani, which in the seventeenth century became one of the most important mercantile city-states in the Malay world due to its unique geographical location (see figure 4.1). Situated in the northern-most region of the Malay-speaking territories, Patani mediates between the northern mainland and island Southeast Asia. It has one of the best natural harbours on the east coast of the Malay Peninsula, and the Tanjung Patani, or Cape of Patani, provides shelter for mariners from the northeast and southwest monsoon before continuing north to Ayudhya or south towards the Straits of Melaka.

The early history of Patani is obscure but the region is said to have been Indianised as early as the second century CE (Wheatley 1961, 285). However, it was not until the sixth century that it became an important trading port of the eastern Indian Ocean and started sending missions to China, which called it *Lang-ya-hsiu*, or Langkasuka (Teeuw and Wyatt 1970, 1). In the eighth century, Langkasuka came under the influence of Srivijaya and it was during this period that the Malay language was introduced to the original Mon-Khmer population of the isthmian parts of the Malay Peninsula (Benjamin 1987, 119). The Srivijayan court culture must have also been adopted by the kings of Langkasuka as suggested by the eighth-century Chinese history, the *Tung Tien*:

> The King and his high officials wear golden cords as girdles, and insert gold rings in their ears. The kingdom (city-state) is surrounded by walls to form a city with double gates, towers and pavilions. When the king goes forth, he rides an elephant. He is accompanied by banners, fly whisks, flags, and drums and is shaded by a white parasol. (Wheatley 1961, 254)

From this record it is apparent that the institution of Hindu-Buddhist kingship was firmly established in Langkasuka and highly likely continued with the court of Patani. By the fourteenth century the concept of the proper alignment and harmony of the temporal world and the gods was in practice and was manifested in the architecture of the Patani palace (Bougas 1994, 17–19). The use of the drums in royal processions shows the preexisting importance of music as part of court culture of Langkasuka and other polities in the region. Music flourished in the Hindu and later Buddhist courts and temples of Southeast Asia (Nicolas 2011, 347) and, according to Chinese records, Srivijayan courts were known to have sent musicians to China as tributes (Hall 1981, 44). Still, the political and cultural transition from Langkasuka to the kingdom of Patani remains unclear. Based on the *Hikayat Raja Langkasuka*, HP and Ibrahim Syukri's (1985) constructions of Patani history, Bougas (1994, 8) supports the idea that Patani was initially the harbour of Langkasuka that grew from a small fishing village into a bustling port city. The ruler of the inland city of Kota Mahligai (Langkasuka?) then decided to move his palace closer to the harbour thus establishing the kingdom of Patani. The eighteenth-century Nakhon chronicles narrate that Patani was one of the Buddhist states incorporated under the rule of Nakhon Sri Thammarat in the thirteenth century (Teeuw and Wyatt 1970). In order to ensure the loyalty of these vassal states, the ruler of Nakhon performed an oath-taking ceremony practiced centuries earlier by Srivijayan kings (Hall 1985, 88). During the ceremony a ruler of a vassal state would drink 'magic' water poured on a stone carved with an oath of allegiance and it was believed that harm would befall any ruler who broke his oath (ibid.). Apart from Srivijaya, influence also came from the Thai state of Ayudhya and the Javanese Majapahit Empire. While Patani was politically subjugated by Ayudhya, it was culturally influenced by Majapahit (Bougas 1994, 11). This can be seen in the practice of certain rituals and ceremonies, the style of dress and headgear; and the performance of *wayang kulit* or shadow puppet theatre with its Ramayana repertoire (ibid.). *Wayang kulit Siam* is still performed today in parts of Kelantan and Terengganu in Malaysia.

THE HIKAYAT PATANI

HP is a Malay historical chronicle documenting the Malay sultanate of Patani. Two separate manuscripts were used in editing the first published version of the *hikayat* by A. Teeuw and D. K. Wyatt in 1970. Teeuw located the first manuscript in the Library of Congress, Washington, DC, titled 'History of Patani, a Kingdom of the East Coast of the Peninsula of Malacca, Near the Siamese Boundary'. Written in Jawi, it was copied in Singapore in 1839 by Abdullah bin Abdul Kadir, famously known as Abdullah Munshi, an accomplished writer of Malay known as the 'father of modern Malay literature'. Siti Hawa (1992, ix) suggests that the manuscript Abdullah copied from could have been obtained in Kelantan the previous year, copied in Singapore and given to Alfred North, an American serving in the American Board of Commissioners of Foreign Mission, who took it back to United States of America. The second manuscript was also accidentally found in 1969 amongst English philologist Walter W. Skeat's (1835–1912) collection now held at the Institute of Social Anthropology at the University of Oxford. A more recent publication of HP was made in 1992 by Dewan Bahasa dan Pustaka, Kuala Lumpur, edited by Siti Hawa Haji Salleh; this only uses the Library of Congress manuscript.

Teeuw and Wyatt (1970) are of the opinion that HP was written by a number of authors who, as in most of the works found in early Malay literature, remain anonymous. The authors maintain elements of traditional Malay historical writing which included myths and legends, *adat istiadat* (customs and ceremonies), laws and beliefs. There is also a customary representation of a Malay city, resembling the ideal Islamic city such as a fortified palace (*kota*), buildings (*balai*), mosques and living quarters inhibited by traders or missionaries from other ethnic groups (*kampong*). Like many other traditional court writings, royal genealogies frame the narrative of HP and it centres on a single court, Patani, from the late fifteenth to the early eighteenth centuries. The HP is divided into six parts by Teeuw and Wyatt (1970, 52) but, in this chapter, emphasis will only be given to Parts 1 and 6:

1. The history of Patani during the Hulu Dynasty (Inland Dynasty)
2. The history of Patani during the Kelantan Dynasty rule, ending with the rule of Aulung Yunus
3. A summary of the Bendaharas of Patani
4. The story of the elephant trainer Cau Hang and Bendahara Datuk Cerak Kin
5. The story of the death of Datuk Sai and the struggle for the position of bendahara during the reign of the Kelantan Dynasty
6. The Undang-Undang Patani

I use Teeuw and Wyatt's English translation for excerpts from the HP in this chapter; translations from other Malay texts are mine.

THE *NAFIRI* AND *NAGARA*

The *hikayat* begins with the rule of King Phaya Tu Kerub Mahajana at Kota Mahligai, a city according to Ibrahim Syukri (1985, 13) situated at Pera Wan (Prawae) in the present-day Yarang district of Patani, Southern Thailand. Archaeological findings show that Prawae was occupied from the twelfth until the seventeenth or eighteenth century when a defensive *kota*, or fort, was built (Welch and McNeill 1989, 41). This first king was succeeded by his son, Phaya Tu Naqpa, who later became the first Muslim ruler of Patani. The story goes that Phaya Tu Naqpa suffered from a disease and was cured by a Sufi *fakir* (ascetic) named Sheikh Said from Pasai. Instead of accepting the king's daughter as a reward, the Sheikh made the king promise to convert to Islam, which he did only after being cured for the third time. Narratives of ruler conversions and miraculous births are common in Malay court chronicles. The *Hikayat Raja-Raja Pasai* (HRP) relates how Merah Silu, ruler of Pasai, was miraculously converted after meeting Prophet Muhammad in a dream and was later taught by Sultan Muhammad, a ruler turned Sufi fakir from India. The role of Sufi fakirs in the conversion of Phaya Tu Naqpa and Merah Silu are substantial in both *hikayat*. Both these rulers later changed their names to Sultan Ismail Syah and Sultan Malik al-Saleh, respectively.

The HP then tells us about a certain Sheikh Safiuddin who settled down in Patani and was later responsible for advising Sultan Ismail's successor Sultan Mudhaffar Syah on matters pertaining to religion. It has been argued on archaeological grounds that the connection between Pasai and Patani led to the Islamization of the latter, based on the tombstones of what are locally believed to be Phaya Tu Naqpa and other sultans that Bougas (1986, 36) has shown were made in Pasai. The accommodative nature of the early proselytising process is evident in the apparently only nominal adherence to Islam of the ruler:

Adapun raja itu sungguhpun ia membawa agama Islam, yang menyembah berhala dan makan babi itu juga yang ditinggalkan; lain dari pada itu segala pekerjaan kafir itu suatu pun tiada diubahnya. (Teeuw and Wyatt 1970, I, 75)

As for the king himself it is true that he became a Muslim inasmuch as he gave up worshipping idols and eating pork; but apart from that he did not alter a single one of his heathen habits. (Teeuw and Wyatt 1970, II, 152)

The implication of the HP is that the establishment of the Malay sultanate was in some part due to Pasai and its migrants living in Patani. This is not surprising as Pasai is considered the cradle of Islam in the Malay world and was seen as a centre of religious authority for the Melaka sultanate. Like Pasai and later Aceh, Patani itself became famed as a centre of Islamic learning in the Malay world, bearing the name *serambi Mekah* (veranda of Mecca). Syed Naquib al-Attas (1969, 27–29) contends that it was these three Malay kingdoms—Pasai, Aceh and Melaka—that played a dominant role in the spread of Islamic theology and philosophy throughout the archipelago. The diffusion of these ideas was due to the emergence of important trading ports and urban centres in the Malay world, resulting in not only the continuous arrival of foreigners from many lands, but also the intra-migration of Malays around the region. Much later in the nineteenth-century state of Perak, J. M. Gullick (1958, 26) notes the migration of Bugis, Keronchi, Rawa, Mandailing and Batak people. Descendants of Melakan, Javanese and Acehnese immigrants formed part of the Malay community in Negeri Sembilan (a state south of Kuala Lumpur, Malaysia) in the same period (ibid.). Although conscious of their own identity, Gullick (1958, 25) suggests that these *anak dagang* (immigrants) and *anak negri* (local-born Malays) still practiced a 'general Indonesian culture'. This interaction and cross-fertilization of ideas helped facilitate the standardization of religion, language and customs, hence creating a sense of cultural unity and cohesion or 'Malay-ness' (Barnard 2001; Matheson 1979; Milner 1982; 2008; Reid 2001).

Sultan Ismail Syah produced two sons and a daughter and both his sons succeeded him to the Patani throne. Apart from Siti Aisyah, who was previously known as Tunku Mahachai, Sultan Ismail Syah's two sons were also given Islamic names by Sheikh Said; the eldest was called Mudhaffar Syah and the youngest Manzur Syah. The instruments of the nobat are first mentioned in the story of the marriage of Sultan Ismail's daughter Siti Aisyah to Raja Jalal, who was made the *bendahara* (prime minister).

> *Raja Jalal itu dijadikan bendahara. Ada dua tahun maka Raja Aisyah laki isteri itu pun dirajakan oleh ayahanda baginda di Sai seperti adat raja-raja besar-besar, ditabalkan dengan nafiri dan negara.* (Teeuw and Wyatt 1970, I, 82)
>
> Raja Jalal was made prime minister. Two years later Raja Aisyah and her husband were made rulers of Sai by her royal father, with all the ceremonies of great rulers, and for their installation the trumpets were blown and the kettledrums beaten. (Teeuw and Wyatt 1970, II, 158)

The mention of the *nafiri* and *negara* shows the importance of the instruments as part of an installation process and, in this case, it also showed the right of a sultan to legitimise his son-in-law as a ruler by giving him Sai as a dominion to rule. Although the Islamization of Patani is ascribed to the influence of Pasai, Patani's nobat, however, is said to be from Melaka as recounted in the *Sejarah Melayu*:

> *Maka Cau Seri Bangsa pun berbuatlah negerilah di sana. Setelah sudah, maka negeri itu dinamai baginda Pak Tani, mengikut nama payang itu, maka disebut orang datang sekarang Petani. Maka Cau Seri Bangsa pun menyuruhkan menterinya Okun Pola namanya, mengadap ke Melaka, memohon nobat pada Sultan Mahmud Syah.* (SM 228:21)
>
> Then Cau Seri Bangsa established a state there. Once completed, it was called Pak Tani, after the fisherman's name, and it is known by people today as Petani. Then Cau Seri Bangsa sent his minister Okun Pola to pay obeisance to Melaka, to ask for a nobat from Sultan Mahmud Syah.

The *Sejarah Melayu* narration continues with Okun Pola and the letter from Patani being accorded the receiving ceremony similar to Pahang, indicating its vassal status. This is further shown by the use of the term *anakanda* (son) by Cau Seri Bangsa in addressing himself and *ayahanda* (father) towards Sultan Mahmud Shah in his letter. The Patani ruler was then *dinobatkan* (installed) in Patani, styled as Sultan Seri Ahmad Syah (SM 229:5). This episode alludes to Melaka's brief control over Patani at the end of the fifteenth century when Siamese influence over the peninsula was undermined by Melaka's growing power. After conquering Pahang and Kelantan, which were under Siamese rule, Melaka managed to extend its influence north of the peninsula, which led to the states of Kedah and Patani requesting the nobat as a sign of submission (Bougas 1994, 13).

There is also mention of continuing with the customs of great kings in HP, in reference to either the practice of previous rulers of Patani or the early Muslim sultanates in the wider Indian Ocean. Since the nobat is said to have been given by the Sultan of Melaka, the 'great kings' could also mean the rulers of fifteenth-century Melaka. In any case, it shows the wholesale adaptation of the *naqqarakhana* and *naubat* tradition of the Islamicate world as a symbol of a ruler's dominion and his prerogative to bestow it upon smaller polities as an acknowledgement of sovereignty or a gift of honour to high-ranking officials. A similar story is told in the SM when Sri Bija Diraja[5] was installed as ruler of Pahang by the Sultan of Melaka in recognition of his success in capturing Maharaja Dewa Sura, the Siamese ruler of Pahang (SM 92:37). Considering his lower standing, Sri Bija Diraja was given the nobat *selengkapnya* (complete), but without the *nagara* drum. In the case of the HP, the use of the *nafiri* and *nagara*, being the most important instrument of the nobat, reflects the importance of the *bendahara* post, in addition to Raja Jalal being the Sultan's son-in-law. It was also a practice of fifteenth-century

Melaka where the use of the nobat was based on the hierarchical nature of the instruments in relation to political stature. However, the ceremony is described in less detail (probably due to its lesser importance) as compared to SM and HRP, where the sitting positions of nobles in the *balairung* (audience hall) and particular *ragam* (pieces) are mentioned.

THE DRUMMING OF SULTAN MANZUR SYAH AND NANG LIU-LIU

Sultan Ismail was succeeded by his eldest son Raja Mudhaffar Syah. During his reign, Patani experienced an increase in economic activities that resulted in a prosperous and peaceful sultanate (Puaksom 2009, 81). Under the new sultan, Patani sought to establish good relations with its neighbours, especially the Siamese state of Ayudhya. Sultan Mudhaffar even went to the extent of residing in Ayudhya for nearly two months, but was deeply offended by the Siamese ruler's offer of a woman for him to marry. This perceived insult led to a war between Patani and Siam in 1563. Although Sultan Mudhaffar Syah managed to enter the Siamese king's palace and forced the king to flee, the Patani forces were repelled and retreated back to Patani led by his younger brother Manzur. However, the sultan and 1,500 of his followers remained in Ayudhya, though their fate were not mentioned in HP. On his return to Patani, Sultan Mudhaffar Syah's younger brother Manzur was installed as the new sultan of Patani.

> *Setelah sampai lalu naik berjalan ke dalam negeri, lalu ke istana kakanda baginda bertakhta di atas takhta kerajaan. Maka genderang tabal pun dipalu oranglah, dan segala menteri pegawai hulubalang pun semuanya menjunjung duli baginda. Setelah sudah maka segala menteri pegawai hulubalang pun semuanya yang mati di Siam bersama-sama dengann kakanda itu pun semuanya digelar baginda akan gantinya pula.* (Teeuw and Wyatt 1970, I, 87)

> After they had arrived the king disembarked and entered the town, and went to his brother's palace where he seated himself on the royal throne. Then the installation drum was beaten, and all the ministers and officials and officers came and paid homage at the feet of the king. After that the successors of all the ministers, officials and officers who had died in Siam together with the king's elder brother were granted titles in their stead. (Teeuw and Wyatt 1970, II, 162)

It appears that this installation ceremony was done hastily. During the absence of Sultan Mudhaffar and his brother Manzur, Patani was left in the care of their brother-in-law the *bendahara* of Sai, Raja Jalal, who was made regent. On his return from Siam, Sultan Manzur Syah was unsure of the *ben-*

dahara's view on him becoming sultan. He sailed past Patani and anchored at Beruas without Raja Jalal's knowledge. Sultan Manzur concocted a story of Johor's impending attack on Sai, so that the *bendahara* stayed clear of Patani and assigned someone to monitor his movements. Without the knowledge of Raja Jalal, Sultan Manzur Syah sailed back to Patani and installed himself as sultan. Raja Jalal learned about his brother-in-law's installation and came to Patani to wait on his new sultan. He later returned to Sai and continued to rule as *bendahara* until his death some time later.

In this story two ceremonies were conducted simultaneously. First there was the installation of the Sultan followed by the menjunjung duli ceremony. The first installation could be an 'informal' ceremony called the pertabalan kerajaan, or 'state installation'. This is done immediately after the death of a Sultan before the body is brought down from the palace for burial. According to Malay royal custom, a deceased ruler cannot be buried until a successor is named and the strict adherence to this adat was evident during the succession crisis of Perak in 1871 when the body of the late Sultan Ali (r. 1865–1871) lay in state for forty days before he was finally buried. In the case related in HP, Sultan Mudhaffar was presumed dead and the ceremony was conducted in the absence of the deceased Sultan's body. In Perak, a mourning period was normally observed after a death of a sultan before a successor was installed as related in the Misa Melayu:

> *Maka adinda baginda Raja Mudalah menggantikan kerajaan kakanda baginda ini menjadi khalifah di dalam negeri Perak. Telah sudah itu, maka diperintahkan jenazah Sultan Mahmud Syah itu, maka dikuburlah dengan sepertinya almarhum di dalam kerajaan negeri Perak. Hatta, maka adinda baginda pun berhentilah nobat dua puluh hari lamanya memberi takziah akan kakanda baginda itu. Telah genaplah dua puluh hari, maka nobatlah baginda Raja Muda digelar baginda di atas takhta kerajaan Paduka Seri Sultan Alaudin Mansur Syah Iskandar Muda Khalifatur-Rahim.* (MM 192: 22–29)

> Then his majesty's younger sibling Raja Muda succeeded the government of his brother to become the caliph of the state of Perak. Later, it was commanded that the body of Sultan Mahmud Syah is prepared, and then buried in accordance with the tradition of the state of Perak. Then his majesty's younger brother stopped the beating of the nobat for twenty days in mourning of his brother. After twenty days his majesty Raja Muda was drummed to the throne styled as Paduka Seri Sultan Alauddin Mansur Syah Iskandar Muda Khalifatur-Rahim.

This passage describes the two-step ascension process of the eighteenth-century Perak court where a successor was first named before the burial ceremony. This was followed by a mourning period of twenty days in which the sound of the nobat was not heard. It is obvious that the mourning period was not observed by Sultan Manzur—not only was the nobat played but he continued with his official installation ceremony (*pertabalan adat*). This could simply be a difference in royal *adat* between Patani and Perak, but it was more likely due to the unsettled political climate that could have pressed Sultan Manzur to officially hasten the establishment of a new *kerajaan*.

The term *menjunjung duli* has two meanings. Firstly, it is a physical act of paying homage to a Sultan by saluting him (which is done annually or biennially as a renewal of pledge of loyalty), normally involving the act of kneeling on the floor and moving forward three times. This act was described in the HP when the rebellious Bendahara Kayu Kelat, after receiving the scarf of Queen Ijau, knelt down and paid homage three times in a row (HP 45:5). Secondly, it is also a ceremony involving the bestowing of royal titles and honours. The *menjunjung duli* ceremony above was a combination of both; while the new Sultan was being paid homage by his nobles, he then appointed the successors of the dead ministers and officials of his brother. This ceremony continued with another installation ceremony:

> *Adapun bedil yang bernama Nang Liu-liu itu pun dipayung dengan payung ubur-ubur ditabalkan tiga hari tiga malam. Dalam tiga hari itu baginda pun tiadalah tabal lagi. Setelah sudah bedil itu ditabalkan, maka baginda pun tabal pula seperti adat raja-raja yang baharu naik raja di atas takhta kerajaan.* (Teeuw and Wyatt 1970, I, 87)

> The cannon Nang Liu-liu was provided with a fringed umbrella and the drums were beaten for it for three days and nights. During these three days no drums were yet beaten for the king himself. After the official beating of the drums for the cannon was finished, only then was the king himself installed to the beat of the royal drums, in accordance with the traditions for kings newly installed on the royal throne. (Teeuw and Wyatt 1970, II, 162)

The sounds of the nobat and *bedil* were a measure of a Malay sultan's authority and prestige (Andaya 2011). The advent of gun technology in the fifteenth century expanded the sonic dominion of Malay rulers established earlier by the nobat. Their ability to aurally control society made them objects of reverence, viewed as animate and bestowed with supernatural powers. The pairing of the nobat and cannon (including firearms) became part of the Malay court *adat* for both solemn and auspicious occasions. The *Hikayat Raja Pasai* notes this pairing in the installation of the first Muslim ruler of Pasai:

> *Maka genderang tabal itu pun dipalu oranglah dan segala bunyi-bunyian pun berbunyilah. Maka bedil nobat itu pun dipasang oranglah dan segala hulubalang dan segala rakyat sekalian menjunjung duli menyembah mengatakan, 'Daulat dirgahayu Syah Alam, zillu fi 'il-'alam'.* (Pasai 32:6)

Then the installation drum was beaten and all the instruments started to sound. Then the signalling cannon was prepared and all the warriors and people paid obeisance proclaiming 'Long live the king of the world, shadow of God on earth'.

The 'installation' of the cannon is a propitiation ritual, as a sign of veneration and of fulfilment of a promise. During his escape from Ayudhya, Sultan Manzur made a promise to the cannon named Nang Liu-liu that, if 'she' could help him fend off the pursuing Siamese, he would have the royal drums beaten for her for seven days. Eventually Nang Liu-liu's shots managed to sink many Siamese boats and frightened the rest from coming close to Sultan Manzur's ship. Similar to state swords, krises and instruments of the nobat, the cannon symbolises Sultan Manzur's *daulat* and is believed to be crucial to the safety and well-being of the state. The drumming of Nang Liu-liu was then followed by the 'official' installation ceremony of the sultan which took place after three days (short of four days as promised). By delaying his own installation, Sultan Manzur showed respect and gratitude to the great *bedil* that helped save his life, in turn restoring Patani's pride. Propitiation rituals are common in Malay courts. In Perak, the *tabal pusaka* ceremony is conducted to officially 'install' the guardian *jinns* of the state and their regalia. Prior to the early 1960s, instruments of the Perak nobat went through a ritual called *berjamu* to 'feed' and appease the spirits said to inhabit them in order to maintain their 'services'. The anthropomorphism of objects, a retention of underlying animist beliefs, is central to the traditional Malay concept of power and the establishment of *kerajaan*.

The Siamese Drums

In an effort to restore Patani-Siam relations and seek pardon from the ruler of Siam, Sultan Manzur Syah sent an envoy, Wan Muhammad, to Ayudhya. On arrival, Wan Muhammad was received by the court of Siam with a ceremony similar to the Melaka Sultanate, a century earlier. Melaka royal protocols dictate that envoys and letters from other states must be received with regalia of the state which included the nobat. Instruments used varied according to the stature of the state they were from. In the SM, it is explained that letters from Pasai and Haru, whose Sultans were considered similar in status with Melaka, were received with full state regalia. This included the full instruments of the nobat—*nafiri, nagara, gendang* and *serunai* flanked by a pair of white state umbrellas (SM 71:26). Letters and envoys from other lesser states were received *dikurangkan hormatnya* (lessen the respect) with just the *gendang* and *serunai* accompanied by a yellow umbrella (SM 71:34). For letters from a Sultan of a slightly higher status, the *nafiri* was played alongside a yellow and a white umbrella. Envoys were received and carried to the palace on elephants, horses or accompanied by foot, according to their status as viewed by the Melaka Sultanate. Before the envoys were sent off, they were given robes of honour and gifts, even those from states of 'lower' status such as Rekan (Rokan) (SM 71:44). The Siamese court ceremony in welcoming envoys and letters is reported in the HP as follows:

> *Setelah sampai ke labuhan pada keesokan harinya maka surat dan segala bingkis pun diarak oranglah dengan gendang nafiri, dan payung iram kekuningan pun terkembanglah kiri kanan gajah menanggung surat itu.* (Teeuw and Wyatt 1970, I, 93)

> After arriving at the port the next day the letter and all gifts were paraded accompanied by *gendang* and *nafiri* and yellow fringed umbrellas were opened to the left and right of the elephant carrying the letter. (Teeuw and Wyatt 1970, II, 167)

The similarity of the *adat* with that of Melaka suggests shared Hindu-Buddhist cultural influences prior to the coming of Islam in Southeast Asia, especially Srivijayan court culture. It might also due to intercultural exchanges during periods of Siamese excursions into the Malay Peninsula. The use of only two instruments and two yellow umbrellas may indicate a 'lesser' treatment accorded to the Patani Sultanate, which is considered a vassal state. The *nafiri* mentioned by the authors of HP could be the Siamese curved metal horn *trae ngawn* used traditionally in court ceremonies, welcoming guests and war. The envoy and letter was well received by Beracau, the Siamese king, and it is reported that Wan Muhammad placed his head under the king's feet as sign of submission. This mission was considered a success when Wan Muhammad, who was given the title *Orangkaya Seri Agar Diraja* prior to his trip by Sultan Manzur Syah, was ceremoniously welcomed from Ayudhya with a letter from Beracau pardoning the deeds of the Sultan's elder brother. This diplomatic triumph was seen as a sign of Sultan Manzur Syah's 'divine power' as ruler of Patani albeit being still under the suzerainty of Siam; as his nobles exclaimed:

> *Daulat Tuanku, barang bertambah-tambahlah kiranya daulat saadat Duli Yang Maha Mulia di atas takhta kerajaan.* (Teeuw and Wyatt 1970, I, 102)

> Hail my Lord, may Your Majesty's divine power on the royal throne increase. (Teeuw and Wyatt 1970, II, 175)

This sentence encapsulates the whole idea of Malay kingship. Here we have the words *daulat, Duli Yang Maha Mulia* and *kerajaan*, which reflect the different cultural and religious influences that were blended together to form what has become a quintessentially Malay concept of power and governance. *Daulat* is seen as the fluid central power that resides in the body of the ruler and the regalia, power that is capable of both good and evil. It is believed that a person who goes against the ruler (*derhaka*) is bound to incur 'divine' retribution (*tulah* or *kena daulat*). The ruler with all this 'divine' power is yet reminded of his mortal self by the honorific *Duli Yang Maha Mulia* (literally, the 'Dust of the Noblest of All') that he is still the 'dust' of the Almighty, a servant of Allah. Lastly, this servant who is bestowed with extraordinary powers by the grace of God is the one worthy of sitting on the throne and manages the affairs of the state (*kerajaan*).

The Timekeeping Ensemble

The years between 1572 and 1584 saw Patani engulfed in political turmoil. The HP relates how two palace rebellions resulted in the deaths of Sultan Patik Siam (r. 1572–1573) and his brother Raja Bambang (1533–1573), both sons of Sultan Mudhaffar Syah. This left the throne open to the six sons and daughters from the line of Sultan Manzur Syah in which Raja Bahdur was chosen as ruler at the age of ten, styled as Sultan Bahdur Syah (r. 1573–1584). From the beginning, there were constant urgings from a court official named Seri Amar Pahlawan to Sultan Bahdur Syah's elder brother Raja Bima to dethrone his younger sibling. Due in part to an insulting incident in which Raja Bima was asked by Sultan Bahdur to dismount from a royal elephant, Raja Bima had made up his mind to kill his brother. After consulting Seri Amar Pahlawan, who promised to let him inside the palace compound, Raja Bima waited until the sound of the nobat was heard.

> *Syahadan tatkala sudah orang nobat subuh juga maka pintu Wang pun dibuka oranglah.* (Teeuw and Wyatt 1970, I, 99)
>
> Then, as soon as the drum for the morning prayer has been beaten, people opened the gate of the royal compound. (Teeuw and Wyatt 1970, II, 172)

In HP we have the earliest account of the use of the nobat for religious purposes in accordance with the practice of Muslim caliphs centuries earlier. Although nobat pieces in the *Misa Melayu* carry the title of certain prayer times such as 'Nobat Suboh' ('Drum for the Morning Prayer') and 'Nobat Isya' ('Drum for the Night Prayer'), there is no mention of the nobat being performed to signal the start of prayer in any early texts. Here we have two instances in which the nobat was played to indicate prayer times, and the *ragam* 'Nobat Subuh' was probably the obvious piece to be played. The drumming during the Friday prayer times could have used other *ragam*, and the signalling of the morning prayer by the nobat also marked the opening of the palace gate. The sound of the Friday nobat even garnered the respect of the rebellious Bendahara on his way to confront the queen:

> *Maka bendahara pun berhenti seketika menengar bunyi nobat palu-paluan pada waktu Jumaat itu.* (Teeuw and Wyatt 1970, I, 99)

> Then the bendahara stops awhile listening to the sounds of the drum during the time of the Friday prayer. (Teeuw and Wyatt 1970, II, 172)

In seventeenth-century Aceh, the Friday prayer was an important weekly event. It was an elaborate *adat* involving a royal procession and the use of the nobat. The *Adat Aceh* describes in detail the sequence of events that needed to be performed including the list of *ragam* or pieces (Ito 1984). This *adat* was rarely practiced by the Sultans of Aceh during the nineteenth century since they were seldom involved in congregational prayers (ibid.). The playing of the nobat in welcoming the Sultan to a mosque is still practiced in Perak today on the morning of Eid al-Fitr. This signalling of prayer times also continues in Kedah where the nobat is played from the Balai Nobat, a tower located in the middle of Alor Setar town, to indicate the start time of certain prayers. In HP there are two instances where the *balai gendang* or drum pavilion is mentioned. Teeuw and Wyatt (1970, 172) translate it as 'pavilion where the mosque-drum was kept', indicating that the drum was used by the mosque to signal start of prayer, similar to the *beduk* drum found in rural mosques in Malaysia today.

After the beating of the piece 'Nobat Subuh', Seri Amar Pahlawan went out to fetch Raja Bima. Once inside he went straight to the audience hall where Sultan Bahdur Syah was about to amuse himself and stabbed him with a *kris*. On witnessing this, Seri Amar Pahlawan followed Raja Bima to the drum pavilion and pierced him with a lance.

> *Setelah sampai ke hadapan balai gendang itu maka Raja Bima pun diradak oleh Seri Amar Pahlawan dengan lembingnya kena perutnya terus ke belikatnya.* (Teeuw and Wyatt 1970, I, 100)

> When he arrived in front of the pavilion where the mosque-drum was kept, Raja Bima was pierced in the stomach by Seri Amar Pahlawan with his lance, penetrating as far as his shoulder blade. (Teeuw and Wyatt 1970, II, 172)

However, in another sentence, the same *balai gendang* is translated as 'the pavilion where the royal drum was kept' (Teeuw and Wyatt 1970, 181). Since *balai nobat* is still to be found today, it is safe to assume that the *balai gendang* (as the alternate use of the word *gendang* and nobat is normal in Malay literature) mentioned in HP was in fact the pavilion that housed the royal drums of the palace. The following is narrated in HP during the arrival of the ruler of Johor to Patani:

> *Setelah sampai ke balai gendang maka Yang Dipertuan pun datanglah. Setelah Yang Dipertuan melihat kenaikan Syah Alam itu maka Yang Dipertuan segera turun dari gajahnya mengiringkan Syah Alam naik ke balairung.* (Teeuw and Wyatt 1970, I, 109)

> When she had come as far as the pavilion where the royal drum was kept the king arrived. When he saw the Queen's mount he immediately dismounted from his elephant, accompanying the Queen on foot to the audience hall. (Teeuw and Wyatt 1970, II, 181)

Whether it was used to store the mosque drums (*beduk*) or nobat, the *balai gendang* was an essential part of traditional Malay fort-city architecture as noted in the nineteenth-century *Hikayat Siak*:

> *Maka segala orang besar-besar pun berkerahlah orang negeri, menebas dan menebang, dan berbuat kota, parit dan istana balairung dan balai gendang dan masjid, pedapuran, penanggah.* (Siak 461)

> Then all the nobles asked the people of the state to clear the land and built a fort, drains and a palace with an audience hall and drum pavilion and mosque, kitchen.

According to Muhammad Haji Salleh (2011, XLIV), in fifteenth-century Melaka, the *balai gendang* was a building or office in which the *bendahara* (prime minister) conducted his daily duties. Readings of Malay chronicles such as *Hikayat Hang Tuah* and *Sejarah Melayu* indicate that the pavilion was also the point where foreign guests or subjects would dismount from their horses and elephants before proceeding on foot to the audience hall. The idea of a separate building within the palace compound housing drums of the state was similar in concept to the *naqqarakhana* (drum house) in Mughal India where a special building was constructed at palace gates for the *naubat* to be played to announce the arrival of guests or the departure of the ruler.

This *balai gendang* must also have been used to announce other religious occasions such as the Eid al-Adha and the coming of Ramadan as noted on the last page of the HP:

> *Dan hari raya haji tabal demikian itulah tiupnya, dan tabal tabal tatkala memegang tiga kali demikianlah tiuplah juga.* (Teeuw and Wyatt 1970, I, 144)

> And at the festival of the pilgrimage, at the beating of the drum, the trumpets should be blown in the same way, and at the beating of the drums on the three

days preceding the commencement of the fast let the trumpets be blown in the same way. (Teeuw and Wyatt 1970, II, 217)

After the deaths of Sultan Bahdur Syah and Raja Bima, Patani was left with four female heirs and saw the beginning of the period of reigning queens. The first queen to rule was Raja Ijau (r. 1584–1616) followed by her sisters Raja Biru (r. 1616–1624), Raja Ungu (r. 1624–1635) and Raja Ungu's daughter Raja Kuning (r. 1635–1688?). During the reign of Raja Ijau, Patani adopted a business-friendly approach that saw an increase in foreign trade. The Dutch and British were allowed to open trading factories and European travellers to Patani spoke highly of the queen (Amirell 2011). After thirty-two years on the throne, Raja Ijau was succeeded by her sister Raja Biru and the new queen continued with the previous trading policies. During this period the queenship, was formally institutionalised by the powerful *orangkaya* of Patani and Raja Biru's ascendancy seemed uncontested (ibid.). Raja Ungu came to the throne in 1624 as a strong leader who had great dislike of the Siamese. While refusing to use the title *Phra Cau*, given by the Siamese to her two predecessors, Raja Ungu styled herself as *Paduka Syah Alam* ('Her Excellency Ruler of the World') and embarked on an expedition against Siamese suzerainty. As part of her political plan, she established close relationships with other Malay sultanates and married her daughter Raja Kuning to the Yang Dipertuan of Johor.

THE JOHOR NOBAT IN PATANI

As with other court chronicles such as *Sejarah Melayu* and *Hikayat Aceh*, the authors of HP also highlight Patani's relationship and rivalries with other influential Malay polities such as Aceh, Pahang and Johor. Such a contest is related in the story of the Yang Dipertuan of Johor, Sultan Abdul Jalil Shah (r. 1623–1677) who married Raja Kuning around 1623. Raja Kuning was the daughter of Raja Ungu, the third of the line of Patani queens who was married to Sultan Abdul Ghafur Mohaidin Shah (1590–1614) of Pahang. Considering the close relationship of Pahang and Johor, it was not surprising to see Patani, too, becoming closely involved with Johor politics. This resulted in the arranged marriage of Raja Kuning to the ruler of Johor, notwithstanding the fact that she was already married to Okphaya Deca, son of the ruler of Nakhon Si Thammarat, who had been away for three years (Teeuw and Wyatt 1970). The HP details the ensuing war between Patani and Siam, as a result of this 'rebellion' by Raja Ungu against Siamese suzerainty, to which Patani had long sent tributes.

In asking for the hand of Raja Kuning, the Yang Dipertuan of Johor sailed to meet Raja Kuning's mother Raja Ungu, the Queen of Patani. The Johor ruler was met by Seri Maharaja Lela at Beruas and as a 'gift' to the queen, the Yang Dipertuan did not beat his nobat within the vicinity of the kingdom of his future wife:

> *Maka Yang Dipertuan Johor pun belayarlah. Setelah sampai ke Beruas maka tiadalah diberi palu gendang nobat itu. Maka titah Yang Dipertuan kepada orang kaya Seri Maharaja Lela, 'Inilah persembah kita kepada bonda kita'. Dan selama Yang Dipertuan duduk di Patani itu tiadalah Yang Dipertuan tabal; dan disuruh oleh Paduka Syah Alam tabal pun tiada ia mahu.* (Teeuw and Wyatt 1970, I, 109)

> Thereupon the King of Johor set sail. When they arrived at Beruas he refused to allow the royal drum to be beaten. And the king spoke to Seri Maharaja Lela, 'This is Our present to Our mother'. And all the time he remained in Patani the King of Johor did not have his drum beaten; he refused even when the Queen asked him to do so. (Teeuw and Wyatt 1970, II, 181)

This perceived act of respect could also be a sign of arrogance towards the sultanate of Patani in a world where territorial boundaries were often marked by the sounds of the nobat (Meilu Ho 1991, 7; Andaya 2011, 26). It was also common practice in the Muslim world for travelling rulers to bring along their instruments as a show of royal extravagance but not without creating a commotion. It was related by Ibn Batutta that the Sharif of Madina, ignorant of the customs of the fourteenth-century Delhi Sultanate, played his drums (*tubul*) and trumpets (*anfar*) while visiting India, much to the consternation of the general populace (Farmer 1987). There was increasing rivalry between Patani and Johor in the sixteenth and seventeenth centuries as the Malay sultanates strived to fill the power vacuum left by the fall of Melaka. The ruler of Johor's perceived arrogance was earlier felt by the queen when he asked to be personally welcomed by her majesty, which prompted her ministers to remark:

> *Daulat Tuanku, sebenar seperti titah Duli Syah Alam itu, kerana orang Johor itu barang bagaimana pun ia hendak membesarkan dirinya juga.* (Teeuw and Wyatt 1970, I, 109)

> Hail my Lady, it is just as Your Majesty says, for these people from Johor, whatever they do, it is always exclusively for the sake of their own importance. (Teeuw and Wyatt 1970, II, 181)

Nevertheless, the marriage was consummated a few months later and the royal couple sailed back to Johor. The death of of Paduka Syah Alam in 1635 prompted the couple to return to Patani where Raja Kuning was installed as the new queen with the title 'Phra Cau'. After the funeral of her mother Raja Ungu, the Yang Dipertuan of Johor sailed back to Johor and left behind his younger brother the Yang Dipertuan Muda and mother to look after his wife in Patani. It was during his absence that an adulterous affair is reported in the HP involving the queen and the Yang Dipertuan Muda of Johor. The marriage of Raja Kuning and the Johor ruler seemed to have been dissolved between 1642 and 1643 and Raja Kuning eventually married her brother-in-law the Yang Dipertuan Muda. The queen's new husband, spending most of his time being entertained by the court dance called *tarian asyik,* was soon attracted to one of the singers named Dang Sirat (or Dang Merta). The HP describes the dance as *asyik tarik-tarikan* which, according to Sheppard (1983, 12), literally means 'absorbed in poetry' and was traditionally performed in the courts of Kelantan, Pahang and Kedah. The *asyik* dance of the Patani court was probably brought from Pahang since it was only during the reign of Raja Ungu, who was married to the Sultan of Pahang that the dance began to be performed. The names of four male musicians and twelve female singer-dancers of the troupe are given in the HP, including three popular songs or dance-stories.

Patronage of the arts was a matter of great pride for Malay sultanates. Besides the nobat, the inclusion of the dance into the court shows Patani's efforts to elevate itself to the same status as Johor or Aceh. Foreign guests were also entertained with the *asyik* dance, which the English traveller Peter Floris described during his visit to Patani in 1611 as 'very pleasaunte to behold'; he had not seen 'better in all the Indies' (Moreland 2002, 87, 63). The Johor prince's fascination with the court dance led to an adulterous affair that ended tragically, and the nobat was at the centre of the whole drama. The dancer Dang Sirat, described as possessing an unpleasant physical disposition, is said to have used black magic to seduce the Yang Dipertuan Muda. She became increasingly bold with her requests and ultimately demanded that she be installed as queen. Interestingly, the Johor prince was also not only advised by his officials from Johor but also the Acehnese, whose sultanate had recently been at war with Johor. In the following passage, it is clear that both the Johoreans and Acehnese shared the same *adat pertabalan* (installation custom) and understood the implications of the drums. The discussion between the Yang Dipertuan Muda and his advisers regarding the installation of Dang Sirat (who asked to be addressed as Encik Puan) is related in the HP:

> *Kita hendak tabalkan di Kedilah; baik hendak pun kita tabalkan di rumah Encik Puan ini, kerana berdekatan sangat dengan istana besar, jadi sarulah ragamnya nobat Johor dengan nobat* Patani *itu'. Maka sembah sekalian menteri, 'Pendapat patik jikalau tuanku tabalkan Encik Puan itu di Kedi, jadi berbandinglah nobat paduka adinda dengan nobat Encik Puan, kalau-kalau*

fadilat nama duli tuanku pada negeri yang lain'. Maka titah Yang Dipertuan, 'Jikalau demikian, di mana baik kita tabalkan Encik Puan ini? Maka sembah segala orang Aceh, 'Pendapat patik di Tambanglah baik, jikalau tuanku hendak berbuat negeri pun dapatlah kerana rakyat pun banyak hampir pada tempat itu, dan segala menteri hulubalang Patani ini mana yang patut kita pindah bawa mudik dengan anak bininya duduk bersama-sama Encik Puan. (Teeuw and Wyatt 1970, I, 118)

We wish to have her installed in Kedi, even though we would prefer to have Encik Puan installed here in her own house; but this is too near to the main palace and the drum of Johor would sound discordant with the drum of Patani'. Then the ministers respectfully reported, 'In our opinion, if my Lord installs Encik Puan in Kedi, then the Queen's drum would be matched with the drum of Encik Puan, so perhaps my Lord's name would be disgraced in other countries'. Then the Prince said, 'In that case where should we have the drum beaten for Encik Puan?' The Achehnese said respectfully: 'In our opinion Tambangan is the right place. Even if Your Majesty should wish to build a settlement it could be done there, as many people live near that place. And all the ministers and officers of Patani, those who are fit to be transferred an taken upstream, let us take them upstream with their families to stay with Encik Puan. (Teeuw and Wyatt 1970, II, 188)

There are interesting points that can be extracted from the story related above. First, there was the 'violation' against the queen by the Yang Dipertuan Muda of Johor—an act that could be seen as more than just a flash of sexual incontinence but an effort at usurping power and consolidating Johor's influence over Patani. This happened at a time when Patani was politically and economically weak, ruled by a queen who had no real political power. The affairs of the state were run by the *orangkaya* (nobles) who had been opposed to her mother's confrontational policies, and it is reported that Raja Kuning was even denied access to state coffers and had to fend for herself. Her vulnerability was taken advantage of by the Yang Dipertuan Muda of Johor and his followers who began to have political ambitions.

Secondly, we see the involvement of Malays from a number of different sultanates in the affairs of Patani; for example, the marriage of Raja Ungu and Raja Kuning to the Sultans of Pahang and Johor respectively. These alliances would have also resulted in the migration of the sultan's subjects or officials to Patani, where new customs and cultural practices were learnt, adopted and possible marriage relationships established. Then there were the Acehnese among the Johor ruler's circle of advisers and followers, probably the result of Johor's earlier reconciliation with Aceh. This shows the need of subjects and officials as part of a political structure to maintain power even though they were in a 'foreign' state; in other words, there existed a *kerajaan* within a *kerajaan*. The Johor prince was also reminded of the importance of a high number of subjects in order to *buat negeri* (establish a state) and even the families of Patani nobles and warriors could be mobilised if necessary. The ability to command a large number of loyal subjects or followers reflects a Raja's greatness and a measure of his wealth. In a world of constant migration and shifting of allegiance, any possible attempt by a competitor to gain political influence through the mustering of subjects must be viewed with grave concern by a reigning ruler. For whatever reason, this fluidity of migration, interactions and shifting of alliances in the Malay world to a certain extent helped to construct a kind of overarching Malay cultural identity.

Thirdly, the prince of Johor had a nobat with him even though he was in Patani and attempted to exercise his perceived 'power' in installing whoever he pleased. The existence of the nobat shows the need to maintain power in a competitive environment. Anderson (1990, 27) points to some of the more esoteric ways in which rulers in Java emphasised their power through the presence of 'strange' and 'wonderful' people—clowns, dwarfs, and so on—at their courts. There also appeared to be at least one 'extraordinary human being' in the household of the prince of Johor, by the name of Dang Jela. She was the servant of the mother of the Yang Dipertuan Muda and is said to be well versed in sorcery and taught Dang Sirat the art.

> *Dan adalah Dang Sirat itu berguru hubatan kepada Dang Jela dan Dang Jela itu hamba kepada bunda Yang Dipertuan, pengasuh pada Yang Dipertuan Muda dan yaitu juru bawa mandi Yang Dipertuan Muda juga.* (Teeuw and Wyatt 1970, I, 116)

> This Dang Sirat had been taught magical charms by Dang Jela, who was a servant of the mother of the King of Johore and was one of the prince's nurses, and it was she whose duty it was to bathe the prince. (Teeuw and Wyatt 1970, II, 186)

Both the Johoreans and Acehnese knew about the *adat istiadat pertabalan* (installation ceremony) and its importance in establishing a *kerajaan*. They understood the concept of the nobat as a ruler's symbol of sovereignty and power, and the importance of displaying that symbol. Discussions also focussed on the proper demarcation of aural boundaries to avoid the overlapping of the sounds of the nobat. Those from Johore, now believed they were superior to Patanis, chose to have their nobat distinguishable (and perhaps louder) than the Patani's in order to *jaga nama*, or 'save face', and not to incur *malu* or dishonour. Name and honour are significant words among Malays and royal subjects, and as a show of allegiance they are duty-bound to uphold the *nama* of their ruler (Milner 1982, 105–7).

The story of Raja Kuning concludes the first part of the HP, which deals with the *Hulu* (Inland) dynasty. The second part looks into the Kelantan dynasty and a brief summary of all the *bendahara* who served under different rulers of Patani. Part 4 of the HP tells the story of Cau Hang the elephant trainer and his grandson Bendahara Datuk Cerak Kin. The activities of Datuk Sai and the *bendahara* power struggle during the Kelantan dynasty are narrated in Part 5. There is no mention of the nobat or any musical activities in the four parts above. It is the last section of the HP, Part 6, obviously written by an expert on court music and customs, that a detailed description and instruction on the nobat is found, which will be analysed next.

MALAY ADAT AND THE PATANI NOBAT

The final part of the HP deals with Malay customs and the nobat ensemble of Patani. By the term *adat,* one would expect a complete array of court customs, etiquettes or a list of ceremonies, but in this case, the main focus of the *adat* is on the Patani nobat. Apart from HP, there are a number of texts that give some attention to the *adat* of the nobat, notably: *Adat Aceh, Adat Raja Melayu, Misa Melayu* and *Adat Resam dan Adat Istiadat Melayu* (Syed Alwi 1986). Although the *Adat Resam* is rather recent (first published in 1960), it is based on royal customs from the nineteenth-century Riau Lingga sultanate, with information gathered from surviving members of the royal family. The HP is one of the only *hikayat* in the Malay literary genre that has a special section on the *adat* which is useful in the study of the nobat. The HP text can be divided into (a) a description of some of the regalia, (b) a list and description of the *ragam* (pieces) of the nobat and (c) instruction on how the pieces are to be played.

Section A: Regalia

The existing instruments in the present Malay nobat ensembles such as *nagara* or *nekara, gendang, nafiri, serunai, gong* and *kopak* are first mentioned in one of the earliest Malay texts—the *Hikayat Amir Hamzah*. Although a translation from a Persian romance, the author of the hikayat described instruments found in the fourteenth-century Malay world in his narration. There is no mention of the term nobat but instruments used in the ensemble mentioned above are clearly named especially in the context of war; for example, the *nagara, gendang, nafiri, serunai* and *gong* are joined with *ceracap* and *dandi* as part of *genderang perang* or the war drum ensemble. Other instruments mentioned in the *hikayat* include aerophones such as *merangu, muri, serdam*, idiophone *kopak* and chordophones *harbab* and *kecapi*.

In another early text, the *Hikayat Raja Pasai*, the *gong, gendang* and *serunai* are named but not explicitly stated as being part of a nobat ensemble. A clearer picture can be found in the *Sejarah Melayu* that names the *gendang, nafiri, serunai* and *nagara* as being part of the *alat kerajaan* (state regalia) that were used in official Melaka court *istiadat*. Thus, these instruments can be said to constitute the basic nobat ensemble of Melaka although one instrument the *madeli* (a type of idiophone) is also mentioned on two occasions. Apart from the nobat instruments, a number of other instruments are also mentioned. These instruments are categorised as *bunyi-bunyian Melayu* (Malay instruments) and differentiated from *bunyi-bunyian Jawa* (Javanese instruments) such as *gendir, sekati* and *gambang* (SM 117:13). This clear distinction between the two sets of instruments suggests an awareness of a distinct cultural identity among the Malays of fifteenth-century Melaka.

In the case of the HP, however, only five musical instruments are mentioned. In addition to the *gendang raya* or big drum, four instruments constituting the nobat ensemble similar to the ones found in the *Sejarah Melayu* are named. These instruments are clearly part of the Patani nobat ensemble from the sixteenth to the eighteenth century. This *hikayat* is the only known text that lists an inventory of the nobat instruments as part of the state regalia of a Malay court:

> *Dan nafiri emas empat dan perak empat butir dan serunai emas dua dan perak dua butir dan gendang nobat dua belas butir dan negara delapan butir.* (Teeuw and Wyatt 1970, I, 144)

> And there were four gold trumpets and four silver trumpets, and two gold oboes and two silver ones and twelve state drums and eight other drums. (Teeuw and Wyatt 1970, II, 211)

There are more instruments mentioned in this section of the *hikayat* than would be found in present ensembles, and they would be more valuable. This was a reflection of the economic prosperity achieved by the kingdom during the height of its power, but also the value placed on these instruments of power. The description of the regalia in HP, although on a smaller scale, mirrors that of Abu'l Fazl, the Mughal Emperor Akbar's (r. 1556–1605) chronicler who detailed the *naubat* instruments of the Mughal court in 1593. Since the demise of the Patani Sultanate, no other Malay sultanate is known to have possessed such a lavish set of royal musical instruments. The idea of a large royal ensemble like Akbar's did not gain wide acceptance among Malay sultanates. The sound of eight *nafiri* blowing and twenty drums beating traversing the quiet soundscape of seventeenth-century Patani would surely have had a tremendous impact on the populace or any foreign visitor hearing them for the first time. Emanating from the source of power, the palace, it truly reflects the majesty of the *kerajaan* and its ruler.

Section B: Repertoire

The terms usually used in classical Malay literature to denote a song or musical piece are *ragam* and *lagu*. Etymologically, *ragam* is also used to describe a variety or diversity of things such as food or flowers, while *lagu* is closely related to music, especially songs and melodies. In HP the nobat pieces are called *ragam*, a term which is still used by nobat ensembles. This is more appropriate since nobat pieces are instrumental and differentiated by the variety of different drums patterns or styles rather than the melody played by the *serunai*. Nobat *ragam* are cited in a number of Malay texts as part of a narrative or a documentation of a court's customs and ceremonies. Some of the pieces mentioned are 'Ibrahim Khalil' ('Hikayat Raja-Raja Pasai'), 'Gendang Adi Mula' ('Sejarah Melayu'), 'Nobat Iskandar' and 'Nobat Ibrahim' ('Syair Seratus Siti'), 'Ibrahim Khalil' ('Adat Raja Melayu), 'Nobat Iskandar' ('Syair Siti Zubaidah') and 'Nobat Iskandar Zulkarnain' ('Hikayat Hang Tuah'). A more recent text documenting the nineteenth-century nobat *adat* of Riau-Lingga (Syed Alwi 1986), lists 'Iskandar Syah Zulkarnain', 'Ibrahim Khalil', 'Arak-Arak', 'Palu-Palu', 'Seri Istana', 'Subuh' and 'Perang' as part of the repertoire. There is also a mention of the use of pieces from Perak and Indragiri to add to the repertoire, but that are not listed since they are not considered part of the official *ragam*.

All the pieces mentioned by Syed Alwi are still performed today by the nobat of Terengganu, a state geographically close to Patani. Other known texts documenting a complete list of repertoire are the *Misa Melayu*, *Adat Aceh* and HP. Table 4.1 lists the *ragam* of the Patani nobat found in the HP.

Compared against the list shown in table 4.1, there are several pieces which are similar in name within the existing Perak repertoire and the obsolete Melaka repertoire as described in the SM. However, looking at the *ragam* of seventeenth-century Aceh listed in the *Adat Aceh*, none of the pieces mentioned bear any similarity to Patani's or, indeed, any of the existing repertoire in the current ensembles. This may strengthen the argument, related in *Sejarah Melayu*, that the Patani nobat originated from Melaka.

Teeuw and Wyatt found twenty-five pieces listed in HP. There are possibly five more that are not specifically mentioned in the list: 'Nobat Isyak', 'Perang', 'Arak-Arakan', 'Nobat Subuh' and 'Raja Berangkat'. Teeuw and Wyatt (1970) were unsure if 'Perang' was indeed part of the repertoire, resulting from different interpretations of the term:

Table 4.1. The *ragam* of the nobat found in the Hikayat Patani

1. Adimula	16. Inanganda
2. Membetung Gendang	17. Kumbang Menyeri
3. Bujang Alulu Dalul	18. Mandi Adam
4. Dendeng Anak	19. Julang Karang
5. Jalin Meminang	20. Kepi
6. Repen	21. Cik Dewa
7. Orang	22. Inang Sultan
8. Jaman Kembang Seri	23. Bara Alam
9. Raja Bayu	24. Baju Antara
10. Kita Mula	25. Belut
11. Burung Di Peti	26. Nobat Isyak?
12. Temeti	27. Perang?
13. Ragam Tumus Raja-Raja Rebih Diwangkara	28. Arak-Arakan?
14. Cakera Alam	29. Nobat Subuh?
15. Seri Paduka	30. Raja Berangkat?

Bab ini membentung gendang namanya, demikian bunyinya: . . . maka lalu perang. (Teeuw and Wyatt 1970, I, 144)

This paragraph deals with the melody called *membentung gendang;* it sounds as follows: . . . and then the melody 'war' is played. (Teeuw and Wyatt 1970, II, 211)

Bab ini jalin meminang namanya, demikian bunyinya: . . . lalu perang. (Teeuw and Wyatt 1970, I, 144)

This paragraph deals with the melody called *jalin meminang*, it sounds like this: . . . then war starts. (Teeuw and Wyatt 1970, II, 212)

'Perang' is mentioned twice more in the HP and, again, Teeuw and Wyatt (1970) differ in their interpretation of line below. I am of the opinion that the proper translation of the phrase *diubung dengan perang* should be "connected to the piece 'Perang'", which makes more sense considering the earlier mention of the piece 'Perang' as a continuation from another piece.

Maka diubung dengan perang pula; tiup panjang pula dua kali pandaknya tiga kali. (Teeuw and Wyatt 1970, I, 144)

And in connection with a state of war too; again blow long twice, short three times. (Teeuw and Wyatt 1970, II, 215)

The Riau nobat in the nineteenth-century did use the *ragam* 'Perang' to end a piece as documented by Syed Alwi (1986, 73):

Adapun lamanya nobat itu dipalu ialah selama 32 tiupan nafirinya. Setelah itu baharulah pada penghabisannya dipukul gendang perang sebagai penutup.

The duration the nobat is beaten is equivalent to the nafiri being blown 32 times. After this, at the end, the war drum is beaten as the ending.

Furthermore, connecting pieces in a 'suite' is a common practice of nobat; the Perak nobat, for example, plays a medley of four pieces depending on the duration of a particular ceremony (Raja Iskandar 2018). Again, in the fourth occurrence of the word Perang, it is translated as 'war melody' clearly supporting its existence as a piece.

Sebagai pula tatkala hendak palu perang itu maka tiuplah panjang pula dua kali. (Teeuw and Wyatt 1970, I, 144)

When people want to play the war melody, blow the trumpets long twice. (Teeuw and Wyatt 1970, II, 215)

Other possible pieces 'Nobat Isyak' (HP 92:4), 'Arak-Arakan' (HP 93:2), 'Nobat Subuh' and 'Raja Berangkat' (HP 93:20) are also mentioned in the HP but are not part of the repertoire. In the case of 'Nobat Subuh', there is no specific mention of the piece or even the term 'Nobat', other than the time of *subuh* (HP 92:11). It could also be that during this time of the day other pieces were also played which did not carry the title. Nevertheless, there is also a strong possibility that the piece did exist since it is mentioned in conjunction with 'Nobat Isyak'. Furthermore, all four pieces are still to be found in the present repertoire of Perak and Selangor, while 'Arak-Arakan' (with slight variations) is found in all existing Malay nobat ensembles. The reason that the other three pieces are not part of the repertoire is unknown.

While the titles of some of the pieces may indicate their functions within a certain context, most however leave us with no clue whatsoever as to their functions or even their literal meanings. No attempts were made by Teeuw and Wyatt (1970) or Siti Hawa (1992) to decipher the meanings of the *ragam*. In looking into the repertoire of the Kedah nobat, Meilu Ho (1991, 69) argues that some of the titles with no semantic meaning could be cyphers of some sort, 'designed to conceal or discourage curious investigation'. Comparing the Patani with the Perak repertoire, I would suggest that there are two types of *ragam*: the *lagu tetap* (fixed pieces) and *lagu berpalu* (beating pieces), where *lagu tetap* are pieces fixed or assigned to be performed for specific occasions, and *lagu berpalu* are pieces selected at random based on their suitability during a particular moment. From the list, it can be assumed that certain pieces, based on their given titles—like 'Adimula' ('Primordial Beginning'), 'Dendeng

Anak' ('Rocking a Baby'), 'Jalin Meminang' ('Asking for the Hand in Marriage'), 'Mandi Adam' ('Adam's Bath'), 'Nobat Isyak' ('Drum for the Night Payer'), 'Nobat Subuh' ('Drum for the Morning Prayer'), 'Perang' ('War'), 'Arak-Arakan' ('Procession'), 'Raja Berangkat' ('The King Leaves')—are those under the *lagu tetap* category. These pieces could be used for specific court ceremonies as indicated (or hinted) by the titles.

Section C: Instruction

The HP also documents how the *ragam* are to be played. It presents a detailed technical instruction to musicians of the nobat more sophisticated than any other found in Malay literature. A mnemonic system was used to describe the rhythmic patterns and the technical aspects of *nafiri* playing. A variety of long and short patterns are given and repeated according to the need of the occasion, similar to the pieces found in nobat ensembles today. The instruction can be divided into two types: one for the drums and another for the *nafiri*. However, no instruction is given on how the *serunai* is to be played.

GENDANG PATTERNS

The HP documents detailed mnemonic syllables for the twenty-five nobat *ragam*. It is clear here that similar to the Perak nobat, pieces are differentiated by the rhythmic patterns or *ragam* and not the melody played by the *serunai*. Syllabic notation is a typical method of learning in societies steeped in oral tradition for aiding the retention of musical information, and drum students normally learn to speak and memorise these patterns before actually playing the instruments. A similar learning method is used in the music of *wayang kulit* and *makyong* in Kelantan. Each of the pieces is given its title and followed by syllables and further instructions, either to repeat (*balik pulang*) or continue with another piece (*terus perang* or straight to the piece 'Perang'). As an example, the first piece is explained in the HP as follows:

> *Bab ini ragam amanyag nobat: pertama adimula amanya, demikian bunyinya: kemetang kemetang kemetitang kar kemetetang kemetang lekat lekat tipekab nang kemetang kekerkam tepat tepat tepat.* (Teeuw and Wyatt 1970, I, 144)
>
> This chapter deals with the melodies of the royal drums. The first one is called adimula (primordial beginnings), and it sounds as follows: *kemetang kemetang kemetitang kar kemetetang kemetang lekat lekat tipekab nang kemetang kekerkam tepat tepat tepatl.* (Teeuw and Wyatt 1970, II, 215)

The syllables of the pieces range from simple three-word *gam gam gemetang* to highly complicated thirty-nine-word mnemonics. In the Perak nobat, sequences of patterns are normally repeated and are often connected to other *ragam*. In the HP, the only connecting *ragam* mentioned is the 'gendang perang'. However, these largely onomatopoetic mnemonics do not include rhythmic indications or speed of pieces. We can only speculate, based on the spaces given between the syllables; for example, *gam tang* could be played slower than *tepegamtang* or *tit tang* than *titang*. It is difficult to decipher and reconstruct the rhythmic patterns of the Patani nobat due to the large number of different syllables and combinations found. Some of the syllables could have been the same but wrongly copied especially those involving the Jawi letters ک (*kaf*, or 'k') and ݢ (*ga*, or 'g'). So the mnemonic *kemetang* could actually be *gemetang* and the same with *ger* and *ker*. Siti Hawa (1992) uses (rather inconsistently) the letter ݢ instead of ک in many instances, for example, *gegergam* instead of *kekerkam*. For this section, I will use Siti Hawa's edition of the HP, which makes more sense considering the close sounding nature of the letters thus reducing what could possibly be repetitions of the same syllable. Except for two, all of the *ragam* start with the first syllable *gem* or *gam* and end with either *gam*, *tang* or *ting*. I will use the 'a' vowel instead of 'e' in some of the syllables, thus *gemetang* will be spelled as *gametang*.[6] There are five types of syllables found as listed in table 4.2.

Table 4.2. The Five Types of Syllables

Monosyllabic	Disyllabic	Trisyllabic	Quadrisyllabic
Gar	Lekat	Tep-e-gar	Gam-e-titang
Gam	Tepat	Tep-e-gab	Gam-e-tang-gam
Gab	Tekat	Gam-e-tang	Tang-gam-e-tang
Ter	Tepit	Tep-e-tang	Tep-e-gam-tang
Tit	Kemba	Tep-e-gam	Tang-e-tepat
Tang	Tang-gar	Ge-gar-gam	
Ting	Gegar?	Tang-e-tang	
Nang	Ti-tang	It-e-cu	
Ngat	Tang-kim		
	Tang-gam		
	Tang-tang		
	Gi-tang		
	Ke-tang		Pentasyllabic
	Kemat		Tepe-gam-e-tang
	Karang		Tang-gam-e-tepat

In order to decipher the onomatopoetic phrases, a comparison with existing nobat ensembles is needed. The only surviving Malay nobat ensemble with written instructions or notation is that of Kedah. Called *dai*, the notations are indicators or symbols written in the Jawi alphabet and icons mainly to guide drum players, with occasional instructions for the other instruments. There are some similarities between the Patani and Kedah notations, especially the ending syllables used, but we can only speculate as to how the former were performed. In the Kedah nobat, syllable *tang* is played by hitting the edge of the drum and *tik* is played by nudging the edge of the drum; both are played using the left hand. On the other hand, *dam* is played by hitting the centre of the drum using a curved stick in the right hand (Meilu Ho 1991, 32). The Perak nobat only uses the monosyllables *tik* and *tam* for left and right hand playing. Similar to the Kedah *dam*, the Perak *tam* also denotes the hitting of the right hand using the stick. When shown the HP drum patterns, a player of the Kedah nobat acknowledged the similarities and was convinced that there existed some form of historical connection between the Kedah and Patani nobat.[7]

In the Patani instruction, amid the non-semantic words and phrases, there appears the di-syllable *gegar*, which in the Malay language means 'shake'. Could this be a special instruction to the drummers to actually shake the drums to produce a musical effect? In the Kedah *dai*, there is an instruction called *guruh* (thunder) in which the drummer would repeatedly play *dam* on the right hand to create a 'thunderous' effect. The term *guruh* is not uncommon in describing the sound of the nobat, as related regarding the nineteenth-century Riau custom compiled by Syed Alwi (1986, 69):

Apabila lepas tiga kali berbunyi tiupan nafiri itu maka berbunyi pula guruh atau ragam nobat itu.

After the *nafiri* is blown three times then the thunder or pieces of the nobat are then sounded.

Another interesting word that appears in the HP is *slui*, which is used in relation to the *nafiri*. In the *dai* of the Kedah nobat there is a similar word, *sloay*, which is an indicator to hit repeatedly the centre of the drum with a stick. It is unsure whether these words are related to each other.

In sum, based on the comparison and the onomatopoetic mnemonics it can be deduced that the syllable *tang* and *ting* are played with the left hand, or without using a stick. This is also similar to the *ting* drum mnemonics of *wayang kulit* and *makyong* drums, that indicates beating at the side of the drums to produce a 'ringing' tone. Deeper sounds such as *gam* or *kam* could indicate the use of a stick, struck in the middle of the drum. The onomatopoetic *lekat*, *tekat*, *tepat* and *tepit* could mean the dampening or muting of the drums. The different variation of sounds furthermore indicates a possible *menyelang*, or 'interlocking', of the drums, similar to the Perak and Kedah nobat.

ON PLAYING THE *NAFIRI*

The HP offers an amazing observation of the detailed playing technique of the *nafiri* with musical and technical instructions. In the musical part, players are advised how to play alongside the drums on a number of pieces or during a particular time. Some of the instructions are for general pieces and some are specific. For example, the *nafiri* player, when playing a piece in which the drum (presumably the *negara*) is supposed to start the piece, has to wait until the first tap is heard. For more specific pieces or time, the HP documents that:

> *Tatkala nobat waktu isyak itu demikian itu juga mulanya; tatkala turun kepada perangin tiuplah beri lanjut sekali dahulu, sudah tiup tiga kali pula tambah.* (Teeuw and Wyatt 1970, I, 144)

> When the drum is beaten in the evening, the beginning should be the same; when it lowers to the *perangin* (the mouthpiece through which air passes?) give a prolonged blow once, after that give three additional blows. (Teeuw and Wyatt 1970, II, 214)

Although the *nafiri* is considered a melodic instrument, it does not function as such within the present context, and is limited to playing single or, in the case of the Kedah nobat, three notes (Meilu Ho 1991, 30). One interesting point about this *nafiri* instruction in the HP is the mention of a specific 'melody' played by the instrument called 'Palu-Paluan'.

> *Sebagai pula, tatkala hari Jumaat tiuplah bersama-sama dengan gendang, tiup panjang dua kali pandak tiga kali panjang pula sekali; tiuplah ragam palu-paluan beri lanjut tiga kali.* (Teeuw and Wyatt 1970, I, 144)

> Another rule, on Fridays we should blow the trumpets together with the drums, blow them long twice and short three times, and then long again once; blow the melody *palu-paluan*; prolong the blows three times. (Teeuw and Wyatt 1970, II, 214)

The only known *ragam* played by a melodic instrument are found in the Perak nobat, called 'Merawan' and 'Senangin' and played by the *serunai*. In the technical part of *nafiri* playing the ideal sound to be produced and correct technique is as follows:

Adapun tatkala tiup panjang itu demikian bunyinya: uting, beri lanjut serta diketarkan. Tatkala tiga kali ditiup demikian bunyinya, yang sama tengah itu dilanjutkan sedikit bunyinya. (Teeuw and Wyatt 1970, I, 144)

Now as regards to a long blow, its sound should be as follows: *uting*, let it be prolonged and let it trill. In the case of three blows let the sound be the same, but the middle one should be protracted a little. (Teeuw and Wyatt 1970, II, 214)

In the passage above, the mnemonic sound of a 'long blow' has two syllables, *u* and *ting*, indicating a use of two notes sliding either down or up. Usually in the Kedah nobat a long *nafiri* blow begins with a higher note (G5) sliding down to (D5), an interval of approximately a perfect fourth (Meilu Ho 1991, 146). In the case of the Patani *nafiri*, based on the mnemonic syllables, it was likely that it started with a lower note. There is also the use of the word *diketarkan* which, from a musical point of view, more closely resembles the musical effect of vibrato or tremolo.

The following sentences deal with the sounds of another 'long blow' and a 'short blow' using a number of extra syllables.

Adapun yang bunyi panjang itu uting ang uting. Adapun yang pandak itu ating ating uting ti u, ujung sekali itu dieret sedikit. Adapun yang lima kali itu berturut-turut senapas senapas. (Teeuw and Wyatt 1970, I, 144)

As for the long blow, its sound is *uting ang uting*. As for the short blows, they sound *ating ating uting ti u*—the last part should be drawn out a little. As for the five consecutive blows, they should be blown in one breath each time. (Teeuw and Wyatt 1970, II, 215)

The aspiring player is further taught how to blow a proper sound using such term as *bulat*, or 'round', to describe the ideal tone.

Adapun barangsiapa hendak belajar maka tiuplah beri kuat-kuat supaya bulat bunyinya. Adapun memasukkan uting itu dipetik-petik lidah sehabis-habis kuat, maka besar bunyinya; lamun kurang pun kurang bunyinya, demikianlah syaratnya membunyikan itu. (Teeuw and Wyatt 1970, I, 144)

Now anyone wanting to learn to blow the trumpet should blow as hard as possible, so that the sound is 'round'. If one has to insert (the long blow) *uting* the tongue should be (moved to and fro) as vigorously as possible, so that the sound be loud. If the blowing is not strong enough, then the sound is insufficient; such is the condition for blowing the trumpet. (Teeuw and Wyatt 1970, II, 216)

Apart from the need to produce a 'round' tone, a student is also advised to use his tongue in order to create an *uting* sound by moving it to and fro. In the Perak nobat the term *petik* (literally, 'snap') refers to the finger movements of a *serunai* player. The use of the tongue and emphasis on blowing strength in playing the *nafiri* is interesting since it mirrors the embouchure technique of brass playing in producing different tones and pitches. Although traditionally limited to a few notes, mostly played as drones, could the Patani *nafiri* have been used to play more sounds and notes? The mentioning of the *ragam* 'Palu-Paluan' specifically played by the *nafiri* could very well answer this question. The variety of sounds (and probably pitches) also shows the *nafiri* as playing a more active role in the ensemble than it does today.

SUMMARY

The discovery of the HP manuscripts, their romanization from the original Jawi and later translation into English help enlighten us about one of the most obscure sultanates in the Malay world. There is not much difference in terms of writing style and theme as compared to other well-known historical literature such as *Sejarah Melayu* and *Hikayat Raja Pasai*. The HP nevertheless provides a chronological narrative of events that is independent of any direct influence from other texts of the same genre and stands above the rest in terms of its historical accuracy, originality and, of course, its musical content.

There are elements of continuity with cultures of the past shown in the retention of Hindu-Buddhist, especially Srivijayan court culture, including art and architecture. Performing arts were used as a symbol of greatness and the nobat could have been used to exhibit Patani's standing as a power to be reckon with in the region, especially to foreign trading powers. This is clear in the description given in the HP of the costly and large ensemble found in the inventory of the court.

The HP is explicit in showing the volatile nature of the sultanate both externally and internally. The authors show no restraint in detailing the seditious nature of the sultanate's officials and the reckless, condescending manner of those from Johore. These anecdotes underlie the larger narrative of Patani's continued efforts in maintaining a good relation with its northern Siamese suzerain while at the same time enhancing relations and strengthening alliances with other Malay sultanates. Patani is portrayed as a rising power in the wake of Melaka's demise, rivalling the contemporary powers of Johor and Aceh, within which emerges scenes of an interconnected world of Malay migrants, merchants, *fakirs*, princes and nobles that form a unified cultural identity, a sense of 'Malay-ness'. While Patani welcomed the diversity of Malays from different parts of the archipelago that made up its population, the sultanate upheld its pride and dignity against any attempt to undermine its sovereignty.

This is shown in the swift response meted out against the power-usurping Yang Dipertuan Muda of Johor and his followers.

The nobat is central to the *kerajaan* in this world, and an essential part in the formation of one. Although lacking in ceremonial details, the nobat is shown in the HP as not just an important component in the running of the state, but an essential one, from marking the time of prayers and religious celebrations and installing new rulers and cannons, to receiving foreign envoys and demarcating territorial boundaries. Like any other Malay polity, the Patani nobat as part of the state regalia powerfully sounded out the ruler's majesty and *daulat*, and was central to its continued existence. It was a source of power, a measure of a ruler's *nama* (name), wealth and prestige. This was particularly reflected in the large size of the ensemble, and the very fact of HP's documentation of a long list of repertoire with meticulous details of the playing instructions. The great financial value of the instruments outweighs present-day ensembles and underlines the wealth and influence enjoyed at the height of Patani's existence as a regional power. Although not denying the fact that relations were made with other Malay sultanates, Patani seemed to chart its own course in establishing its own cultural identity amid the larger Malay world.

The Melaka Empire is largely absent from the HP's conceptualizations of this world, probably a sign of Patani's deliberate disassociation from Melaka's legacy. Patani is a Malay sultanate among the many but a *different* one. Perhaps ironically then, the *Sejarah Melayu* clearly states the Patani nobat's Melaka origin. Historically, the HP does not document the origins of the Patani nobat. But by looking at the repertoires of Patani and Perak (the latter of which is certainly derived from Melaka), we observe pieces with similar titles. Even the Melaka piece 'Adimula' mentioned in the *Sejarah Melayu* was part of the Patani repertoire.

Nor does HP reveal any clue to the later fate of the Patani nobat. The ensemble and other regalia were most likely confiscated by the Siamese after their 1785 subjugation of Patani. Another possibility is that the regalia was transferred to Kelantan, but looking at Kelantan's present-day court ensemble the *gendang besar*, there is no semblance of the nobat ensemble described in the HP. *Gendang besar* is more akin to a *makyong* ensemble than a nobat and the only aspect that parallels the Patani nobat was the size of the ensemble used during the installation of Sultan Ismail Petra in 1979, involving eight musicians.

The HP, like many other court chronicles, is an immortalisation of various events and customs involving Malay rulers, their families and nobles. This was done for the benefit of future generations, for them to understand, remember and learn from past achievements and mistakes. Despite the mythological origins and miraculous conversions of Malay rulers bestowed with *daulat*, they are still portrayed as mortal beings that made wrong judgements, lost battles and died miserable deaths. Archaeological evidence and non-Malay records may prove the existence of the rulers of the Patani sultanate but the sight and sounds of the Patani nobat can only remain in our imagination.

Nonetheless, it is clear that the court ensemble portrayed in the HP would have produced what Schafer (1994, 10) terms a *soundmark*, a unique sound that identifies a community, in this case the people of Patani, but also with deep connections to the larger Malay world. The Patani-ness of the sound is evident in the unique titles of the *ragam* and rhythms documented, but at the same time, its nobat remains identifiable as one among a number of Malay nobat, many of them interrelated through Melaka, from Patani to Riau and Aceh to Brunei. As the centuries roll by, the nobat becomes more and more truly a *Malay* soundmark. There are hints—the recognition of difference between *bunyi-bunyian Melayu* (Malay instruments) and *bunyi-bunyian Jawa* (Javanese instruments), for instance—that this nascent process of identity formation was in part the result of increasing encounters with outsiders, especially Europeans as suggested by Leonard Andaya (2001; 2008). This is the subject of the next chapter, in which we shall look at an aspiring seventeenth-century sultanate across the Straits of Melaka–Aceh.

NOTES

1. This chapter is derived in part from the article, Raja Iskandar Bin Raja Halid, 'The *Nobat* in Early Malay Literature: A Look into the *Hikayat Patani*', *Indonesia and the Malay World* 46, no. 135 (2018): 168–97; copyright © editors, *Indonesia and the Malay World*; reprinted by permission of Taylor & Francis Ltd, http://www.tandfonline.com, on behalf of editors, *Indonesia and the Malay World*.

2. This idea was used by Meilu Ho (1991) in her study of the Kedah nobat where a structural parallel between the *nahara-serunai* and sultan-chief relationships is made. She contends that although the *nahara* is seen as the most important instrument of the nobat, but as a musical ensemble the *serunai* is the chosen human and musical leader. This may be true only to the Kedah nobat, but the same cannot be said about the other remaining ensembles. In the Perak nobat, for example, performance is led by the *nengkara*.

3. Anderson argues that the Javanese concept of power is in opposition to Western political theory where it is not the exercise but the accumulation of power that matters. He further contends that a substantial part of traditional Javanese literature 'deals with the problem of concentrating and preserving of Power rather than its proper uses' (23).

4. The survey of early Malay literature is made possible by the Malay Concordance Project, an online service initiated by Dr. Ian Proudfoot of the Australian National University.

5. Seri Bija Diraja is a title given to the fourth most senior nobles in the fifteenth-century Melaka sultanate after Bendahara (prime minister), Penghulu Bendahari (finance minister) and Temenggung (defence minister). Together with the Laksamana (admiral), he is in charge of military campaigns.

6. 'Gam' has a more downbeat feel, as compared to 'gem'.

7. Personal communication with the deputy leader of the Royal Nobat of Kedah in Alor Setar, Kedah, August 2013.

Chapter Five

The *Adat Aceh* and Seventeenth-Century European Encounter

The arrival of the Portuguese on the shores of Melaka in 1511 marked the beginning of a long era of European colonization of the Malay world.[1] Melaka was in Portuguese control for almost 130 years until the city was wrested from them by the Dutch in 1641. The Dutch control of Melaka lasted 184 years before it was handed over to the British after the Anglo-Dutch Treaty in 1824, which effectively divided the Malay world into two: the present-day territory of Indonesia and the Malay Peninsula and Straits Settlements. For more than four centuries, the European-Malay encounter had a huge economic, political and social impact on the peoples of the region. It also saw the start of critical European inquiry and scholarship of Southeast Asia which has continued to this day.

The aftermath of Melaka's fall saw the emergence of new sultanates and revitalisation of existing ones. It opened the door for the quest for political and economic supremacy among Malay polities which involved intense maneuverings that often led to war. This process has been discussed by Leonard Andaya who further argues that the increasing contact between indigenous peoples and the Europeans in the sixteenth century helped to stimulate 'ethnic formation' in the Straits of Melaka (2008, 4). This encounter and the increase in economic activities in the region, stimulated the collective notion of Malay identity especially among different intra-migrating ethnic groups who tend to identify themselves with the larger more powerful Malay community (see chapter 4).

Scholarly debate on the nature of Malay identity or 'Malayness' covering both sides of the Melaka Straits has been going on for decades (Milner 2008; L. Andaya 2001; 2008; Barnard 2001: 2006; Reid 2001; Fee 2001; Shamsul 1996: 2001; Matheson 1979). In his analysis of debates on identity in Malaysia, Shamsul (1996) outlines a number of critical challenges, the most important of which relates to what he terms the 'conceptual' problem of perception: the 'static' and 'dynamic' notions of identity (476). He further argues that identity formation takes place within the context of 'authority defined' and 'everyday defined' social reality, which coexist and are intricately bound at any given moment (477). Sociologist Lian Kwen Fee (2001, 877) views the construction of Malay identity as the reaction to external political and economic influences, which the ruling elites and intellectuals took advantage of to mobilise the support of the masses for their own aims—a process of ethnic formation that included the rise of nationalism and invention of traditions. Although these discussions are largely focussed on the colonial and postcolonial period, it can be argued that this process started in the early modern period, as reflected in the customary writings of court chronicles and manuals by established Malay sultanates. This took place before the ethnic classification of peoples based on the Enlightenment view of European travellers and later colonialists that resulted in the publication of travelogues and 'colonial knowledge' (Reid 2001, 303; Fee 2001, 863; Shamsul 2001, 357). Katherine Brown (2000, 3) argues that European travel writings were published with certain set of aims—among others—to increase the prestige of individuals, nations and competing companies.

Malay sultanates held elaborate ceremonies and celebrations where music mediated notions of Malay identity and supremacy; and documented them in manuals of *adat*. Musical performance became a vital tool in developing a coherent sense of collective identity and the establishing of social and political boundaries. The focus of this chapter is the kingdom of Aceh. While the history of sixteenth- and seventeenth-century Aceh is intertwined with the history of the wider *dunia Melayu*, indigenous and foreign literatures provide little information on its musical heritage, especially court music. Situated in the cradle of Islam in the region, it was inevitable that the religion was integrated into the fabric of its society, helping mould a more 'Islamised' Malay identity. But there are two questions that remain. How far did Islam go in shaping Malay-Acehnese culture, especially with regard to court customs and ceremonies? And what impact, direct and indirect, did European imperialist expansion have on Aceh and, by extension, other Malay sultanates, and how did responses to these encounters affect court practices—especially the nobat institution?

This chapter explores the *adat* of the court of Aceh to reveal, on the one hand, the richness of its musical tradition and, on the other, the influence of the religio-political developments in the post-Melaka period in the shaping of Malay-Acehnese cultural identity. I consider how the ruler possessed not only political power but also absolute control over religious and sonic space. Europeans too, while initially mere passive observers, would eventually entangle themselves in the dynamics of Malay politics and encounters involving sound-worlds will be discussed against the evolving nature of Malay identity and culture. I shall begin with brief background on the initial European encounter, the impact of Melaka's fall and the rise of Aceh as a new regional power.

FIRST ENCOUNTER: MELAKA AND THE PORTUGUESE

Considered a successor to the Srivijaya Empire, Melaka began to assert itself as an important port by the middle of the fifteenth century. Its strategic position in a narrow strait that connected the Indian Ocean with the South China Sea made it a thriving commercial centre. Melaka's importance to international maritime trade was well summarised by Tome Pires (1465–1524) when he declared that 'whoever is Lord of Malacca has his hands on the throats of Venice' (Suma Oriental). Melaka became not only the center of commerce but also Islamic learning and the enculturation of Malay identity (Barnard 2001; L. Andaya 2001). According to historian Leonard Andaya:

> So dominant was the image of Melaka that the name Melayu and all things Malay came to be equated with Melaka. What was Melakan was Malay, what was truly Malay was Melakan. (33)

At its peak, Melaka was admired throughout the *alam Melayu* as a symbol of Malay greatness which laid the basis on which later Malay sultanates measured themselves. Under court patronage, the arts and literature flourished, while royal customs and ceremonies were firmly established and documented. The Melaka sultanate was immortalised in a number of Malay court chronicles, which included among others the *Sejarah Melayu* and *Hikayat Hang Tuah*. Melaka's expansion and the subsequent spread of the nobat to other states in the Malay world were narrated in the *Sejarah Melayu* (SM 92:33; 173:24; 190:12; 228:21; 229:39) as explained in chapter 3. The narrations not only reveal the geographical influence of the Melaka sultanate (Pahang, Kampar, Beruas, Petani and Kedah) but also detail the customary use of the nobat in bestowing honour or prestige on lesser polities as a symbol of suzerainty over them. This Malay court *adat* or custom of bestowing drums and robes of honour (*khil'at*) was likely influenced by the Muslim courts of South Asia and the Middle East (see Gordon 2003, 2).

Melaka's reputation as a growing regional power and an important trading port of the East reached King Manuel I of Portugal, who sent a mission to establish ties with the sultanate. Led by Diogo Lopes de Sequeira, the Portuguese became the first Europeans to reach the shores of Melaka and Southeast Asia in 1509. The Malays' first encounter with the *Peringgi*[2] is recounted in the *Sejarah Melayu*:

Maka segala orang Melaka pun berkampunglah melihat rupa Peringgi itu, sekaliannya hairan melihat dia. Maka kata orang Melaka ia ini Benggali putih; maka pada seorang Peringgi itu, berpuluh-puluh orang Melaka mengerumun dia, ada yang memutar janggutnya, ada yang menepuk kepalanya, ada yang mengambil cepiaunya, ada yang memegang tangannya. (SM 230:14)

The people of Melaka gathered to see how the Frank looks like, everybody was bemused. Then said the Melakans, 'he is a white Bengali!', then tens of Melakans began to surround him, some twisted his beard, some tapped on his head, some took his hat, some grasped his hand.

The Portuguese were initially welcomed by Sultan Mahmud Shah (r. 1488–1528) but he was later warned by Muslim traders in Melaka of the possible threat posed by the Europeans. Convinced by the warnings, Sultan Mahmud captured and killed some of de Sequeira's men, and attempted to attack their ships (Ricklefs 2001, 26). Two years later, another mission was sent to Melaka. This time it was led by Alfonso de Albuquerque and after several failed negotiations, the Portuguese eventually attacked and conquered Melaka in 1511. Sultan Mahmud Shah and his family escaped the onslaught and moved south to Johor. After several failed attempts to recapture Melaka, Sultan Mahmud was forced to flee to Pahang before sailing to Bentan, where he established a new capital. According to C. C. Brown's translation of the *Sejarah Melayu* (Brown 1952), the Melaka state regalia, including the *pedang kerajaan*, was safely taken to Bentan. In the year 1526, Bentan was attacked and finally razed to the ground by the Portuguese, which forced Sultan Mahmud to move to Kampar, Sumatera. It is further stated in the SM that the gold and valuables of Melaka were saved during the onslaught.

The fall of Melaka resulted in the establishment of two new sultanates, Perak and Johor. Both considered themselves rightful successors to the Melaka Empire, based primarily on the fact that their founders were both sons of the last Sultan of Melaka, in addition to common mythic ancestors, religious and cultural ties. However, the rise of these Malay polities, especially Johor, did not go down well with Aceh, a Malay sultanate which was growing in power by the early sixteenth century. Aceh, together with Pasai, Pidie, Daya and Lamuri were small kingdoms independent from Melaka in northern Sumatera, a region where Islam was first introduced in the thirteenth century.[3]

Melaka's rise as an economic, cultural and religious center could be attributed to its long relations with Pasai, which according to Groeneveldt (1960, 87) shared the same language, way of dressing and ceremonies as the former. For economic and political purposes, Melaka's first ruler Parameswara married a princess from Pasai, leading to his conversion to Islam and the introduction of the nobat to the Melaka court. Although Melaka rose to prominence as an Islamic sultanate in the fifteenth century, Pasai was still considered superior as a centre of Islamic learning and acted as spiritual guide to the Melaka sultanate. Pasai's connection to the Islamic kingdoms in India was evident when the Sufi traveler Ibn Battuta, acting as an envoy of the Sultan of Delhi, visited the sultanate during the reign of Sultan Malik al-Zahir (r. 1297–1328). During his stay in Pasai, Ibn Battuta witnessed a court ceremony in which music was played, writing:

> We dismounted at the usual place (where the lances were) and the sultan rode into the palace, where a ceremonial audience was held, the sultan remaining on his elephant opposite the pavilion where he sits (at reception). Male musicians came in and sang before him, after which they led in horses with silk, caparisons, golden anklets, and halters of embroidered silk'. (Gibb [tr.] 1929, 276)

With the demise of the Melaka sultanate and the annexation of Pasai in 1524, Aceh began to establish itself as the center of Islamic scholarship, and more importantly took over the mantle of Malay supremacy, famously becoming known as 'the veranda of Mecca'. According to Leonard Andaya (2008, 125), Aceh's edge over Johor as Melaka's successor was due to its strong economic and cultural relationships with great Islamic kingdoms in the Middle East and India, and 'came to offer new standards of Malayness based on Islamic models in literature, in court administration, and in behavior'.

ACEH AS THE NEW MALAY-MUSLIM CENTRE

The Portuguese were seen as a serious threat to the Malay world. After the defeat of Melaka, resistance against the Portuguese continued with the Acehnese. A *jihad* (holy war) was launched against the 'infidel' Portuguese, and Aceh began to assume the responsibility as not only defenders of the Malays but also of Melaka as center of the Malay world (Hadi 1992; L. Andaya 2001, 2008). Muslims passing through the Straits of Melaka began to shift their trade and religious activities from Portuguese-occupied Melaka to other ports in the region, including Patani, Palembang, Brunei, Banten, Makasar, Banjarmasin and Aceh (Reid 2001, 300). Due to its strategic location and abundance in natural produce, Aceh rapidly rose in prominence. Under the rule of Sultan Alaudin Ri'ayat Syah al-Qahar (r. 1537–1568), Aceh began sending envoys to the Ottoman Empire in order to strengthen its relations with the wider Muslim world. In response, the Ottoman Sultan sent a certain Lutfi as an ambassador to Aceh in 1564, who after two years returned to Istanbul with a letter from Sultan Alaudin requesting military aid (against the Portuguese in Melaka) and pledging his kingdom's subservience to the Turkish Empire (Alam and Subrahmanyam 2005, 212–13).

Islam continued to play a dominant role in the affairs of the kingdom and as a center of Islamic learning, Aceh attracted many foreign *ulama* (religious scholars) to its shores. During the reign of Sultan Ali Riayat Syah (r. 1571–1579), an Egyptian scholar of the Shafie *madhab* (school of thought) arrived from Mecca and taught metaphysics. This was followed by the arrival of two scholars from Mecca in 1582 during the reign of Sultan 'Ala al-Din (r. 1579–1586). One was a Sufi named Sheikh Abu al-Khair and the other Sheikh Muhammad Yamani who taught Islamic theology. Leonard Andaya (2008, 124) comments that:

> Building upon Pasai's reputation as a center of Islamic knowledge, Aceh demonstrated its Islamic cosmopolitanism by adhering to the latest religious and secular fashions from the Islamic world. Scholars, traders, and foreign envoys from Muslim lands brought their wares, tracts, and ideas to Aceh. They enticed the ruler and the people to institute changes that would update their society in the image of their illustrious coreligionists in the Ottoman, Safavid, and Mughal Empires. As was characteristic of Southeast Asia, Aceh only selected those aspects that were compatible with the society.

It was not long before Aceh began receiving foreign visitors apart from Muslim scholars from the Middle East and South Asia. In 1592, English trader James Lancaster came just a few miles from the shores of Aceh before heading to the island of Penang on the west coast of the Malay Peninsula. Having plundered a few Portuguese ships along the Straits of Melaka, Lancaster sailed back to England only to return later to Aceh in 1602. However, Lancaster's visit was preceded by another Englishman, John Davis, who became the first English to set foot on Aceh in 1599.

THE EUROPEANS' ENCOUNTER WITH THE NOBAT

John Davis's arrival as navigator of the Dutch fleet commandeered by Cornelis de Houtman marked the beginning of English-Acehnese interactions. He was kindly received by Sultan Alaudin Riayat Syah who wanted to know more about Queen Elizabeth and England's defeat of the Spanish Armada in 1588. Aceh's admiration of England was viewed positively by the English and subsequently a letter from Queen Elizabeth to the Sultan of Aceh was brought by Lancaster on seventh of June 1602 as part of the first voyage of the English East India Company. He and his crew were first received at the port of Aceh by two Dutch merchants, who brought them to their factory and advised them on local customs and manners. Acknowledging the arrival of foreign guests, the Sultan then sent his officials to summon them for an audience at the palace. In accordance to Malay royal customs in receiving foreign ambassadors, a procession was held to accompany the envoys, letters and gifts to the palace. The ceremony involved a number of officials, guards, elephants, and the nobat. It was reported by Lancaster (1940, 91) that the Sultan:

> sent six great elephants, with many trumpets, drums, and streamers, with much people, to accompany the generall to the court, so that the presse was exceeding great. The biggest of these elephants was about thirteene or fourteene foote high; which had a small castle upon his back, covered with crimson velvet.

This was one of the earliest accounts of the Malay nobat by a European traveler. Lancaster's entourage was also entertained by the Sultan at his court where they drank rice wine followed by the ruler's 'damosels' dancing and playing music.

Lancaster's visit was followed by Thomas Best who was accorded the same ceremony, this time receiving gifts and a letter from Sultan Iskandar Muda in 1613. Ralph Croft, one of Best's men, wrote:

> The present and letter was brought to our house by a nobleman riding upon an ollephantt, accompanied with other towe of the Kinges chiefe nobles, with muzick plaieing before them alongst the streets, as ther customes is in such affaires which concernes the Kinge. (Best 1934, 167–68)

In 1621, a French general, Augustin de Beaulieu, arrived in Aceh on a mission to obtain a trading license and permission to build a factory from Sultan Iskandar Muda. Similar ceremonial reception was accorded to the Frenchman by the Acehnese nobilities:

> The other two Orankays rode upon Arabian horse before the elephant that carried the letter. Before them were fourteen or fifteen men, without which nothing could be presented to the king: six trumpets, six drums, and six hautboys led the van, which sounded till we arrived at the castle, about a league off. (731)

Beaulieu's account clearly states the instruments and number of players involved. The trumpets, drums and hautboys mentioned could be the *nafiri*, *gendang* or *nengkara* and *serunai* as these instruments were commonly used by Malay sultanates in the region (see chapter 3 for details of fifteenth-century Melaka's ceremony). This is probably the first account of the number of players involved in a procession, but it is uncertain if the number changed through time. Although there were minor variations in the accounts given by these European travellers (for example, the number of elephants used) the ceremony continued to be performed during Iskandar Thani's reign (1636–1641). According to Peter Mundy (1919, 118), he 'sente 5 or 6 Elephants to bringe them to Courte, where haveinge dyned and beinge invested after the Malayan manner'. Based on these accounts, a slight difference is apparent between the seventeenth-century-Acehnese and fifteenth-century-Melakan ceremonies, including the fact that the state umbrella was not used in Aceh. However, both sultanates used the full nobat to indicate the importance of the letter being presented.

These accounts by various seventeenth-century European travellers show the Aceh Sultanate's attention to royal ceremonial details as a manifestation of its economic and political power. Aceh's royal ceremonies, both secular and religious, were conducted similarly to other great Indian Ocean Muslim kingdoms at the time. These involved street processions, which were seen as important visual and aural reminders of the ruler's authority and presence. A seventeenth-century Acehnese sultan's weekly procession to the mosque can be seen as an important reminder of his power as the daily *adhan* (call to prayer) was for the greatness of Allah.

Fortunately, we do not have to rely solely on European accounts for descriptions of the Acehnese nobat of this time. Details of these royal ceremonies were codified in a court record known as the *Adat Aceh* (AA). Like the *Hikayat Patani* (HP) and *Sejarah Melayu* (SM), the AA is a written testament of a Malay sultanate's greatness, a reminder of its esteemed genealogy and guide for proper royal conduct. These shed a different light on European encounters with the nobat.

THE *ADAT ACEH*

The AA is a manual detailing the royal affairs of the Acehnese state. It was compiled in three main stages beginning in 1607, followed by the second stage in 1645/1646 and lastly in 1708/1709 (Hadi 2004, 119). It was copied in the nineteenth century to provide the English authority in Penang the necessary information to draft an Anglo-Acehnese commercial treaty. The Malay manuscript was kept at the India Office Library until it was published in facsimile in 1958 by Gerardus W. J. Drewes and Petrus Voorhoeve, under the title *Adat Atjeh*. It was not until 1976 that the *jawi* manuscript was transliterated into Romanised Malay by Teungku Anzib Lamnyong and published in Aceh. The AA received considerable attention by scholars looking into the history of Aceh but the text itself has only been thoroughly studied by Takeshi Ito (1984).

The AA is divided into four parts:

1. Regulations for Kings
2. Genealogy of the Kings of Aceh
3. Religious and court ceremonies
4. Administrative rules and practices at the port

Four religious events are mentioned in Part 3 of the AA: the coming of Ramadan, the Friday prayer and the celebration of *Eid al-Fitr* and *Eid al-Adha*. The details of the ceremonies may be summarised below.

Majlis Tabal Pada Hari Memegang Puasa (Start of the Fasting Month Ceremony)

Ramadan is the ninth month of the Muslim lunar calendar and is considered the holiest month for adherents of the faith. It is observed as the month of fasting, an obligatory act for able-bodied persons, which is prescribed as one of the five pillars of Islam.[4] The coming of the month is based either on the visual sighting of the crescent moon (*hilal*) on the twenty-ninth evening of Syaaban, or astrological calculation (*hisab*). If the moon is sighted, Ramadan will be celebrated on the evening itself since in Islamic (and Jewish) tradition, a new day starts after sundown. The Aceh Sultanate acknowledged the marking of the coming of Ramadan as part of the ceremonies of the court codified in the AA in the seventeenth century. It is interesting to note the use of the word *tabal*, in the ceremony. The Arabic loanword meaning drum and by extension, installation, as the ruler was 'drummed in'. The sequence of the ceremony is explicitly laid out in the AA and music played an important role.

The AA states that on the eve of the thirtieth of Syaaban, the Shahbandar Seri Rama Setia brought a tribute of clothing to the Sultan. He placed it on a ceremonial platform[5] called *biram* situated outside the *dalam* or royal enclosure and watched the coming of the new moon. The next day, or on the first of Ramadan, royal insignia named Raja Tajuk Intan Dikarang was carried in a procession to the palace. The Shahbandar then offered seven bowls of flowers to each of the three burial complexes of the Sultan's ancestors. The ceremony continued as narrated in the AA:

> *Kemudian maka berdirilah Bentara Blang kemudian ditiup oranglah nafiri tujuh ragam serunai pun tujuh ragam juga, kemudian dipalu oranglah genderang dong*[6] *tujuh kali tujuh ragam.* (AA 50a: 2–5)

Then Bentara Blang[7] stands up, followed by the blowing of the *nafiri* in seven tunes, the serunai in seven tunes too, then the standing drums are struck seven times in seven tunes.

Although the royal ceremony marking the coming of Ramadan is not prescribed in Islam, the number seven used is prevalent in the Qur'an and Hadith (sayings of Prophet Muhammad) as a number particularly associated with Islam (e.g. Qur'an, 65:12 and 67:3). Major acts of worship such as the *tawaf* (circumambulation) of the Ka'abah and *sa'ie* (walking back and forth) between Safa and Marwah during the Hajj are done seven times. The prostrating position of the daily prayer also requires seven parts of the body to touch the ground. Could the use of the number be said to give the Aceh court rituals higher religious significance and legitimacy from the Islamic point of view? This contrasts with some of the royal ceremonies of the Perak[8] and Riau courts, as successors to the Melaka ruling house. According to Winstedt (1925), the old Melaka constitution practiced in Perak, Pahang and Negri Sembilan was shown to have used the numbers 4, 8, 16 and 32 derived from Hindu-Buddhist cosmology. The nobat is still played to mark the coming of Ramadan in Perak today, after the *Asar* (mid-afternoon) prayers on the three last days of Syaaban.

The ceremony continued with tributes and the insignia Raja Tajuk Intan Dikarang carried by the Shahbandar brought into the palace following the Sultan's command. The *cap* or royal seal was then brought in and witnessed by the *hulubalang* (district chiefs) in accordance to their rank. The head of the royal drums then requested a specific piece to be played:

> *Kemudian dari itu maka sembah Keujruen Geundrang Seri Udahna Kembaran mohon titir Ragam Adani tabal Paduka Seri Sultan, maka sabda yang maha mulia yang dibawa Megat maklum Keujruen Geundrang Seri Udahna Kembaran, maka mohon palu Genderang Berangkat seperti adat majlis yang telah lalu.*
> (AA 51a:10–11; 51b:1–4)

> Then from there Keujruen Geundrang Seri Udahna Kembaran asks for the piece Ragam Adani tabal Paduka Seri Sultan be played, then his majesty's command is conveyed by Megat to Keujruen Geundrang Seri Udahna Kembaran, then asks that the piece Gendang Berangkat be played as was done in ceremonial customs previously.

Ito (1984, 219) interprets the sentence '*maka mohon palu genderang berangkat*' as asking for 'the drumsticks to be delivered'. I would suggest though that '*palu genderang berangkat*' is the beating or playing of the piece of 'Genderang Berangkat' ('Departure Piece'), since nobat pieces are often preceded by the term *Genderang* or *Gendang* in addition to *Ragam, Lagu* and *Nobat* (see chapter 3). If the word were 'drumsticks', then the term *pemalu*, or 'beater', would be more appropriate here. The playing of 'Gendang Berangkat' is clearer in another sentence found later in AA which says *maka dipalu oranglah Gendang Berangkat kemudian berangkatlah Syah Alam* (AA 54b:9–10)—'[the piece] Departure Piece was beaten then Syah Alam departed'. A piece entitled 'Gendang Berangkat' is still played today in the courts of Perak and Selangor, and probably in seventeenth-century Patani (see chapter 4).

The ceremony continues with the beating of the royal drum:

Setelah sudah berangkat Syah Alam maka naik sembah bentara mohon dipanggil salih dan segala alat pawai, bagi segala hulubalang pun duduklah mengadap ke balai pedang. Kemudian maka turun jua ke balai pedang sebelah dan ke balai keujruen tandil sebelah maka dijunjungkan sabda kedua mereka; insya Allah Taala, sabda yang maha mulia menitah raja nobat Ibrahim Khalil tabal Paduka Seri Sultan yang di dalam tetap di dalam yang di blang tetap ke blang, pada naik sembah Paduka Maha Menteri dan Seri Ratna Perdana dimohon sebut Ibrahim Khalil seperti majlis yang telah lalu. (AA 51b:4–11; 52a: 1–3)

After the Syah Alam departs then the herald comes to request all the swords and regalia, the district chiefs then sit facing the Hall of Swords. They come down (officials) to the Hall of Swords and the Hall of the Guard respectively then both carry the royal command; God willing, his majesty commands that the drum Ibrahim Khalil is struck for Paduka Seri Sultan—what is inside remains inside what is outside remains outside. Paduka Maha Menteri and Seri Ratna Perdana then make obeisance and request the drum Ibrahim Khalil (be beaten) as was done in ceremonies previously.

According to Drewes and Voorhoeve (1958), Ibrahim Khalil refers to the name of the big royal drum played during the installation or *pertabalan* of the Sultan. In this case, the drum is also used to mark the coming of Ramadan, hence the term *tabal* used to name the ceremony. The drum is also mentioned in *Hikayat Raja-Raja Pasai* (HRP) where chiefs would face the instrument during the installation ceremony. According to *Adat Raja-Raja Melayu* (ARM), which records the royal customs of the Melaka sultanate, the Melaka installation drum was also called Ibrahim Khalil and was used during a royal wedding celebration. An important ceremony such as the *pertabalan* must be accompanied by a special *ragam* or piece such as 'Nobat Tabal' in the present-day courts of Perak and Selangor. In the case of AA, an installation piece 'Ragam Adani' is played on the drum Ibrahim Khalil. In nineteenth-century Riau the name Ibrahim Khalil referred to the piece played by the nobat ensemble during the installation of the sultan and the paying homage (*menjunjug duli*) ceremony. Today the piece is played by the nobat of Terengganu which was originally from Riau (see chapter 3).

Ibrahim Khalil is a shorter name of Ibrahim Khalilullah or Ibrahim the friend of Allah, Khalilullah being an epithet given to Prophet Ibrahim, one of the most revered figures in Islam. This was based on the verse from the Qur'an (4:125):

> Who can be better in religion than one who submits his whole self to Allah, does good, and follows the way of Abraham the true in Faith? For Allah did take Abraham for a friend.

The name Ibrahim Khalilullah appears in numerous early Malay texts including *Hikayat Amir Hamzah*, one of the oldest Malay texts about the heroics of Amir Hamzah, the uncle of Prophet Muhammad. In Kedah, the nobat was traditionally known to have been derived from the tradition of Prophet Ibrahim and was passed down to Iskandar Zulkarnain (Aziz Deraman and Ramli Wan Mohamad 1994, 32).

One of the earliest accounts of the inauguration of the coming of Ramadan was made by Houtman who witnessed the ceremony in 1599:

> After witnessing the new moon [Ramadan], all the officials with their best garments headed towards the court, as if they were going to perform the prayer. Right in front of the court entrance stood one of the highest rank officials who dressed in a long white robe and held a gilded shield in his left hand and a drawn sword in his right hand. Then he held up the sword over his shoulder. All the drums were then beaten and the trumpets blown, and all flintlocks were fired, so were seven harquebuses[9] located outside of the palace. Indeed, this marks the coming of the fasting month. (Quoted in Hadi 2004, 121–22)

The playing of music and firing of arms in royal celebrations were already in practice earlier in Pasai and Melaka as recorded in the HRP and ARM and contemporary Patani (see chapter 4). In celebrating royal installations, marriages and births, a ceremony called the *Istiadat Meletak Kerja* (Start of Work Ceremony) would be held. The nobat was played and cannons fired to announce this ceremony and followed by *berjaga-jaga* or night vigils, which could last from a few days to a few months. The use of both the royal ensemble and firearms described by Houtman reflected the importance placed by the Acehnese court on religious observation, on par with secular celebrations. This was in addition to the use of the installation drum Ibrahim Khalil and the use of the term *tabal*. It is also interesting to note the seven harquebuses fired as compared to the sixteen cannons used by the Melaka sultanate.

Two other ceremonies were performed during the month of Ramadan, which were held on twentieth and twenty-seventh nights of Ramadan where the *genderang jaga-jaga* were sounded to mark the beginning of two nights of vigils or *berjaga-jaga*. The first one was called *lailat al-Qadar*, or the 'night of destiny'—the night it is believed the Qur'an was revealed.

Hari Raya Puasa (The Celebration of Eid al-Fitr)

The end of Ramadan is celebrated with a day called Eid al-Fitr, which falls on the first of Syawal, the tenth month of the Muslim calendar. One of the features of this celebration is the *sunat* or recommended congregational prayer at the mosque on the morning of Eid al-Fitr, performed anywhere between sunrise and midday. Similar to the obligatory Friday prayer, the Eid al-Fitr prayer includes a sermon given by a *khatib*[10] at the mosque. In seventeenth-century Aceh, the Sultan's attendance at the Bait ar-Rahman mosque was an elaborate ceremony which involved a grand procession. The ceremony began with the *penghulu bilal* (chief of the muezzin) calling for the *tongkat khutbah* (staff used during the sermon) at the *dalam* (royal enclosure). The use of the staff by the *khatib* while delivering the sermon is recommended but not compulsory in Islam. It was based on a *sunnah* (practice) of the Prophet who used to hold a staff or bow while delivering a sermon on the pulpit. It is not widely practiced now in the Middle East but is common in the Malay world to this day.

Besides helping the *khatib* to focus and encourage proper conduct, the staff can be viewed as a symbol of the speaker's power, a license to deliver a religious message to the masses. The request for the staff by the chief of the muezzin was a symbolic gesture acknowledging the religious, as well as political, authority of the Sultan. The act showed the ruler's absolute power over religious matters: any public address needed his initial blessings. The official in charge of the drums, Seri Udahna Kembaran, then requested that the *genderang dong* be beaten. Again, this showed that the Sultan's power transcends the visual or physical into the audible.

Once all the chiefs and nobilities had taken their positions in accordance to their ranks in the Hall of Swords, the Kadi Malikul Adil then invited the Sultan to perform the prayer at the mosque. The piece 'Gendang Berangkat' was then played while the sultan departed in a procession accompanied by Sufi faqirs, imams and religious persons reciting the *takbir* and *dhikir*. An account was given by Sebald de Weert (1567–1603), a captain of the Dutch East India Company (VOC) who witnessed the procession of 'Eid al-Fitr in 1603:

> Thus the young king ('Ali Ri'ayat Shah) went to the mosque, accompanied by many nobility, a great number of elephants and a small number of horses; in addition, several thousand people, carrying arms, standards, arrows and flintlocks, also followed on foot. There was tremendous noise of various instruments, such as horns, trombones, kettledrums and cymbals. (Ito 1984, 227–28)

The description given by de Weert of the musical instruments involved in the procession and the 'noise' that they produce is worth discussing. The horns, trombones and kettledrums could be the *nafiri, serunai* (or other wind instruments) and *nengkara* or *gendang*. Weert's account of the 'noise' produced reflects his lack of understanding of the nature of the Malay nobat processional music that could be 'thunderous' in nature. This could also due to the ensemble's militaristic roots from the wider Islamicate world of the time. Drums and horns were originally used in battles not in a strictly musical sense but to produce crude and loud noises to demoralise opponents. This was incorporated into non-military purposes which included royal processions and religious celebrations. Abu'l Fazl described the procession of the Mughal Emperor Akbar:

> The noise of the drums and the melodies of the magician-like musicians gave forth news of joy. Crowds of men were gathered in astonishment on the roofs and at the doors. (AN 3:549)

The noisy nature of processions and celebrations is widely reported in early Malay literature. It is narrated in the *Misa Melayu* (MM) that:

> *Maka gendang serunai gong canang pun berbunyilah malam siang tiada berhenti: terlalu gegak gempita riuh rendah tiada disangka bunyi lagi'*. (MM 84:7)
>
> The gendang serunai gong canang were played continuously day and night; too loud, noisy, boisterous (and) the sounds were unmistakable.

Once the sultan reached the mosque a different tune is played:

> *Apabila sampai hadarat Syah Alam ke dalam diwal mesjid maka tatkala itu genderang pun dialih oranglah murinya*[11] *pada Ragam Siwajan*. (AA 55b: 1–3)
>
> Once the Syah Alam reaches within the walls of the mosque then the *muri* in the drums (ensemble) changes (the tune) to Ragam Siwajan.

This passage introduces a new instrument (*muri*) which played a new tune called 'Ragam Siwajan'. The sentence '*dialih oranglah murinya*' implies that the instrument was part of the ensemble that played during the procession. It is however uncertain whether the new tune was as 'noisy' as the processional tune described by Weert. Musical ensembles used in a procession, apart from being described as being *gegak gempita* (thunderous), may also be portrayed as *merdu* (sweet, soft and melodious) in Malay literature. The *Hikayat Hang Tuah* (HHT) notes, for instance:

> *Maka segala bunyi-bunyian daripada gendang, serunai, nafiri, madali, merangu, sekati, kopok, ceracap empat puluh bagai ragamnya itu pun berbunyilah terlalu merdu bunyinya*. (HHT 150:27)
>
> Then all the instruments, from *gendang, serunai, nafiri, madali, merangu, sekati, kopok, ceracap* forty types of pieces sounded so melodious.

There is no indication how the piece Ragam Siwajan sounded either in the AA or eyewitness account. We can only speculate that since the muri was playing the melody, the piece could be a *merdu* one. Furthermore, the sultan had reached the door of the mosque and was on his way inside. Loud music would seem inappropriate and could easily disrupt the members of the congregation who were offering *tahiyat al-masjid* prayers.[12] Once the ruler was inside a curtained space in the mosque the herald gave a signal for the music to stop. After the prayers, the Sultan was then greeted by his subjects and sat briefly on a platform before leaving the mosque in a procession. The sequence of events is mentioned in the AA and a new instrument and piece are also introduced:

Maka hadarat Syah Alam pun semayam di mahligai kerajaan maka berbunyilah medeli[13] *di halaman astaka itu dengan Ragam Biram maka khidmatlah bentara yang membawa salih itu dan segala pegawai dan segala balatentara pun sekalian mengikut seperti bentara itu juga. Setelah itu maka diragam oranglah Genderang Berangkat kembali dari mesjid ke dalam Kota Dar al-Dunia dengan izni, maka berangkatlah mereka itu sekali lagi serta berundurlah sekalian mereka itu bersaf-saf.* (AA 57b: 10–11; 58a:1–6)

Then the honorable Syah Alam sat on the royal throne (and) the medeli was sounded in the vicinity of the pavilion with (the song) Ragam Biram then the herald carrying the royal sword started to perform his duties and followed by all the officers and soldiers. After that (the piece) Genderang Berangkat was played from the mosque to Kota Dar al-Dunia and they departed and returned (to the palace) in rows.

The musical sequence for the celebration of Eid al-Fitr as described by the AA and an eyewitness account can be summarised as follows:

1. The musical ensemble consisted of the *nafiri, serunai, muri, medeli, nengkara* and cymbals.
2. The official in charge of the drums, Seri Udahna Kembaran, requests that the *genderang dong* be beaten.
3. The piece 'Gendang Berangkat' is played when the sultan departs in a procession towards the mosque.
4. A different tune called 'Ragam Siwajan' is played once the sultan reaches within the walls the mosque.
5. Once the sultan exits the mosque and sits on a dais, the *medeli* then plays the tune 'Ragam Biram'
6. The piece 'Gendang Berangkat' is played again when the sultan leaves the mosque and heads towards the palace.

Hari Raya Haji (The Celebration of Eid al-Adha)

The culmination of the *hajj* is the celebration of Eid al-Adha which falls on the tenth of Dhu al-Hijjah, the twelfth month of the Muslim calendar. It is also known as *Hari Raya Korban* or the feast of the sacrifice, in commemorating Prophet Abraham's sacrifice of his son Ismail in fulfilling God's command. The celebration begins with the recommended congregational Eid al-Adha prayer at the mosque followed by the sacrifice of animals. Similar to the Friday and Eid al-Fitr prayers, a grand royal procession was held to accompany the ruler to the mosque to perform the prayer. In seventeenth-century Aceh, Eid al-Adha was considered the greater of the two Eid but has now become a minor celebration as compared to Eid al-Fitr throughout the Malay world. In the AA, the procession ceremony was named as *Adat Majlis Hadarat Syah Alam Berangkat Sembahyang Hari Raya Haji ke Masjid Bait ar-Rahman* (His Highness Syah Alam's Departure for the Eid al-Adha Prayers to the Bait ar-Rahman Mosque Ceremony).

The ceremony started at dawn with the Penghulu Payung Amat Diraja (official in charge of ceremonial umbrellas) ordering the erection of ceremonial umbrellas along the road from the palace to the Bait ar-Rahman Mosque. When all the state regalia and dignitaries were in place at the palace, the head of the royal ensemble then requested that the piece 'Gendang Berangkat' be played. The AA gives a list of groups involved in the procession which include the royal family, district chiefs, religious officials and commoners. Similar to the Eid al-Fitr celebration, the procession was accompanied by the 'noisy' Gendang Berangkat but was overshadowed by the sounds religious chanting:

> *Sekalian mereka itu mengiring ke kiri kanan gajah yang dikendarai oleh Kadi Malikul Adil itu serta takbir dan zikirullah dengan amat sangat nyaring suaranya, tiadalah dapat diperikan lagi fasahat lidahnya dan latafat suara mereka itu. Kata yang empunya cerita ini dari pada barang suara itu maka Seri Sultan pun tiadalah mendengarkan segala bunyi-bunyian yang gegap gempita lagi sebab mendengar orang takbir dan zikirullah, maka tatkala itu Johan Syah Alam pun beriba-iba mengucap zikirullah serta membaca tasbih dari pada manikam yang berbagai warna cahayanya itu, maka kelakuan baginda tatkala itu terlalu 'asyki lagi zauqi dan wijdani[14] akan Allah Taala menzahirkan kebesaranNya dan kemuliaanNya baginda itu akan khalifahNya.* (AA 66b:5–11; 67a:1–6)

All those accompanying on the left and right side of the elephant ridden by Kadi Malikul Adil were chanting the *takbir* and *zikirullah* with such loud voices, the fluency of their tongues and gracefulness was their voices were indescribable. According to the narrator of this story, the Sultan no longer heard the loud instruments anymore due to him listening to those voices reciting the takbir and zikirullah, while the Johan Syah Alam himself was reciting the zikirullah using prayer beads made of glittering precious stones of multiple colors, then his highness was in the state of extreme infatuation, feelings of fulfilment and ecstasy in manifesting the greatness of Allah and His magnificence, his highness is His caliph.

The sultan's obliviousness to the accompanying music narrated here shows his deep religious ardor, initiated by the repeated chants of his subjects and is typical of Malay court chronicles (see MM 95:13). As in the Eid al-Fitr ceremony, once the procession reached the entrance of the mosque, the piece 'Ragam Siwajan' was played (AA 83a: 5–6). The drums (*genderang*) and all other instruments (*segala bunyi-bunyian*) then parted from the main procession and moved to the right (AA 83b: 1–3). Another piece called 'Ragam Kuda Berlari' was then played continuously while the Sultan made his way into the mosque greeted by state nobility and finally by Kadi Malik al-Adil (AA 83b: 9–10). Once the Sultan was inside the curtained royal enclosure of the mosque to perform his recommended prayers, the music stopped playing.

After the congregational prayers the ritual of the sacrifice was performed during which the instruments of the ensemble are clearly stated:

maka adalah di antara fakih yang banyak itu seorang fakih yang tua berdiri di hadapan qurban melihatkan uratnya maka tatkala itu gong, genderang, medeli, ceracap pun dipalu oranglah lagunya Kuda Berlari dan lagi nafiri dan serunai dan margu itupun ditiup oranglah terlalu azimat bunyinya, maka apabila sudah lagunya, Syah Alam sikin pada leher qurban itu hingga adalah tercucur darahnya kadar sedikit maka segera disambut oleh Syekh Syamsuddin sikin itu dengan tiada terangkat dari pada leher qurban sikin di tangan Syah Alam itu, maka Syekh Syamsuddin pun menyudahkan dia. (AA 89b: 5–11, 90a: 1–4).

then among the many fakih was an old one standing in front of the sacrificial animal observing its veins and at that particular moment, the gong, drums, medeli, ceracap started to play the song Kuda Berlari and the nafiri and serunai and margu were blown with such loudness, then after the song stops, Syah Alam cut the neck of the sacrificial animal until blood oozed out a little and the knife was immediately held by Syekh Syamsuddin[15] without lifting it from the neck of the animal and he then completed the slaughter.

The Sultan then sat on a raised platform watching the sacrifice ritual continue to be performed. After the first symbolic slaughter, the ruler's sacrificial act was represented by Kadi Malikul Adil who continued to slaughter the animals to the sounds of the ensemble:

Maka tatkala itu Kadi Malikul Adil pun diperwakilah Juhan Alam menyembelih qurban, setelah itu maka bunyi-bunyian pun dipalu oranglah dari pada gong, genderang dan takbirlah seperti adat tatkala Syah Alam menyembelih qurban itu. Maka segala fakih pun menghabiskanlah segala qurban itu disembelihlah, maka segala bunyi-bunyian pun berbunyilah sekali lagi hingga tiga kali. (AA 90a: 9–11; 90b: 1–4)

Then Kadi Malikul Adil was assigned to represent Johan Alam to slaughter the animals, after which the gongs, drums were beaten and the takbir was chanted in accordance to the ceremony of Syah Alam's slaughtering of the animals. Thus all the fakih completed the sacrificial rituals then all the instruments were sounded again three times.

A similar Eid al-Adha procession to the one described by the AA was witnessed by the British traveler Peter Mundy who visited Aceh in 1637, during the reign of Sultan Iskandar Thani. According to Mundy's account, about five hundred young buffaloes (based on local report) were sacrificed and the meat distributed to the people.

After the sacrificial rituals were done, the ruler and his entourage then headed back to the palace:

Maka Syah Alam pun semayamlah ke atas mahligai kerajaan itu maka berbunyilah medeli, ceracap di halaman astaka itu dengan Ragam Biram Medeli, maka khidmat bentara yang membawa salih itu serta dengan segala raja-raja dan segala hulubalang dan segala pegawai dan segala balatentera sekaliannya mengikut serta tertib bentara itu juga. Setelah itu maka diragam oranglah Genderang Berangkat kembali dari mesjid ke dalam Kota Daruddunia itu dengan izni. (AA 91a: 1–8)

Then the Syah Alam rested on the state throne while the *medeli, ceracap* played 'Ragam Biram Medeli' in the courtyard of the *astaka*, then the herald brought the state sword followed by all the royal family, district chiefs, officers and army personnel. After that, the tune Genderang Berangkat was played from the mosque returning to Kota Daruddunia with the permission [of Allah].

Once the procession reached the field or garden called the Medan Khayali, a sequence of events ensued where a number of new songs were played:

Maka apabila sampailah Syah Alam itu ke karang dialihkan oranglah segala ragam genderang itu kepada Ragam Sani. Apabila sampailah ke Medan Khayali maka dialihkan orang pula murinya genderang itu kepada Ragam Mahligai, hingga sampai ke pintu maka dialihkan orang murinya genderang itu dari pada Ragam Mahligai kepada Muri Dari Mesjid, maka turunlah segala raja-raja dan kadi dan segala pegawai yang di atas gajah itu masing-masing mengampir gajah istana mengiringi di tanah lalu masuk ke dalam Kota Daruddunia. Maka tatkala itu segala kanak-kanak yang membawa segala bunyi-bunyian yang indah-indah seperti yang telah kami sebutkan pada cerita kami yang dahulu itupun hampirlah, sekalian mereka itu pun menyambut baginda itu dengan meniup segala bunyi-bunyian maka muri genderang pun dialihkan oranglah sekali lagi kepada Ragam Siwajan lalu ke halaman mahligai Jitakandran. Maka apabila sampailah penganjur itu ke halaman mahligai Jitakandran itu maka menyimpanglah segala mereka itu ke kanan serta khidmat. Apabila sampailah gajah istana itu ke halaman mahligai Jitakandran maka berdirilah segala mereka itu masing-masing pada tarafnya maka muri genderang pun dialihkan oranglah kepada Ragam Kuda Berlari, maka khidmatlah bentara yang membawa salih itu ke atas kepalanya. (AA 92a: 6–11; 92b: 1–11; 93a: 1–5)

When the Syah Alam arrived at the courtyard the tune was changed to Ragam Sani. When he reached Medan Khayali the tune was changed to Ragam Mahligai, until he reached the door and the muri changed from Ragam Mahligai to Muri Dari Mesjid, then all members of royalty and the chief judge and all officers dismount from their elephants and approached the palace elephant accompanying it on foot and went into Kota Daruddunia. Then the children who were playing those beautiful instruments as mentioned before moved closer to welcome his highness by blowing the instruments and the tune played by the muri of the genderang [group] was once again changed to Ragam Siwajan until they reached towards the courtyard of the Jitakandran mansion. Once they reached the courtyard, the group then moved to the right. When the palace elephant reached the courtyard, all [the nobles] stood according to their ranks then the muri changed to Ragam Kuda Berlari then the herald placed the state sword above his head.

This passage is important. First, there are a number of new pieces introduced that are not mentioned earlier during the Eid al-Fitr celebration. Second, there is the mention of '*segala kanak-kanak*' (all the children) indicating that musicians playing the muri or the muri ensemble were children. Third, there is also the use of the adjective '*bunyian yang indah-indah*' (beautiful sounds) to describe the sound or music played as 'beautiful', which confirms the earlier assumption that the piece 'Ragam Siwajan' played by the muri was a 'merdu' one. It also raises the question as to whether there were different ensembles involved in the ceremonies:

1. The 'Muri Ensemble' comprising children playing 'melodious' tunes
2. The 'Nobat Ensemble' comprising adults playing 'loud' pieces
3. A combination of both with each taking turns in playing different songs

Apart from writing the account of what he called the Buckree Eede, Mundy also produced a sketch of the procession (see figures 5.1).

Figure 5.1. Peter Mundy's sketch of Sultan Iskandar Muda's procession in 1637. *Source*: Hakluyt Society.

Figure 5.2. An enlarged part of Peter Mundy's sketch of the musical ensemble. *Source*: Hakluyt Society.

Mundy's sketch of the procession and the musical ensemble is probably the oldest visual depiction of a Malay nobat. In his description of the court ensemble, Mundy (1919, 123) wrote:

> Att his Issuing Forth the Musick played, some of them by turns and other alltogether, as Hautbois, straight trumpets, and others in forms of great hunting horns, Drummes (the 3 latter of Silver); another Copper Instrument called a gung, wheron they strike with a little wooden Clubbe, and allthough it bee butt a small Instrumentt, not much More then 1 Foote over and ½ Foot Deepe, yett it maketh a Deepe hollow humming sound Resembling thatt of a great bell: all the afforesaid musick Discordantt, Clamorous and full of Noise.

Mundy's description of the music being played 'by turns' can either indicate a sequence of instruments playing a particular piece or a group of musicians taking turns performing. Nobat pieces found in Malay courts today are divided into sections where an instrument, either a *nafiri* or *serunai*, indicates the start of a piece and is followed in turn by other instruments such as the *nengkara* and *gendang*. Based on the type and number of instruments used described by Mundy, it was highly likely that groups of the same instruments, for example the 'straight trumpets', played alternately with the 'great hunting horns' and also 'alltogether' or simultaneously. Since Mundy and other European travellers could not have access to the mosque and court compounds, there was no mention of any drastic change of pieces or musical style when moving from public to more exclusive spaces in their accounts.

The first group of blowing instruments described by Mundy were *hautbois* (shawms), straight trumpets and great hunting horns. Like other European observers, he was of course using European instruments as the basis for his descriptions. Mundy used the term *hautbois* to describe the *serunai*, considering the similarities in terms of shape, size and color of the two instruments. Hautbois or oboe was the most important wind instrument in European art music of the seventeenth century and its technological advancement was mainly attributed to a number of French instrument makers (Swain 2013, 205). Straight horns clearly referred to the nafiri. One interesting instrument mentioned by Mundy was the great hunting horn, probably referring to the medieval *olifant* or ivory hunting horns made of elephant tusks (see figure 5.2). It is not surprising if the Acehnese royal ensemble had used ivory horns considering the large number of elephants available in the kingdom. A similar instrument can also be found in the naubat ensemble of the sixteenth-century Mughal court based on Abu'l Fazl's book *Ain-i Akbari* (figure 5.3).

Figure 5.3. A sketch of a *naubat* instrument from *Ain-i Akbari*, by Abu'l Fazl. *Source*: Abu'l Fazl ibn Mubarak. 1873. Ain-i Akhbari, vol. 1. Translated by Blochmann. Calcutta: The Asiatic Society of Bengal.

Mundy also mentioned the use of silver drums but did not describe what type they were. Based on his sketch, they were likely portable double-headed barrel drums but no *nengkara* is visible. Could the lack of details in his description of these instruments indicate his lack of enthusiasm of the instruments due to their prevalence in European music, thus rendering them less 'exotic'? Nonetheless, one 'exotic' instrument caught his extra attention: a copper *gung*. Based on his description, the gong was likely a small portable *tawak* or *tetawak* prevalent in traditional Malay music. Like de Weert before him, the processional music was described by Mundy as 'full of noise'.

The musical sequence for the celebration of Eid al-Adha as described by the AA can be summarised as follows:

1. The ceremony began with the official in charge of the drums, Seri Udahna Kembaran, requesting that the piece 'Gendang Berangkat' be played.
2. The royal procession towards the mosque started with the accompaniment of 'Gendang Berangkat'.
3. The tune 'Ragam Siwajan' was played once the sultan reached within the walls the mosque.

4. Another piece called 'Ragam Kuda Berlari' was then played continuously while the Sultan made his way into the mosque greeted by state nobility. The music stopped once the Sultan was inside the curtained royal enclosure of the mosque to perform his recommended prayers.
5. After the prayers and before the start of the sacrificial ceremony, 'Ragam Kuda Berlari' was once again played to mark the start of the ritual.
6. The music stopped once the ruler started to slaughter the first animal and continued for three times when the religious official Kadi Malikul Adil continued with the ritual.
7. While the ruler rested on the state throne, the *medeli, ceracap* played 'Ragam Biram Medeli' in the courtyard of the *astaka*.
8. The herald then brought the state sword followed by all the royal family, district chiefs, officers and army personnel. The tune 'Genderang Berangkat' was then played to accompany the Sultan's return to Kota Daruddunia from the mosque.
9. When the royal elephant reached the great square Jitakandran all the nobilities stood in accordance to their ranks while the muri played the tune 'Ragam Kuda Berlari'.
10. When the Syah Alam arrived at the courtyard the tune was changed to Ragam Sani.
11. When he reached Medan Khayali the changed the tune to Ragam Mahligai.
12. Once the Sultan reached the door and the tune of the muri changed from Ragam Mahligai to Muri Dari Mesjid.
13. All members of royalty, the chief judge and all officers then dismounted from their elephants and approached the palace elephant accompanying it on foot and went into Kota Daruddunia.
14. Then the children who were playing those beautiful instruments moved closer to welcome his highness, blowing the instruments, and the tune played by the muri of the genderang [group] was once again changed to 'Ragam Siwajan' until they reached the courtyard of the Jitakandran mansion.
15. Once they reached the courtyard, the group then moved to the right. When the palace elephant reached the courtyard, all [the nobles] stood according to their ranks then the muri changed to 'Ragam Kuda Berlari' then the herald placed the state sword above his head.

The complexity of this ceremony reflects the heightened significance of Eid al-Adha as the most important religious event in Aceh. The text shows the use not only of different pieces as markers for specific rituals but also different groups of musicians. There is an indication of the contrasting nature of the pieces, between the 'noisy' 'Gendang Berangkat' to signal the start of the procession and the 'melodious' 'Ragam Siwajan' played at the mosque. In an event involving thousands of people, these pieces became crucial aural signals to mobilise the procession and reminders to indicate the progressive stages of the whole ceremony.

THE FRIDAY PRAYER

In Islam, Friday is considered the most sacred day of the week. It is a day where it is compulsory (*wajib*) to attend the congregational prayer called the *sembahyang jumaat* at the mosque. In seventeenth-century Patani, the weekly prayer was marked by the sounds of the nobat, but in Aceh it was an elaborate and grand occasion that involved a royal procession. This procession was witnessed by Ralph Croft, who wrote:

> Our Generall went to the court, according to the Kinges desire unto him the daie before; where we see the Kinge in most royall estait, comeinge unto his church in most rich array, accompanyed with his nobles and chief of his kingdome. From the church [he] retourned unto a grene before his palace gait, wher he did sitt in a rich chaire of state of pure gold. (Best 1934, 168)

According to the AA the royal processions to the masjid ceremony started with the herald requesting the appropriate Friday regalia be brought down. The chief muezzin then called for the sermon staff followed by the beating of the *genderang dong* by Seri Udahna Kembaran, official in charge of the drums.

The musical sequence for the weekly Friday prayers as narrated in the AA is summarised as follows:

1. Official in charge of the drums, Keujruen Geundrang Seri Udahna Kembaran, requests that the *genderang dong* be beaten.
2. A different tune called 'Ragam Siwajan' was played once the sultan reached the doors of the mosque.
3. While the sultan sits on a dais at the mosque, 'Ragam Kuda Berlari' was played
4. The drums (no specific tune was mentioned) were played to accompany the sultan on his way back towards the palace.
5. Once the procession reached the Balai Pedang, the ensemble then played the piece 'Ragam Siwajan'.

Table 5.1. List of Songs Found in the Adat Aceh

1. Genderang Berangkat
2. Ragam Siwajan
3. Ragam Kuda Berlari
4. Ragam Sani
5. Ragam Biram Medeli
6. Ragam Adani
7. Ragam Mahligai
8. Ragam Kembali Dari Masjid/Muri Dari Masjid

From the list provided in table 5.1, the title 'Gendang Berangkat' is still found in the nobat repertoires of Kedah, Perak and Selangor.

Only the *genderang*, *gong*, *nafiri*, *nengkara* and cymbals from this list survived in the remaining nobat ensembles in the Malaysian and Brunei courts (see chapter 3). The instruments *muri*, *medeli* and *margu* (or *merangu*) which are ubiquitous in traditional Malay texts are now extinct (Nicolas 1994, 163, 165, 167). It has to be stressed however, unlike the ethnographic descriptions by European travelers such as Peter Mundy, instruments mentioned in the AA and early Malay literature in general can also be viewed as literary device— elements of story-telling (ibid.). Thus, musical instruments and scenes of merriment may not necessarily be based on actual observations but on stories passed down through other texts or oral tradition, or simply on literary convention.

SUMMARY

The inclusion of the nobat in religious ceremonies and celebrations, and its sounding to mark prayer times gave it moral credence and higher spiritual affiliation. This is evident through narrations in the *Adat Aceh* where the indigenised nobat was used in important religious observations such as the

Table 5.2. Instruments listed in the Adat Aceh

1. Genderang Dong
2. Genderang
3. Gong
4. Nafiri
5. Muri
6. Medeli
7. Nengkara
8. Ceracap
9. Margu
10. Cymbals

annual *'Eid* celebrations and weekly Friday prayers, which was conducted on a grand scale. This was done as a show of power in a region where there was growing European encounter and also in following the practice of contemporary Islamic empires such as the Mughals and Safavids.

European intervention and growing economic and political power gave rise to intense rivalry among Malay sultanates, especially after the fall of Melaka. These polities such as Aceh sought to be centers of Malay culture and the nobat was brought to the center of attention. This was evident in the public aural and visual display of the ensemble and its numerous references in Malay court chronicles and manuals, including European accounts. These observations documented by some early European travellers provided invaluable information on Acehnese court culture involving the nobat. We are also enlightened to the perception and interpretation of these Europeans of the sights and sounds they experienced.

Instruments, repertoire and size of the ensemble evolved throughout the centuries in correlation with economic and political development. While the regional sultanates maintain the nobat's symbolic nature, each of them seemed to chart their own unique trajectories. New songs were composed, instruments added (or discarded) and ceremonies developed to reflect local culture while maintaining the collective sense of identity of the larger Malay world. The AA shows the unique characteristic of the Acehnese nobat which involved the use of indigenous instruments and the playing of 'melodious' pieces while nearing the mosque (see table 5.2). This was high unlikely to be practiced by other nobat ensembles in the region.

Literature, in the form of court chronicles and manuals was an immortalization of various events and customs involving the nobat. For generations these texts became a source of pride and symbol of cultural supremacy for Malay rulers and the *Adat Aceh* is a testament of this. The Johor sultanate's completion of the *Sejarah Melayu* in 1612 was seen as an attempt to claim leadership of the Malay world once held by Melaka. Aceh viewed this as a provocation and subsequently invaded Johor and captured its sultan, his family and the author of *Sejarah Melayu*, Tun Seri Lanang (L. Andaya 2001, 47). The weakening of Aceh in the middle of the seventeenth century saw Johor reasserting itself as the successor of Melaka and center of Malay culture. The nobat continued to be played in the courts of Johor, Perak, Kedah and later in eighteenth-century Selangor. However, the ensemble was never to be performed again in processions on the same scale as the Acehnese but remains to this day as a symbol of a Malay ruler's power and sovereignty. European encounter with the nobat continued with the English and Dutch colonisation of the Malay up to the middle of the twentieth century, which will be discussed in the next chapter.

NOTES

1. This chapter is derived in part from an article, Raja Iskandar Bin Raja Halid, 'The Adat Aceh: A Window into a Seventeeth-Century Malay Soundscape', *Indonesia and the Malay World* 49, no. 145 (2021): 395–411. copyright © editors, *Indonesia and the Malay World*; reprinted by permission of Taylor & Francis Ltd, http://www.tandfonline.com, on behalf of editors, *Indonesia and the Malay World*.

2. The Malay word *peringgi* or *feringgi* was derived from the Persian *farangi* meaning foreigner. It could originally be an Arabic term *firinjiyah* or *alfranj*, which referred to the Franks of Western Europe in the Middle Ages.

3. According to Arun K. Dasgupta (1962, 188), the region of north Sumatera, although in contact with the Srivijaya Empire based in the south, was relatively free from Hindu-Buddhist religious influence. He further argued that Islam gained a foothold on an area which was geographically remote to a largely Indianised region.

4. The five pillars of Islam are: (1) *Shahada* or declaration of faith; (2) *Salat* or the five daily prayers; (3) *Zakat* or giving of alms; (4) *Sawm* or fasting in the month of Ramadan; and (5) *Hajj*, or the pilgrimage to Mecca, for those who can afford it.

5. This is according to Takeshi Ito (1984), but in Acehnese the word *biram* can be understood as a two-headed mythical snake, red precious stone and elephant.

6. Drewes and Voorhoeve (1958) suggest that *genderang dong* was probably an upright drum similar to the one used in a Batak orchestra. According to Kartomi (2012, 289), in Acehnese music *dong* means a standing position as opposed to *duek* or sitting. In seventeenth-century Aceh, the *genderang dong* could also be a drum played in a standing position especially during a procession as practiced by nobat ensembles in present day Malaysia.

7. According to Takashi Ito (1984, 41), the term *bentara* used in Aceh is a confusing one, but he contends that bearers of the title could probably be those concerned with palace matters, similar in rank as a junior *orang kaya* (nobles). In the Melaka court, *bentara* was the royal herald, higher in rank to the eunuchs and concubines.

8. There are *adat* in Perak which required the nobat to be silenced for seven days after the death of a sultan and the *berjaga-jaga* (night vigils in preparation for a royal celebration) was done for seven days and nights (see *Misa Melayu* 32:29 and 70:5).

9. A muzzle-loaded firearm used in the fifteenth to seventeenth centuries.

10. A *khatib* is a general term used for the person giving a sermon during the Friday and two Eid prayers. He could be the imam of the mosque, a religious scholar or political leader. The *khatib* would normally use the *tongkat khutbah* or sermon staff, holding it with his right hand while giving a sermon on the pulpit in following the *sunnah* of Prophet Muhammad.

11. *Muri* is frequently mentioned in early Malay literature but is now obsolete (Nicolas 1994, 163). According to Wilkinson (1901, 662) the instrument was "a sort of flute or clarionet of metal (in contradiction to a bamboo-flute or *bangsi*)'. Teeuw et al. (2004, 350) describes *muri* as a 'kind of flute or flageolet'.

12. *Tahiyat al-masjid* prayers are offered once a person steps into a mosque before sitting down.

13. *Medeli, mudelli, madali* or *mandeli* is a wind instrument, which is now extinct (Wilkinson 1901).

14. The Arabic words *zauki* or *dhauki* (fulfilment) and *wajdini* (ecstasy) were also used in a seventeenth-century Sufi text from Pasai, see A. H. Johns (1957).

15. Syekh Syamsuddin al Sumatra'i or Sumatrani was the Grand Mufti of Aceh. Also known as Syamsuddin of Pasai, he served under Sultan Saidil Mukammil (1596–1604), Sultan Ali Riayat Shah (1604–1607) and Sultan Iskandar Muda (1607–1636).

Chapter Six

From British Colonialism to Independence

> Imagine yourself transported to a land of eternal summer, to that Golden Peninsula, 'twixt Hindustan and Far Cathay, from whence the early navigators brought back such wonderful stories of adventure. (Swettenham 1895, ix)

> Malaya, land of the pirate and the amok your secrets have been well guarded, but the enemy has at last passed your gate, and soon the irresistible Juggernaut of Progress will have penetrated to remotest fastness, slain your beasts, cut down your forests, 'civilised' your people, clothed them in strange garments, and stamped them with the seal of a higher morality. (Ibid., x)

> To begin to understand the Malay you must live in his country, speak his language, respect his faith, be interested in his interests, humour his prejudices, sympathise with and help him in trouble, and share his pleasures and possibly his risks. Only thus can you hope to win his confidence. Only through that confidence can you hope to understand the inner man, and this knowledge can therefore only come to those who have the opportunity and use it. (Ibid., 1)

The above quotes are from British administrator Sir Frank Swettenham's book *Malay Sketches*, published in 1895. Considered an expert in matters related to British Malaya, Swettenham's condescending tone can be seen as an encapsulation of the post-Enlightenment colonial worldview and British imperial plans in Malaya. He constructed a narrative of change, using the pirate and amok trope, which according to Eddie Tay (2011, 25) sought to underline the inferior nature of the natives that provided a hospitable environment to the colonial enterprise. Malaysian sociologist Lian Kwen Fee (2001, 864) views

Swettenham as part of the group of scholar-administrators who considered the Malay 'race' to be incapable and weak, hence the need for them to be 'civilised'. This was in contrast to the earlier view of the Scottish Enlightenment group that considered all human beings to have equal capabilities (ibid.). An important part of this civilising process was the documentation, classification and publication of 'facts' that shaped what Bernard Cohn (1996, 5) terms 'investigative modalities'. Malaysian anthropologist A. B. Shamsul (2001, 357) argues that a systematic application of some of these 'modalities' (which included historiography, observations, travelogues, surveys), limited the natives' ability to 'define their world'. He further contends that British colonization was also a 'cultural invasion in the form of the conquest of native 'epistemological space" (ibid.).

British hegemony also led some Malay rulers to submit to the 'civilised' British model of governance and way of life for their own benefit, while implicitly serving colonial interests (Andaya and Andaya 2001, 151). This ignited debate among the Malay community who began to raise questions regarding Malay identity or 'Malayness' (ibid.). But how far did the Malay ruling elites go in serving their states' interests (including their own), without compromising the Malay *adat* (customs), tradition and values? How much did this encounter and power interplay affect Malay royal customs, especially the nobat institution, considered an important part of court regalia? Also, to what extent did this process, especially through British colonial policy of non-interference in matters of religion and Malay customs, affect the culture of the Malays? How had the institution been used to fulfil imperial aims?

The British foray into the Malay world began when trader James Lancaster, on his first voyage to the East Indies, landed on the island of Penang in 1592. In February 1601, as a special envoy of Queen Elizabeth, Lancaster commanded the first fleet of the newly established East India Company and managed to secure an alliance with the Sultanate of Aceh. A number of English travellers followed, including Peter Floris, John Smith, Peter Mundy, Thomas Forrest and Thomas Best. However, it took nearly two centuries until the British finally gained a foothold in the Malay Peninsula. Capitalising on the ongoing conflict between Kedah and Siam, Captain Francis Light promised Sultan Abdullah Mukarram Shah of Kedah military protection in return for leasing Penang to the East India Company in 1786. This marked the beginning of British occupation of the Malay Peninsula. With the later inclusion of Province Wellesley (1798), Singapore (1819), Melaka (1824) and Dinding (1874), these colonies were incorporated into what was known as the Straits Settlements, following the Anglo-Dutch and Pangkor Treaties of 1824 and 1874, respectively.

The period between 1819 and 1874 saw the creation of what Barbara and Leonard Andaya (2001, 117) described as a 'New World', which was largely shaped by European imperial plans, British-Dutch rivalry and indigenous conflicts. Not only was the Malay world artificially divided between what are known today as Malaysia and Indonesia, this upheaval also resulted in the establishment of the independent states of Johor and Pahang. The 1874 signing of the Pangkor Treaty with Perak was seen as the beginning of direct British intervention into the political affairs of the Malays and the start of the Resident system. Considered as a 'protected' state under the treaty, the Sultan's political and economic power became the prerogative of the Resident except in matters relating to Malay customs and religion. Although sultans were given this autonomy, the nature of this authority later became increasingly problematic, especially in the realms of Islamic and secular law (Iza Hussin 2007, 784–85). Religion and custom, according to Barbara Andaya (2001, 163), although excluded from British control, 'were the fundamental and frequently the only justification for Malay political action. The division between religious and secular, so clear-cut to Europeans, was simply an alien concept to Malays'.

The growing interaction between the Malays and British throughout the nineteenth century inevitably had an impact on the former's culture and identity. European civilization began to be highly regarded and emulated by Malay elites as a symbol of modernity and success; and it did not take long before Western culture permeated throughout urban society in the Malay Peninsula. This imitation of the coloniser, as part of a process of being 'reformed', is what Homi Bhabha (2007, 121) terms 'mimicry'. Sultan Abu Bakar of Johor, for example, was criticised for his strong affinity to anything Western and his 'Malayness' was thus questioned. Concerns were raised by Malay Muslim scholars in Riau regarded the decline of traditional custom and one scholar, Raja Ali Haji, openly criticised Malays who wore European clothes (Andaya and Andaya 2001, 153). The British, despite their military superiority, economic power and European ideals, still relied upon the 'uncivilised', ancient symbolic customs of the Malay sultanates to achieve their imperialistic aims. In the meantime, Malay elites too took advantage of the British by accommodating their traditional customs for their own economic gains and political legitimacy (Iza Hussin 2007, 765–66). The idea that identity is fluid and constructed expediently could not have been more pronounced during the last century of British rule in the Malay Peninsula.

The prevalence of European culture especially among Malay ruling elites was responsible in part for the hybridization of Malay court customs to suit the changing political and social environment of colonial rule. This period also saw the rigorous research, documentation and publication of materials on Malay studies by British scholar-administrators, travellers and reporters as part of (or at least facilitated by) the imperial project. From newspaper reports and journal papers to travelogues and film documentaries, these materials provide invaluable insights into Malay culture of this period. They need to be read critically, however: for a variety of now well documented reasons, colonial observations could be patronising in nature.

This chapter considers the British intervention into the political affairs of the Malay Peninsula in the nineteenth and twentieth centuries, which clearly led to the gradual erosion of the rulers' powers and subsequent impact on Malay court culture. It explores the British colonial documentation of the nobat within the context of colonial political manoeuvrings and the response of Malay ruling elites who, while consolidating their political legitimacy, reassessed their own cultural identity anew.

BRITISH INTERFERENCE AND THE PERAK REGALIA

The Treaty of Pangkor was the culmination of two major events in Perak: the conflict between two Chinese secret societies known as the Larut War and the issue of royal succession after the death of Sultan Ali in 1871. Raja Abdullah, who was Raja Muda, or 'heir apparent', at the time, went against royal custom by not attending the burial of the late sultan.[1] Consequently, the Malay chiefs decided that Raja Ismail, the Raja Bendahara, be installed as sultan instead. On the advice of his business associates, Raja Abdullah wrote a letter to Andrew Clarke, governor general of the Straits Settlement, requesting British intervention with a promise to accept a British resident in return for him being recognised as ruler of Perak. The British saw this as an opportunity to gain control of a rich tin-producing state. Raja Ismail, dethroned and humiliated by the British who bestowed upon him the newly introduced title of Sultan Muda, was predictably absent during the signing of the treaty and kept the state regalia with him (Barlow 1995, 59). Since the regalia were crucial in the installation of Raja Abdullah, the new British administrators had to regain possession and a mission was sent to persuade Raja Ismail. This was not dissimilar to the event in Riau when the Dutch had to take possession of the regalia from Tengku Hamidah in order to install Tengku Abdul Rahman as Sultan of Riau-Lingga in 1823.

This meddling in the royal customs of Perak was marked by a misunderstanding of the importance of the regalia with serious political consequences. J. W. W. Birch's report to the Colonial Office suggested that: 'As regards the regalia, the country can get on very well without it, or, as soon as it can afford

Figure 6.1. Plate from Winstedt and Wilkinson's (1934) article 'A History of Perak' showing some items of the Perak state regalia, which included the nafiri. *Source*: MBRAS.

it, a new set can be procured, but it is difficult to convince these native chiefs of this' (CO 273/88, Birch to Colonial Office: Report on Perak, 2 April 1875). Birch also reportedly said 'it concerns us little what were the old customs of the country nor do I think they are worthy of any consideration' (Winstedt and Wilkinson 1934, 104). This perceived disregard of local customs and misunderstanding of the critical importance of the state regalia cost J. W. W. Birch, Perak's first British Resident, his life: he was murdered near Pasir Salak in November 1875. This incident started what was known as the Perak War, which lasted two years and saw a number of casualties on both sides. Sultan Abdullah was convicted for the murder and exiled to the Seychelles with his family in 1877; and Raja Yusuf was then appointed as the twenty-seventh Sultan of Perak. With the help of the Sultan of Kedah, Raja Ismail finally returned the Perak state regalia at the end of the war but a number of items were reportedly lost in the meantime (Winstedt and Wilkinson 1934, 165).

THE NOBAT AND COLONIAL SCHOLARSHIP

This episode in the early stages of direct British involvement in indigenous affairs enlightened them on the importance and significance of the regalia to a Malay ruler's political legitimacy. The 'magic powers' of the regalia would be discussed in detail by William Skeat in his book *Malay Magic* (1900), a result of a number of years' worth of ethnographic work. This encounter also saw the development of a closer relationship between the British and Perak court that would facilitate closer scrutiny of matters relating to the state. The study of the peninsula and its people was imperative since according to Swettenham at the time, 'the characteristics, customs, peculiarities and prejudices of the Malay had yet to be learned' (1895, 228).

One important step towards a sustained study encompassing the whole region began when in 1877 a group of British scholar-administrators formed a society to 'promote the collection and record of information relating to the Straits Settlements and the neighbouring countries' (JSBRAS 1, 1878, III). The society published the *Journal of the Straits Branch of the Royal Asiatic Society* (JSBRAS), which was later known as the *Journal of the Malaysian Branch of the Royal Asiatic Society* (JMBRAS) (see Choy 1995). Although scholarly in nature, articles in the journal were written without too much jargon (ibid.), in order to make them accessible to the general European expatriate population with interests in the Orient. The journal, and other British documentation such as newspaper reports and travel writings, constituted part of 'colonial knowledge', which A. B. Shamsul (2001, 357) argues would later shape Malaysian historiography and the concept of Malay identity or Malayness. Colonial publications also served as a symbol of prestige and influence among competing European powers in Asia (Brown 2000, 3).

It did not take long before Malay court customs began to be documented. The first article relating to Malay performing arts appeared in the second publication of JSBRAS in December 1878. Written by Swettenham, it describes a 'nautch' performance, which involved dancers and musicians performing at the Bendahara of Pahang's house. The journal's authors at the time seem to have been particularly drawn to the realms of the exotic and supernatural, especially in relation to court customs and traditional beliefs. W. E. Maxwell, for example, an officer who was involved in the military operations during the Perak War, wrote an article about a 'mysterious document' that was part of the Perak regalia called *chiri* (Maxwell 1881). The document was read out during a sultan's installation by the Toh Seri Nara Diraja, the herald known as the *orang muntah lembu* (literally, 'people of the bull's vomit') who came from the same lineage as the *orang kalur*, players of the Perak nobat; this subject was to be covered in greater detail later by William Linehan (1951). It was not surprising that this interest in the 'superstitious' beliefs and magic of the Malays was later to become associated with the nobat and court regalia.

One of the most dramatic accounts of the 'mysterious' nature of the nobat was given by Skeat in *Malay Magic*. In explaining the 'peculiar sanctity of the regalia', Skeat (1900, 41) relates a few stories he encountered:

> Drops of perspiration, for instance, would form upon the Trumpet when a leading member of the Royal House was about to die (this actually happened, as I was told, at Langat just before the death of Tungku 'Chik, the late Sultan's eldest daughter, who died during my residence in the neighborhood). . . . Then one Raja Bakar, son of a Raja 'Ali, during the rethatching of the house at Bandar, accidentally trod upon the wooden barrel of one of the State Drums and died in consequence of his inadvertence. . . . When therefore, a hornet's nest formed inside one of these same drums it was pretty clear that things were going from bad to worse, and a Chinaman was ordered to remove it, no Malay having been found willing to risk his life in undertaking so dangerous an office an unwillingness which was presently justified, as the Chinaman, too, after a few days' interval, swelled up and died.

Works on Malay magic and court regalia were further carried by R. O. Winstedt (1925). Peppered with similar dramatic incidents, the telling of such stories was also indicative of the power British officials had over Malay ruling elites, given the ease with which they gained their 'secrets'. Claims were often made of being the first to witness or record a hitherto unknown event; for example, Swettenham (1878, 163) asserts that the 'Malay nautch' he witnessed had so far been 'undescribed'. Winstedt (1925, 84), too, states that 'the *séance* to "revive" (*memuleh*) the Perak regalia has never been described'. He describes the ritual in a particularly dramatic fashion:

> Then the two chief magicians did obeisance to the regalia, offered delicacies to 'the thousand genies' and poured upon the royal drums and into the royal trumpets drink, which vanished miraculously as though imbibed. (Ibid.)

Winstedt (1945, 140) also reveals the Perak royal secret, whispered to the ear of a sultan during his installation:

> In Perak, when the Sultan has entered the palace and taken his seat on the throne, his chief herald, Sri Nara-diraja proclaims the royal title and, as a Brahmin whispers into the ear of his pupil the name of the god who is to be the child's special protector through life, so the herald whispers to his new lord the State secret, Vicitram, the name of the lord of that Meru in old Palembang, ancestor and guardian of Perak royalty.

Apart from the exoticization and dramatization of the nobat in colonial writings, Europeans also made note of the close relationships they established with the Malay royal households (as if following Swettenham's advice on the importance of gaining the Malay's confidence in order to understand him).

To illustrate his close relationships with the Selangor royalty, Skeat (1900, 42) writes that:

> Both these strange coincidences were readily confirmed by the present Sultan on an occasion when I happened to question the authenticity of the story, and as His Highness is one of the most enlightened and truthful of men, such confirmation cannot easily be set aside ... having occasion to visit the Raja Muda at his house at Bandar, I took the opportunity of asking whether there was any objection to my seeing these much debated objects, and as His Highness not only very obligingly assented, but offered to show them to me himself, I was able both to see and to handle them, His Highness himself taking the Trumpet out of its yellow case and handing it to me.

Another sample of the trust gained from Malay rulers can be seen in a story related by R. J. Wilkinson (1932, 79) on the installation of Sultan Idris of Perak:

> After he has been purified the new Sultan dons his royal dress and insignia and proceeds to take his seat upon the dais-throne. There he must sit absolutely still while the State Band plays five, seven, or nine *man*. Seven is the usual number. What is a *man*? Nobody knows; it is what the band plays at this time. Why must the Sultan never stir? Let Sultan Idris answer: 'When I was installed', said he, 'the widow of Sultan Ali came up and put a pad on my shoulder where the gold chain of the Sword of Alexander rested. She told me that the ghostly enemies of the State would be likely to pull at the chain so as to get me to make some unlucky movement. All this is mere superstition, of course; but I humored her. And I am bound to add that I felt three inexplicable tugs while the band was playing the seven *man*.

These accounts show, albeit from a biased European perspective, the apparent high level of trust gained from the Malay ruling elites and their willingness to share their cultural heritage with their colonial overlords. This was a far cry from the earlier 'experiment' with Resident Birch; no doubt Swettenham would have seen this as an important diplomatic improvement.

ABU BAKAR'S NOBAT TUNE

Although Johor did not come under direct British rule until 1914, the latter's influence on the establishment and development of the state was immense. When Stamford Raffles arrived in Singapore in 1819, he saw the potential of the island as a strategic base for British economic expansion in the region. Singapore was then governed by the Temenggong of Johor, who was under nominal rule of the Johor-Riau Empire based in Daik, which was under Dutch control. Taking advantage of the local political disputes at the time, Raffles finally managed to secure Singapore by installing Raja Husain as Sultan of Johor; an act that greatly displeased the Dutch. After the signing of the Anglo-Dutch treaty in 1824, the British officially possessed Singapore and Johor slowly began to disassociate itself from Riau. In the meantime, Temenggong Ibrahim of Singapore had his own political ambitions and began negotiating with the British. His close affiliation with the British bore fruit when he solidified his political position after the death of Sultan Husain in 1835. His son Ali succeeded as Sultan of Johor but was confined within the small area of Muar while Temenggong Ibrahim was given powers to administer much of the state by the British. During his reign, Temenggong Ibrahim also delegated some of his duties to his son Abu Bakar, who was trained in a mission school in Singapore.

Temenggong Ibrahim died in 1862 and was succeeded by Abu Bakar, who was already a well-known figure among the elites of Singapore. Known for his fluency in English and taste in European culture, not surprisingly, Johor was soon governed in the mould of a Western bureaucracy. He began to get international recognition by travelling abroad and was received by Queen Victoria, who became a close friend. In 1868, with the approval of Sir Harry Ord, Governor of the Straits Settlement, Abu Bakar proclaimed himself as the Maharaja of Johor. Abu Bakar's reign is considered by historians as the period of both Westernization and modernization, hence the title 'Father of Modern Johor' bestowed upon him (Rahimah Abdul Aziz 1997, 3; A. R. Tang Abdullah 2008, 209). The British was so impressed by Abu Bakar's abilities and his Western demeanor that Sir Harry Ord viewed him as the 'only Rajah in the whole peninsula or adjoining states who rules in accordance with the practice of civilized nations' (Trocki 2007, 155).

With the backing of the British, the ambitious Abu Bakar finally gained the ultimate recognition he wanted—to be Sultan of Johor. In was reported in a Straits Settlement correspondence:

> Whereas His Highness the Maharajah of Johore has made known to the Governor of the Straits Settlements that it is the desire of his chiefs and people that he assume the title of Sultan, it is further agreed that, in consideration of the loyal friendship and constant affection His Highness has shown to the Government of Her Majesty the Queen and Empress, and of the stipulations contained in this Memorandum, he and his heirs and successors, lawfully succeeding according to Malay custom, shall in future be acknowledged as His Highness the Sultan of the State and territory of Johore, and shall be so addressed. (CO 882/4/22 1885)

Abu Bakar's proclamation as sultan did not go down well with many Malays. He was viewed with suspicion for his Temenggong and Bugis origins, and Western lifestyle. Nevertheless, Abu Bakar was installed at the Istana Besar in Johor Bahru on 29 July 1886. It was reported in the *Straits Times* (1886, 6):

> At a quarter past three o'clock the herald droclaimed [*sic*] the approach of the Sultan and five minutes after His Highness dressed in a pale yellow sarong and baju, entered, the Insignia bearers at once advanced to march out of the room, followed by the Sultan attended by a number of Malay ladies, and the procession towards the *Pancha Persada* commenced. The Band struck up a Malay tune called 'Nobat' and a salute of 17 guns was fired from the flag staff battery. A strip of yellow cloth was laid down from the reception room to the *Pancha Persada* and thence to the Sultan's rooms for him to walk on. In about five minutes the Sultan had reached the platform, where he was received by the Malay ladies already referred to. Here on the platform were bowls of fragrant waters. The Tuan Hakim, as Emaum Besar, blessed the waters, and the ladies who were nearest to him, delegated to the office, sponged His Highness's arms and face—the Band at this time playing a Malay tune called *Lagu Bersiram*. In about ten minutes this washing process was gone through. His Highness was then sprinkled over with gold shred to fine pieces, and leaving the platform enveloped in a purple sarong, the Band playing the *Nobat*, while a second salute was fired from the battery on the hill—he proceeded towards his own rooms to dress for the subsequent proceedings.

The report shows the hybrid nature of Johor's royal ceremony under Sultan Abu Bakar. While certain fundamental customs were maintained, such as the bathing ceremony on the *Pancha Persada*, Western influence was obvious in the use of the military band in accompanying the ceremony, instead of the traditional nobat ensemble. There are a number of reasons for this. Firstly, Sultan Abu Bakar was a descendant of a Temenggong, which was lower in rank as a Sultan and was not entitled for a nobat, which was kept by the Riau-Lingga Sultan. Similarly, the Bendahara family ruling the state of Pahang was not accorded the nobat since they are not of royal lineage and a vassal state of Riau-Lingga.

Sultan Abu Bakar's use of music in marking certain important stages in his installation ceremony was in line with traditional Malay court customs but instead of using the traditional nobat ensemble, a Western style military band was used. However, probably in order to please the more traditional Malay elites and not totally detaching himself from Malay court customs practiced in Riau, a song called 'Nobat' was played. The fusion of both the modern and traditional encapsulates the 'accommodating' process of Malay ruling elites in trying to be 'the recognisable Other' while at the same time attempting to construct (or reconstruct) their own cultural identity. This process was best described in a report by the *Straits Times Weekly Issue* on 12 August 1886 titled 'Institution of Orders of Knighthood in Johore' where a court ceremony 'was conducted with all the ceremony and form of ancient Malay usage, to which was added a little of the pageant attendant on such circumstances in Europe' (*Straits Times Weekly Issue* 1886, 3).

It was after Abu Bakar's death in 1895 that an actual nobat ensemble was played at the palace. The *Singapore Free Press* and *Mercantile Advertiser* (9 September 1895, 3) reported that the ensemble was brought from Riau and played 'weird funeral music' during the lying-in-state ceremony at the throne room. It is however interesting to note that the nobat did not accompany the cortege to the cemetery, as according to normal court customs but was instead accompanied by the Johore Band, which played Mendelssohn's 'Marche Funèbre' and Beethoven's 'Funeral March'. The band was conducted by bandmaster M. Galistan, who was largely responsible for its establishment, under the instruction of the late sultan himself (*Singapore Free Press*, 9 September 1895; *Straits Times*, 8 April 1930; also, see chapter 3 of this book). A similar 'fusion' and the reconstruction of Malay court customs can be seen nearly seventy years later in Kuala Lumpur.

TERENGGANU'S NEW NOBAT AND COLONIAL INTERFERENCE IN SELANGOR SUCCESSIONS

The Anglo-Dutch treaty of 1824 effectively dismantled the Johor-Riau-Lingga Empire, resulting in the creation of the independent states of Johor and Pahang as well as the economic powerhouse of colonial Singapore. It demarcated the lines between British and Dutch control but it was not until 1857 that the Riau-Lingga sultanate officially separated from Johor. Prior to the treaty, the Johor-Riau Empire, considered the successor of the Melaka Sultanate, covered parts of southern Malay Peninsula, southeast Sumatera and the Riau islands. Terengganu had long been connected to Lingga through political and family ties. Upset at not being officially installed as Sultan of Lingga in 1821, Sultan Abdul Rahman left for Terengganu with his son and was sheltered by Sultan Ahmad of Terengganu (Matheson 1972, 121). Abdul Rahman's son Tengku Besar Muhammad married Sultan Ahmad's daughter Tengku Teh and was bestowed with a son named Mahmud. Sultan Abdul Rahman was finally returned by the Dutch to Lingga and installed with full regalia in 1823 but left much of the administration to his son Tengku Besar Muhammad. Sultan Abdul Rahman passed away in 1832 and succeeded by his son Muhammad. When Sultan Ahmad, Muhammad's father-in-law passed away in 1826 a succession dispute ensued and one lost contender Omar was banished to Lingga and sheltered by Sultan Muhammad. Omar went back to Terengganu and overthrew his cousin Sultan Muhammad to become ruler in 1839. Sultan Omar would later return his favor to Sultan Muhammad by sheltering his son Mahmud at his court in Terengganu two decades later. Lingga's nobat was also used during the wedding celebration of Sultan Zainal Abidin III's eldest son (Sheppard 1989). This close relationship between the two sultanates would continue until the last sultan of Lingga was dethroned by the Dutch in 1911.

Terengganu remained free from British intervention until the Anglo-Siamese Treaty was signed in 1909. Former vassal states of Perlis, Kedah, Kelantan and Terengganu came under direct British control at this point. One of the consequences of the event was the transfer of the nobat from Lingga to Terengganu. However, it was not until 1917 that nobat was finally transferred to Kuala Terengganu and first used during the installation of Sultan Muhammad Shah II in 1918. However, nothing much has been reported about the Terengganu palace and the nobat during this early period, possibly due to the 'less close' relationship between the British and Terengganu compared with other sultanates (see the 1917 report by British Agent J. L. Humphreys in the *Straits Times*, 29 October 1918, 2). The Terengganu nobat received a passing mention in a report on the installation of Sultan Ismail Nasiruddin Shah at the Istana Maziah, Kuala Terengganu in 1949. The *Straits Times* (4 June 1949, 4) reported:

> Then after the assembled chiefs and dignitaries had answered 'selamat sempurna' the modern microphone gave way to a blue robed royal trumpeter and the drums of the Nobat (royal musicians).

Selangor received its first British Resident in 1875 during the reign of Sultan Abdul Samad (r. 1857–1896). During this period, the nobat ensemble was no longer active. It was reported that the previous ruler, Sultan Muhammad (r. 1826–1857) ordered that all the regalia destroyed on the advice of Sheikh Abdul Ghani, a religious scholar from Sumatera (Wan Mohd Amin 1966, 89). It is unclear if the nobat was also destroyed but the institution ceased to function during the reign of Sultan Abdul Samad (r. 1857–1896). J. M. Gullick, in a letter in 1989 (ANM 2001/0020668) to Mubin Sheppard, was of the opinion that the regalia destroyed as mentioned by Wan Mohd Amin were perhaps the personal insignia used to install the ruler. This was because the state regalia were still intact, including a pair of *gendang* and the *nafiri*, which were described by Skeat (1900).

According to Wan Mohd Amin (1966, 91), who was *Penghulu Adat* (head of customs) at the time, instruments of the Selangor nobat were still around but in a sorry state. He recalls:

Orang-orang Kalau yang menyelenggarakan nobat itu tiada lagi. Mana-mana yang telah mati, tinggallah anak cucunya tiada disurohkan belajar lagi, maka kerana itu menjadi lapoklah kulit-kulit gendang, tinggal balohnya (rangka gendang) sahaja.

The Kalau people who managed the nobat were no longer around. Whoever died, their sons and grandsons were not asked to learn anymore, thus the skins of the drums decayed, only the wooden frames were left.

In preparing for the installation of Sultan Ala'uddin Sulaiman Shah (r. 1898–1938), the nobat instruments were not in playing order and certain articles of the state regalia had to be re-made. With the approval of the Selangor Resident and Resident General, new sets of crowns were ordered for the Sultan and his consort. It was also decided with the consent of the Sultan, that a request would be made to Sultan Idris of Perak to send his nobat and *orang kalur* to Selangor for the installation. Wan Mohd Amin (1966, 94) wrote:

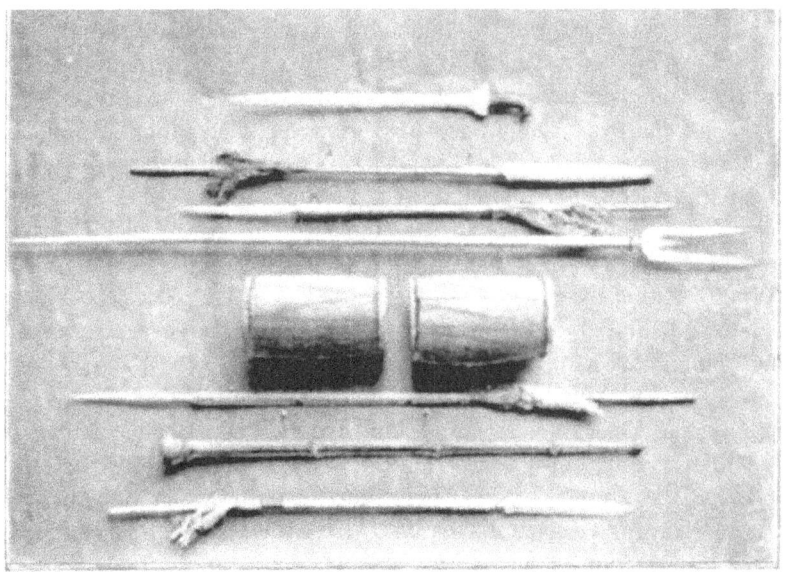

Figure 6.2. The plate from Skeat's book showing models of the Selangor state regalia, which included a pair of *gendang* and a *nafiri* (Skeat 1900, 40). Source: MBRAS.

> *Kerana pada masa yang terdahulu, pada masa Sultan Salahuddin bertabal, nobat dari Perak juga di-gunakan. Maka keputusan meshuarat itu sakalian-nya telah sa-bulat suara bersetuju supaya Raja Haji Mahmud di-tugaskan pergi itu. Hal ini telah di-persembahkan pada Ka-bawah Duli Tuanku, dan sa-telah di-persetujui oleh baginda maka pergi-lah Raja Haji Mahmud membawa surat kepada Duli Yang Maha Mulia Sultan Idris Shah. Tiga hari sahaja lama-nya Raja Haji Mahmud pergi itu maka ia pun balek-lah dengan membawa nobat bersama2 dengan orang2 Kalau-nya sa-ramai lapan orang.*

> Because previously, during the installation of Sultan Salahuddin, it was the nobat from Perak that was used. So the meeting unanimously agreed that Raja Haji Mahmud was assigned to go. This matter was conveyed to His Highness [Sultan of Selangor], and after consent was granted, Raja Haji Mahmud brought the letter to His Majesty Sultan Idris Shah [of Perak]. After just three days Raja Haji Mahmud brought back the [Perak] nobat accompanied by eight orang Kalau.

The meeting involved the Selangor royal family and members of the installation organising committee. Mention of the Perak nobat being used during the installation of Sultan Salahuddin, referring to the first Sultan of Selangor shows the strong historical ties that bound both states, with the nobat seen as a symbol of that bond. The Sultan of Perak gladly gave his permission since it strengthened and enhanced Perak's status as the 'elder' of the two states.

The nobat *adat* was again restored during the installation of Sultan Ala'uddin Sulaiman in October 1903 and it was reported that the installation was successfully conducted although it had been nearly fifty years since the last sultan was installed and sounds of trumpets were heard outside of the throne room (*Straits Times*, 12 November 1903, 6). According to Wan Mohd Amin (1966), during the installation, the nobat played the pieces 'Iskandar' and 'Ibrahim Khalilullah', which were originally called 'Gendang Berangkat' and 'Lenggang Encik Kobat' in Perak (see chapter 3).

Sultan Ala'uddin's rule however was marked by a succession dispute between three of his sons, Tengku Musa Eddin, Tengku Badar Shah and Tengku Alam Shah. According to royal *adat*, Tengku Musa, being the eldest, was the rightful heir to the throne and was appointed to the post of Raja Muda or heir apparent in 1920. He was later dismissed by the British, on the instigation of the Resident, Theodore Samuel Adams, due to 'misbehavior'. Tengku Alam Shah was then appointed to the post in July 1936. The Malays viewed this as a clear breach of the Selangor royal *adat* and considered that the Resident should have consulted the sultan and nobles before the decision was made (Buyong Adil 1971, 162). Tengku Musa Eddin was then appointed Tengku Kelana Jaya in charge of royal customs and ceremonies. The *Straits Times*, in its report on Sultan Alam Shah's coronation in 1939, however, defended the Resident's decision:

> As Sultan Alam Shah was crowned in accordance with a ritual that differs but little from that used for the coronation of his ancestors on the banks of the Langkat river, many must have remembered that he was chosen by the British Government from among the late Sultan Suleiman's sons as the man best fitted to be a modern ruler. A modern Malay, versed in administration and understanding English, Sir Alam Shah yet conforms to the ancient tradition and *adat* of his race and family. When he was appointed Raja Muda or Crown Prince, some Malays feared that he was too 'Europeanized' and that in choosing him for ultimate succession to the throne of Selangor the British authorities sought to disturb the customs and traditions which mean so much to every Malay, whether his home is in court or kampong. How unnecessary were such anxieties was established at this coronation. (27 January 1939, 14)

British meddling in Selangor did not stop there but continued with a request to the Sultan of Terengganu that a nobat ensemble be sent for Sultan Alam Shah's installation ceremony, instead of from Perak. A letter in the Arkib Negara Malaysia dated 29 December 1938, written by Tengku Kelana Jaya, elder brother of Sultan Alam Shah, was sent to Sultan Badrul Alam Shah on behalf of British Resident Stanley Wilson Jones. It is interesting to note that Tengku Kelana Jaya, who was earlier dethroned and humiliated at the instigation of the British Resident, was now writing a letter on his behalf requesting a nobat from Terengganu to install his younger brother. In an excerpt, Tengku Kelana writes:

> *Adalah beta dengan beberapa hormatnya beri maklumkan kepada Seri Paduka sahabat beta yaitu Tuan British Residen Selangor telah memohon sekiranya Seri Paduka sahabat beta boleh memberi pinjam nobat Seri Paduka sahabat beta.* (ANM 1957/0339361)
>
> I with utmost respect wish to inform my acquaintance Your Highness that the Honourable British Resident of Selangor asks if my acquaintance Your Highness can lend my acquaintance Your Highness's nobat.

The nobat was eventually sent to Selangor for Sultan Alam Shah's installation, as confirmed by a number of notes and letters from the Terengganu palace in the Malaysian National and Terengganu State Archives (see figure 6.3) and reports from the *Straits Times*.

Figure 6.3. A memo from the Sultan of Terengganu's private secretary to the state secretary, dated 18 January 1939, requesting an advance of $252.00 for the nobat players' trip to Selangor. *Source*: Arkib Negara Malaysia, ANM 1957/0339361W.

The use of the Terengganu nobat was mentioned in the *Straits Times*:

> When the late Sultan was crowned, orang kalau were borrowed from Perak. On this occasion they have been lent by the courtesy of His Highness the Sultan of Trengganu. (25 January 1939, 1)

Another report stated:

> The voice of the Court Chamberlain, Panglima Dalam announced the arrival of the Highnesses. And this was the signal for the nobat to strike up the Piece of the Prophet Ibrahim (Lagu Ibrahim Khalilullah). (*Straits Times*, 29 January 1939, 14)

Although Tengku Kelana's letter to the Sultan of Terengganu requested the Terengganu nobat, it is uncertain whether it included the instruments or just the players. There was no mention of the instruments being transported to

Selangor and used in the installation in any of the palace letters or reports from newspapers. The beautifully crafted silver drums are unlikely to have been left unnoticed by reporters. Even though Terengganu players were used for Sultan of Selangor's installation, the piece 'Lagu Ibrahim Khalilullah' mentioned in the above report was not part of the nobat of Terengganu's repertoire, known there as 'Lagu Ibrahim Khalil'. It was a Selangor piece (but played as 'Lenggang Encik Kobat' in Perak) and the Terengganu players must have learned it prior to the ceremony. For unknown reasons, Tengku Kelana Jaya once again requested the Terengganu nobat in 1941 but the request was unable to be fulfilled due to certain problems faced by the Sultan of Terengganu at the time (Jelani Harun 2008, 17).

REPORTS ON THE NOBAT

The importance of Perak to the British can be seen in the amount of coverage of this rich sultanate. A special report was given by the *Straits Times* on the installation of Sultan Abdul Aziz of Perak in 1939 (2 March 1939). A whole page was allocated to an article entitled *Ancient State Drums to Beat in Astana* that explains the importance of the nobat and included four photographs and a description of the ensemble. The article also quotes from Winstedt's *History of Perak* regarding the details of the installation ceremony in which the nobat featured heavily.

As part of a postwar plan for a centralised government in the Malay Peninsula, an idea was presented to the British War Cabinet in 1944 for the establishment of the Malayan Union. Under this new entity, the Malay states and the Straits Settlements of Penang and Melaka were brought under a single administrative rule governed by a British Governor. The Malay Rulers, uncertain of their position and threatened by the British for their 'disloyalty' during the Japanese occupation, agreed to the Union although in effect it would diminish their powers except over matters relating to religion and Malay customs. The nine Malay sultans would surrender their full sovereignty to the British Crown and citizenship rights would be extended to non-Malays. The Malayan Union posed the greatest existential threat to the centuries old Malay monarchy since, for the first time, the sultans (other than pertaining to religion and culture) had to concede all political powers to the British Crown. The Malay populace saw this as an attempt to abolish the Malay monarchy altogether and vehemently opposed the idea.[2]

One of the most vocal opponents to the federation was Onn Jaafar, a Malay aristocrat from Johor who was one of the founding members of United Malay Nationalist Organization (UMNO). Formed in 1946, this movement would later be led by a member of the Kedah royal family—Tunku Abdul Rahman Petra. This Cambridge-educated lawyer would later be the first prime minister of Malaya and almost single-handedly changed the Malay system of monarchy forever. The Malayan Union idea was eventually scrapped and after much negotiation the Federation of Malaya was formed. On 1 February 1948, the nobat was played at the Istana Iskandariah, Kuala Kangsar to inaugurate the formation of the Federation (*Straits Times*, 4 February 1948). The playing of the nobat to announce the formation of the new federation can be seen as a sign of relief and delight on behalf of the Malay sultans, especially Sultan Abdul Aziz of Perak (1887–1948), who was really concerned about issue of Chinese citizenship.

British documentation of Malaya was brought to a new level with the advent of film, which was used as newsreels. One of the earliest films of the nobat was made by Pathé News (known today as British Pathé) during the birthday celebration of Sultan Yusuf of Perak in 1952 (figure 6.4). It was the first time that the ceremony was conducted on a field in Ipoh, the capital of Perak and not at the Iskandariah Palace in Kuala Kangsar (sembangkuala.wordpress.com). It can be assumed that the pomp and ceremony were orchestrated to be visible on an unprecedented scale to the general population; even the *menjunjung duli* (oath of allegiance) ceremony was done outdoors including the playing of the nobat. Like Malay sultans centuries earlier, this public ceremony can be seen as visual and aural display of royal power, but this time with the inclusion of a British Resident by the sultan's side.

Figure 6.4. A still from a film by British Pathé showing the nobat of Perak in 1952. *Source*: YouTube.

THE (RE)INVENTION OF TRADITION

'I was one of the architects of Malaya's Independence and also the institution of Kingship' (Tunku Abdul Rahman 1978, 75). The term 'Kingship' here refers to the Malaysian constitutional monarch, the Yang Dipertuan Agong, a post created during the independence of Malaya. After Malaya's first elections in 1955, in which the Alliance Party won, Tunku began his efforts to negotiate Malaya's independence from the British. The nine Malay rulers were, however, apprehensive about the idea since they were unsure what their position in the new nation state would be. They would oppose any attempt towards independence unless issues pertaining to their status were addressed. In order to avoid a confrontation between the people (who wanted independence) and their rulers, to whom they still pledged allegiance, Tunku had to formulate a solution. He met with the nine rulers and an agreement was made that the rulers would be represented in the independence negotiations in London. The two delegations agreed to sail from Singapore to Karachi together in order to sort out any differences and speak with one voice in the independence negotiations with the British. It was during this voyage, which started on 1 January 1956, that the idea of a rotating head of state was raised by Tunku and agreed upon by the representatives of the rulers. Inspired by the system employed in Negeri Sembilan,[3] Tunku proposed the implementation of a unique rotational constitutional monarchy post for the independent Federation of Malaya. The conference of rulers held in June 1957 agreed on the title of 'Yang Di-Pertuan Agong' (literally, 'He who is made Supreme') instead of 'Yang Di-Pertuan Besar' (literally, 'He who is made Majestic'), which was proposed earlier (*Straits Times*, 21 June 1957, 7). In August the same year, the conference of rulers elected Tuanku Abdul Rahman, the ruler of Negeri Sembilan as the first Yang di-Pertuan Agong. Tuanku Abdul Rahman was selected after Sultan Ibrahim of Johor turned down the post despite being the longest serving ruler among members of the council.

This post combined the old Malay feudal system and Western constitutional democracy. Rulers were still installed based on royal lineage and seniority in their respective states, while democratically selected by their fellow rulers for the post of Yang Di-Pertuan Agong. As head of state, the post would be held for five years and based in Kuala Lumpur, while a regent was appointed as acting ruler in the home state during the duration of the appointment. No other country in the world practices such a system and it was a challenge for the appointed ruler to command the same respect and adulation received by long-serving hereditary rulers of countries such as Britain, Japan and Thailand.

THE FIRST INSTALLATION

On 31 August 1957, the Federated States of Malaya officially declared independence from British rule. The installation of the first Yang Dipertuan Agong was conducted in September the same year. Since no palace has ever been built, there was not a proper place to hold the ceremony. There was also a sense of urgency in trying to finalise the whole process of independence and the legitimization of Malaya as a sovereign state. The Tunku admitted that the organising committee faced a problem in finding a suitable place for the installation and royal banquet. He recalled that:

> There was no building big enough or prestigious enough for the purpose in Kuala Lumpur . . . we bought a mansion in Ampang Road and build an annexe in the form of a large hall which is still known as Dewan Tunku Abdul Rahman. The annexe had to be completed within seven weeks and the builders, working 24 hours at a stretch completed the job in time. (Tunku Abdul Rahman 1983, 2)

In accordance with Malay royal customs, the Yang Di-Pertuan Agong needed the essential regalia as symbols of his power and authority, and the finest craftsmen from Kelantan and Terengganu were commissioned to make them, while some were ordered from London. Due to time constraints, the throne of the Yang Dipertuan Agong could not be constructed in time for the installation and, according to Tunku, they 'had to make do with a pair of handsome leather chairs adorned with the coat of arms of the Federation of Malaya painted on the upright portion at the back' (ibid., 2). However, the most essential part of the regalia—the nobat—was not included in the new regalia, and it was decided that the nobat of Kedah would be used for the first installation.

Being a royal himself Tunku knew about the history of the nobat and understood its importance in Malay court tradition. He wrote:

> It was unthinkable to hold the installation of the first Yand Dipertuan Agung of the country without the accompaniment of the Nobat, in keeping with the ancient and traditional Malay custom. So I asked the Sultan of Kedah to lend the Kedah orchestra for this purpose and it has continued to be used all these years. It was also used at the funeral procession of the first and second Yang Dipertuan Agung (When the Barisan Nasional was formed, PAS members objected on religious ground to the use of the Nobat at the funeral). (Ibid., 3)

However, as a British educated, 'modern' Malay, Tunku needed to balance tradition and the realities of a progressive and multiracial country. This was reflected in the novel deployment of forty warriors dressed in the costume of ancient Malacca consisting of Malays, Chinese, Indians and Eurasians during the installation ceremony. Minutes from the Merdeka Celebration committee meetings, dated 2 and 4 January 1957, show that members of royalty advised on details of the installation ceremony and decisions made by the committee had to go through the Malay rulers for final approval. A diagram of the Balairong Seri also shows the efforts made by the committee to uphold traditional Malay court customs, in this case the position of the *singgah sana* or dais directly facing the nobat and sitting positions of royal guests (figure 6.5). This was similar to the floor plan of the Balairong Seri of the Iskandariah Palace in Perak but certain new sitting positions were added. However, film recordings show that the actual Balairong Seri used for the installation differed from the one proposed, especially the Yang Dipertuan Agong's entrance and the position of the nobat ensemble. Tunku Abdul Rahman's ideas were aptly described as a 'blend' in the headline of the *Straits Times*, which read 'Malaya's King Installed: Ceremony Was Brilliant Blend of the Old and the New' (3 September 1957). The historical event was also filmed by Pathé News, including a newsreel about the making of the regalia.

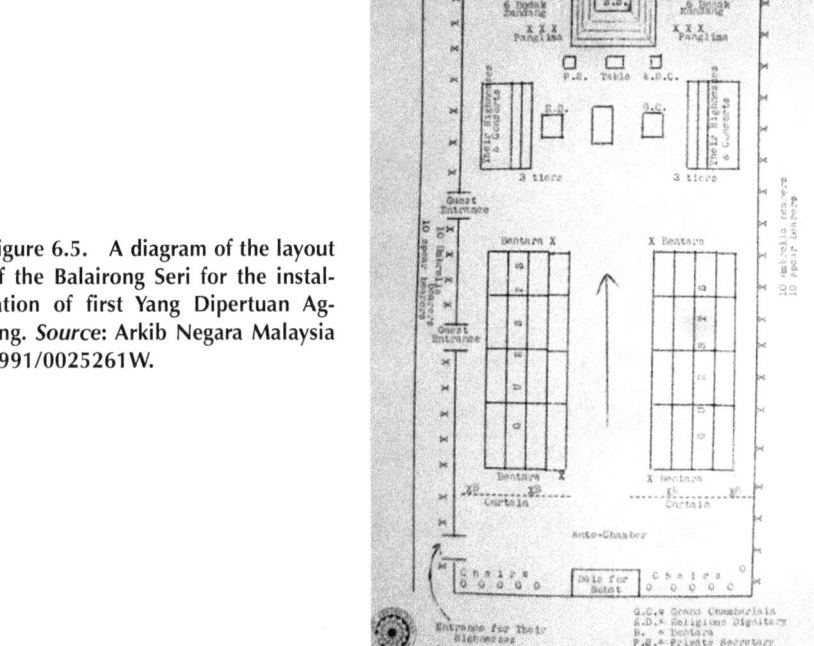

Figure 6.5. A diagram of the layout of the Balairong Seri for the installation of first Yang Dipertuan Agong. *Source*: Arkib Negara Malaysia 1991/0025261W.

THE NOBAT AND POST-INDEPENDENCE MALAYA

Malay court ceremonies continued to be documented by the British even after independence. In 1959, Pathé News made a newsreel on the installation of the sultan of Kedah at the Balai Besar in Alor Setar, where the sight and sound of the Kedah nobat was briefly presented (figure 6.6). In the state of Perak, special coverage was given by the *Straits Times* on the installation of Sultan Idris II of Perak in 1963. Similar to previous reports and articles on the sultanate, such as the installation of Sultan Abdul Aziz in 1939, the nobat continued to be highlighted.

The British presence in post-independence Malaya was crucial in safeguarding their colonial interests while helping the newly established state in matters of governance. This was evident in the continued existence of British companies and expatriates in Malaya years after independence (Harper 2001, 363). While many British officers returned to their homeland to retire, one scholar-administrator decided to stay behind who would leave an indelible impact on Malay cultural preservation and documentation. His name was Mervyn Cecil ffranck Sheppard (MCff Sheppard), later known as Tan Sri Dato' Dr. Haji Mubin Sheppard.

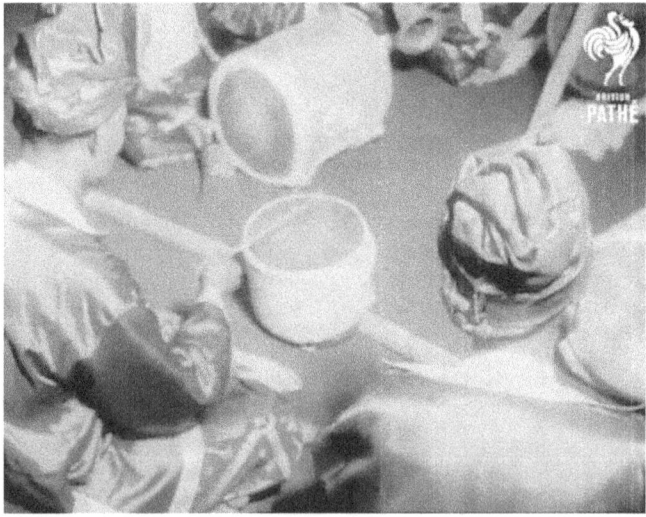

Figure 6.6. A still from a British Pathé newsreel showing the nobat of Kedah playing at the Balai Besar in 1959. *Source*: YouTube.

MUBIN SHEPPARD AND THE MALAY NOBAT

Tan Sri Dato' Dr. Haji Mubin Sheppard (1905–1994; figure 6.7) was a unique figure in many ways. Born in Ireland and a convert to Islam, from 1928 he was successively a civil servant under British rule, Malayan rule and the government of Malaysia. Just prior to Malayan independence, in 1950, Sheppard was acting British advisor to Kelantan and later advisor to Negeri Sembilan in 1956. At the end of November 1955, he informed Tunku Abdul Rahman and High Commissioner Sir Donald MacGillivray that he wanted to continue serving in Malaya after independence (Sheppard 1979). Sheppard, however, made a resolution that his service to the country would be voluntary and determined to make Malaya his home. He recalls:

> When I returned to Petaling Jaya everyone I met asked me what I was going to do. I had made only one firm resolution before I left Ireland. I did not wish to accept any further paid employment. Any work which I did in future would be voluntary, and would, I hoped, be of service to some section of the Malayan public. I was content to make my home in Malaya and for the present, I planned to concentrate on Muslim missionary work and cultural research. (Sheppard 1979, 237)

Sheppard's career as a historian and archivist began right after independence when he was appointed as 'First Keeper of Public Records' at the Arkib Negara or National Archives of Malaysia, followed by a number of appointments which included director of the National Museum of Malaya, journal editor of the Malaysian Branch of the Royal Asiatic Society (JMBRAS) and executive committee member of the Malayan History Society. He was a prolific writer; for half a century, Sheppard produced more than a hundred articles and books on Malay history, art and culture (see Barlow 1995b).

One of his first articles on the nobat was published in the magazine *Malaya in History* in 1958 titled, simply, 'The Nobat', featuring the nobat of Kedah during the installation of the first Yang DiPertuan Agong a year earlier. This was followed by another article in the same publication entitled 'The Kedah and Perak Nobat' in collaboration with Tunku Nong Jiwa and Raja Badri Shah, respectively members of Kedah and Perak royalty (T. N. Jiwa et al. 1962). These were written just after Malaya's independence when for the first time, the nobat was thrust into national and international limelight through the media. Sheppard saw the need for the nobat to be further exposed to the general public, especially those not from the royal towns of Alor Setar, Kuala Terengganu, Kuala Kangsar and Kelang. His worry and aspiration for the nobat were expressed in the last paragraph of his article (1962, 11):

Figure 6.7. Tan Sri Dato' Dr. Haji Mubin Sheppard.
Source: http://www.mbras.org.my.

The Nobat has been filmed and broadcast. It has become a familiar sight and sound to thousands of people of all communities in Malaya. History, centuries old, survives through the patient skill of the Orang Kalur. Is this the last generation of a long and privileged line or may we hope that among the youths of the 1960s one or two will be found to study the unrecorded rhythms and transmit them to posterity?

Sheppard believed in the preservation of tangible and intangible heritage, and his close connections to Malay ruling elites helped to facilitate his efforts. During a trip to Istana Kolam Terengganu in 1966, he saw abandoned gamelan instruments and with the approval of the Terengganu palace, Sheppard managed to revive the joget gamelan Terengganu and had it performed for the first time to the public at Universiti Malaya. Next door in Kelantan, together with ethnomusicologist William Malm, Sheppard managed to record *makyong* performances resulting in ninety hours of audiovisual materials (Sheppard 1979, 255). When news of the existence of an old *nafiri* from the Riau sultanate emerged in Singapore, Sheppard, who was curator of Muzium Negara (National Museum) at the time, went to investigate (*Straits Times*, 20

March 1966, 11). His meeting with Tengku Embong Fatimah, niece of the last Sultan of Riau-Lingga, gave him additional insights into the history of the Riau nobat, which would later be used in his writings.[4]

Besides Kedah and Perak, Sheppard also managed to gain access to the Terengganu nobat, and was fascinated with what he saw and heard. A number of photographs of the Terengganu nobat found in the Arkib Negara[5] are attributed to Sheppard and used in his book *Taman Indera* (1972). The book was a result of more than ten years of ethnographic work and showed his deep knowledge of and affection for Malay culture. By this time, Sheppard had covered all four existing nobat ensembles in the Malay Peninsula and acknowledged the existence of one in Brunei. Apart from his admiration for the designs of the silver Terengganu nobat, he was also fascinated by its sound:

> Those who have heard the Nobat drums of Trengganu agree that there is a majesty in their tone, incomparably more melodious than that of their wooden prototypes in Kedah and Perak. (Sheppard 1972, 20)

Despite his access to Malay sultanates and members of royal families, Sheppard could not gather much information on the history of the nobat. During his tenure as editor of JMBRAS, Sheppard edited a short article on the nobat by Affan Seljuq (1976) that describes the historical connection between the Malay nobat and similar ensembles found in the ancient Iranian court. Sheppard continued with his research throughout the late 1980s and corresponded with scholars including Barbara Andaya, Shukor Rahman, John Miksik, Virginia Matheson and J. M. Gullick.[6] Sheppard wanted to fill some gaps on the historical development of the Malay nobat and was particularly interested in the Selangor ensemble. In a letter to journalist Shukor Rahman, Sheppard wrote:

> I shall be grateful if you will let me know where I can find the information about R.W. Duff's[7] action in calling for the Regalia of the late Sultan Abdul Samad in 1989 (sic) at Kuala Langat. I have been trying, with little success, to find out what happened to the Selangor Nobat, which was probably a complete set of instruments, following the model of the Perak Nobat, seems to have disappeared. It seems possible that these historic instruments were lost during the inter-regnum between the death of Sultan Abdul Samad in 1898 and the installation of Sultan Sulaiman (in 1902). (ANM 2001/0020669)

No letter from Shukor was found in response to Sheppard's enquiry. However, the same question must have been put to J. M. Gullick, who responded that during an inspection of the Selangor regalia at the Jugra Istana (sultan's old palace) by J. H. M. Robson, ADO of Kuala Langat at the time, there was no mention of the nobat. Gullick however quoted Skeat's account of the nobat he saw at the Raja Muda's residence at Bandar (see Skeat 1900), but whether the nobat was the original set from Sultan Salahudin's time was never discussed.

On the fate of the Melaka nobat, Sheppard consulted historian Barbara Andaya who 'had no real answer' but speculated that the instruments could have been lost at sea when one of the Portuguese ships sank in the Straits of Melaka, based on accounts by Portuguese historian Barros (ANM 2001/0020664). Sheppard also wrote to archeologist John Miksik and historian Virginia Matheson seeking information on the Riau nobat (ANM 2001/0020675; ANM 2001/0020679). Both Miksik and Matheson provided photographs of the Riau-Lingga nobat now housed in the museums of Pekanbaru (figure 6.8) and Tanjung Pinang in Indonesia.

Three decades after publishing his first article on the nobat, Sheppard wrote his last, titled 'History of the Malay Nobat', published by the *New Straits Times* on 18 September 1989. It was written to commemorate the installation of the ninth Yang Dipertuan Agong, Sultan Azlan Shah of Perak. Although modest in its scope and depth, Sheppard managed to cover the history of all four remaining nobat ensembles of Peninsular Malaysia and more importantly, present it in the simplest way, and to the widest possible audience—through a daily newspaper. Largely based on his previous writings, Sheppard managed to update certain information, especially on the Terengganu-Riau nobat. Surely, his research and writings on the nobat were not definitive, nor were they highly academic, but his affinity and endless curiosity on the subject was apparent.

Figure 6.8. One of the photographs of the Riau-Lingga nobat sent by John Miksik to Mubin Sheppard. *Source*: Arkib Negara Malaysia, ANM 2001/0020675.

From Lancaster, Croft and Mundy to Wilkinson, Skeat and Winstedt, Sheppard was a part of the long history of British writings on the Malay nobat, which resulted in a mixture of responses that offer glimpses of European ethnocentricity, Enlightenment objectivity and a possible hint of colonial empathy. In a period of three centuries, the sound of the nobat evolved from 'noisy' to 'melodious', from one British observer to another. Sheppard symbolises the end of an era, a culmination of British colonial scholarship in the Malay Peninsula. He went beyond what was prescribed by Swettenham; not only did he sympathise with the natives but became virtually one of them. Sheppard wore the *baju melayu* and *tengkolok* on occasions, embraced Islam and devoted his remaining life towards Malay cultural studies and preservation. After sixty-sixty years of service to Malaya and later Malaysia, Tan Sri Dato' Dr. Haji Mubin Sheppard died in 1994 at age eighty-nine in Kuala Lumpur.

SUMMARY

Despite the colonial policy of non-interference in affairs relating to the religion and customs of the Malays, transgression was inevitable in a number of instances especially relating to royal succession issues. In addition, the British, with their military supremacy, sophistication and superiority of attitude, relied upon the 'uncivilised', ancient symbolic customs of the native Malay rulers to achieve their imperialistic aims. These 'guarded secrets' had to be unlocked to better understand 'the inner man' and facilitate the efforts of managing him. Thus, the study and documentation of the Malay world became a crucial part of the British imperial project. Besides political control, the ability to examine and acquire the 'secrets' of the natives and disseminate them displayed the coloniser's diplomatic and political triumph. This 'colonial knowledge' was fascinated with magic and traditional beliefs, and their association with royal customs and ceremonies—which can be viewed as a continuation of the long history of European exoticization of the Orient. There was also constant reiteration in newspaper reports about the fine balance between 'the old and the new' in Malay court customs. This was seen as a justification for a benign British rule in which Malay traditional customs could still survive side by side with modernity, represented by European values introduced by the British.

British colonization of the Malay Peninsula was a precarious, yet illuminating period for the Malay ruling elites. Despite the subordination and ensuing humiliation, Malay rulers saw before them a superior polity whose culture was worth emulating in its modernity and tastes, something that might redeem their pride and respect on a globalising stage. In a conversation with

Hugh Clifford, Sultan Idris of Perak, awed by what he experienced in England remarked:

> It is a splendid thing to think that one belongs to such an Empire—that one is part of it! None of my forebears, stowed away in their forests, enjoyed the greatness that is mine, in that I am myself a portion of something so very great! (Clifford 1929, 194)

With Britain's growing political and economic control over the nineteenth century, it did not take long before European culture and ideas permeated society. More 'Westernised' Malay rulers were clearly favored by the British and many rulers therefore had their children English educated and 'Europeanised'. Whether one considers this a form of Stockholm syndrome,[8] mimicry or strategic essentialism[9] (or a combination of them), these ruling elites deftly manoeuvred their way into the modern world by accommodating certain traditional *adat* or customs to satisfy both local subjects and British colonialists for their own economic gains and political legitimacy. This encounter, a superimposition of a dominant culture rooted in post-Enlightenment thought that underlines reason and questioning, triggered profound cultural shifts. It functioned as a point of juxtaposition through which the Malays could re-examine, reinvent and consolidate their own identity.

Dutch-British partition of the Malay world also saw direct colonial involvement in the court *adat* involving the nobat. The ensemble was performed to receive Dutch residents in Riau, which eventually led to the construction of a Western style nobat instruments (with tuning pegs similar to the timpani) that forever changed the look and sound of the Riau nobat. The 'silver nobat' is now under the patronage of the Terengganu court and was played on national TV during the installation of the thirteenth Yang Dipertuan Agong, Sultan Mizan Zainal Abidin in April 2007.

Meanwhile, Malay culture continued to be viewed with fascination. Edward Said originally argued in *Orientalism* (1978, 1) that 'the Orient was almost a European invention'. To the British, the Malay Peninsula was not just another colonial conquest but also, to borrow Said's words, 'a place of romance, exotic beings, haunting memories and landscapes' (ibid.). This sense of romanticism interestingly resulted in some degree of empathy on behalf of certain colonisers interested in the nobat. Apart from economic and political interests, the British maintained its presence after decolonization, in order to stay relevant at least in the psyche of the Malays. It can be argued that British imperialism was not totally exorcised but simply took different forms, one of which was in the realm of cultural research, documentation and conservation, epitomised by the efforts of one individual—Mubin Sheppard.

British 'colonial knowledge'—achieved through observations, research and writings—provides an invaluable, objective look into the history of the Malay world, although criticised as being a 'cultural invasion' (Shamsul 2001). It offers another source besides well-known early Malay literature which is often questioned in terms of its historical accuracy. Knowledge about the Malays was important for British imperial plans as Swettenham emphatically stated and resulted in a corpus of books, records, articles, artefacts stored in archives, libraries and museums across the UK and Malaysia. The British, albeit all their colonial misdeeds, contributed immensely towards the understanding of Malay history and culture.

NOTES

1. The late sultan lay in state for thirty-two days until the chiefs decided to put him to rest. It is customary that a successor is named before the dead ruler is laid to rest. Raja Abdullah's reluctance to attend the obsequies was due to his fear of being attacked by another claimant to the throne, Raja Yusuf.

2. Apart from the issue of royal power, the Malays were offended by the high-handed manner in which the sultans were asked to sign the agreement and also on the granting of citizenships to Chinese immigrants which were seen as a political and economic threat to the Malays.

3. In Negeri Sembilan, the ruler or Yamtuan Besar is selected by a council of chiefs called the *Datuk-Datuk Undang* among the four leading princes of the ruling family.

4. Sheppard in his later article mentioned about his interviews with members of the Riau-Lingga royal family who were more than seventy years of age (Sheppard 1989). In the 1966 *Straits Times* report (1966, 11), it was mentioned that Tengku Embong Fatimah 'is more than 70 years old'.

5. ANM 2001/0025628, ANM 2001/0025629, ANM 2001/0025630, ANM 2001/0025631, ANM 2001/0025632, ANM 2001/0025633.

6. Barbara Andaya (ANM 2001/0020664), Shukor Rahman (ANM 2001/0020669), John Miksik (ANM 2001/0020676), Virginia Matheson (ANM 2001/0020678) and J. M. Gullick (ANM 2001/0020668, 2001/0020667, 2001/0020665).

7. R. W. Duff succeeded W. W. Skeat in 1898 as a district officer in Selangor.

8. A psychological phenomenon in which captives have feelings of empathy towards their captors and is often attributed to the captives' instinctive defense mechanism for survival.

9. A term introduced by theorist Gayatri Spivak that refers to a strategy in which ethnic groups temporarily 'essentialise' themselves to achieve certain objectives.

Chapter Seven

Conclusion

The evolution and spread of the Muslim court military/ceremonial ensemble over the past millennium is integrally associated with the ascendancy of Muslim polities via a complex web of connections across Central Asia, the Middle East, North Africa, and South and Southeast Asia. Newly-found power meant that rulers needed fitting emblems of their authority and the new Muslim dynasties began to emulate the splendor and pomp of royal ceremonies practiced by conquered or rival empires. This included, rather prominently, the use of musical ensembles. From the confines of a caliph's palace, the *nauba* concept developed into an institution of major importance that would be used for timekeeping, military and symbolic purposes. Only a privileged few were given the authority to own and play these aural symbols of sovereign power—drums, cymbals and trumpets—to mark prayer times, announce important events and terrify in battles. The ensemble in its numerous variations would emerge as a pan-Islamic symbol of power, normally paired with flags or other emblems of kingship. Through military conquest, political alliance and trade, the ensemble developed into a distinctly Islamicate institution by accommodating and absorbing indigenous influences while maintaining its core symbolic and practical functions. This can be seen in the fusion of different musical instruments found in various ensembles across Southeast Asia, South Asia and the Middle East throughout the centuries. In the case of the Malay nobat, the *nafiri*, *nengkara* and *serunai*, ubiquitous in the ceremonial/military ensemble of the Middle East and South Asia, were fused with the local rattan-laced double headed *gendang* and bronze or copper gong, as well as other indigenous blowing instruments, to create a musical entity unlike any other in the Malay world.

The coming of Islam and the introduction of the nobat to the Malay world was the result of expanding commercial and religious activities across the

Indian Ocean. Once introduced to the Malay sultanates, nobat further enhanced existing court ceremonies introduced by earlier Hindu and Buddhist dynasties and the institution came collectively to symbolise Malay power and sovereignty. The nobat became a tool for political alliance, subjugation and allegiance, most notably at the height of the Melaka sultanate in the fifteenth and early sixteenth centuries. Its instruments were part of the court regalia and the institution was revered as the epitome of a sultan's *daulat* or divine essence and crucial in the legitimization of a ruler. Although Malay polities understood the significance of the nobat within the wider Malay world, aspiring sultanates tended to chart their own cultural trajectories. Since a musical performance 'communicates' through a 'language' that constructs meanings, the sight and sound of the nobat inevitably became signs and symbols that represent the concepts, ideas and feelings of he who commanded the performance. The Malays were thus culturally attached to the nobat due to its association with courts that provided them with protection, meaning and a sense of identity. This mutually accepted and understood cultural practice was thus used to mark out and strengthen one's identity vis-à-vis other different Malay subgroup.

This was shown by the Patani sultanate and how the nobat was used to shape Malay-Patani identity as documented in the *Hikayat Patani*. Like other Malay port cities in the region, there was an influx of migrants from other parts of Malay world into Patani. This seems to have required a clear and conscious effort of differentiation that helped characterise Patani identity against other Malay sultanates. Patani nobat pieces, which were almost entirely different from those of the other known ensembles, were meticulously documented and instruments of the ensemble described in detail. Similarly, Aceh went through a process of identity formation, but this time perhaps even more strongly through the need to reassert Malay power after the fall of Melaka to a non-Malay entity, the Portuguese. The nobat thus became a generally recognised representation of royal power not only among competing Malay sultanates but also by colonising foreign powers. The elaborate ceremonies involving the nobat detailed in the *Adat Aceh* were a testament of Aceh's power and demonstration of its pervasive Islamicate influences.

These displays of uniqueness are not just evident in early Malay texts but also in the repertoires and instruments of surviving nobat ensembles today. Even the ceremonial uses of these ensembles differ from one other. The issue of musical change according to Nettl (1992, 522) could include a number of factors, for example the problem of oral transmission and migration. Nettl argues that movements of different groups and high level of interactions between migrants could increase the possibility of musical change; this resonates well with the historical development of the Malay nobat in the context of intense circulation of Malay ethnic subgroups and non-Malay communities in the early modern Straits region. Nevertheless, while musical difference is evident, there were still elements of continuity and similarity between nobat ensembles due to cross-cultural influences and its sheer ritual power as bestower of *daulat* on a Muslim Sultan. If one looks at the *Hikayat Patani* and the Kedah nobat musically, as I have here, similarities between these two chronologically distant ensembles emerge in terms of playing techniques and piece structure. This may have been due to their close geographical proximity and the shared Thai influence over the two northern sultanates.

The Malay *bahasa* or language, written in Jawi and embodied in early court literature, was also a potent symbol of ethnic identity throughout the Malay world. Together with *agama* (religion) and *raja* (royalty), it forms what is known as the three pillars[1] of 'Malayness', which are prevalent in the narratives of the texts themselves although A. B. Shamsul (1996b, 17) argues that this is a recent construct. The concept of Malayness and *kerajaan* that has been thoroughly discussed by Milner (1982, 2008) underlies some of the observations presented in this research. It can be argued that the nobat's centrality in the triangulation of *bahasa*, Islam and *kerajaan* in many of these narratives, especially those relating to court *adat* (customs), made the nobat institution itself a non-negotiable part of the pan-Malay idea of identity—a fourth pillar of Malayness. In essence, the nobat's association with the royal institution, which oversees matters relating to the Malay *adat* and Islam to this day, makes it a quintessentially 'Malay' art form.

By the middle of the twentieth century, the nobat of Patani, Aceh and a number of other Malay courts on the Indonesian side of the Malay world gradually stopped to be performed.[2] The remaining and still functioning nobat housed in four sultanates on the Malay Peninsula together with five other sultanates (or Malay states) later merged with the British Straits Settlements Penang and Melaka to form the Federation of Malaya. These nobat housed in the courts of Kedah, Perak, Selangor and Terengganu did not go unnoticed by the British when they began to interact with these royal households in the nineteenth and early twentieth centuries. This encounter would later result in the documentation of the nobat and other Malay court practices as part of the British imperial plan, but also in certain changes to the nobat institution.

COLONIAL KNOWLEDGE, POWER AND MALAY IDENTITY

The arrival of Europeans and their subsequent colonization of the Malay world brought the nobat and its unique link with Malayness into the limelight. The nobat institution was documented, albeit in a limited and often shallow way, as part of the colonial project of 'cultural espionage' disguised under scientific, historical and popular anthropological discourse. The scrutiny of this symbol of Malay royal power itself symbolised British colonial superiority. However, unlike the more readily appreciated music of performances such as *tarian asyik* or *joget gamelan*, the nobat remained outside the scope of what was acceptable as 'music' in the ears of Europeans. It was seen largely as an exotic ensemble that produced 'noise' and 'strange music', and hence there was no real effort to study and analyse its musical structures. The nobat's interest in colonial eyes was largely due to its close association with magic and the supernatural, elaborate rituals and pompous ceremonies (especially in installing British-approved rulers)—a spectacle of oriental exoticism that so fascinated Europeans and affirmed their prejudices about Oriental despotic rule. While stereotyping and signifying the indigenous Malays or the 'Other', the British were, through their treatment of nobat as weird, noisy, magical spectacle, defining themselves.

British administrators began to understand that the nobat was not merely a superficial part of the Malay court regalia. While promoting British values would greatly benefit the coloniser, the British became more careful in their handling of Malay traditional customs and beliefs after Birch's assassination. Although Western music and instruments were introduced across Britain's Southeast Asian colonies, which greatly influenced other forms of local music making, the nobat remained virtually untouched due to its critical ritual role. It nonetheless continued to function even in the most fast-developing Westernised court surroundings, in which rulers appropriated European-style attire, customs and ceremonies. In a globalising world of cultural exchanges—or rather in this case an asymmetrical imposition of a dominant culture—the nobat stood out for its 'timelessness'. It represented the 'old' in the oft-repeated colonial narrative of the successful mixture of the 'old' and the 'new' in the ongoing discourse of Malay cultural development under British rule. The nobat was caught up in the struggles of identity formation at a time when the Malay elites were seeking to balance tradition and Western-style modernisation on their way towards independence from the British; aroused in part by a rising tide of Malay nationalism from below.

While the ruling elites' growing acceptance of British culture helped consolidate their political and economic interests, the continued maintenance of certain aspects of Malay court culture was also considered imperative. Beneath the Western suits and ties, a strong sense of 'Malayness' was espoused in the inherent belief that not only were the nobat and other articles of the court regalia 'abstract' forms of symbolic power, but in fact capable of exerting 'physical' power. This belief underlined the Malay concept of *daulat* and a ruler that was truly *berdaulat* had to be in possession of the nobat or articles of the regalia. Any act of *derhaka* or disobedience against a *raja berdaulat* would incur *tulah* or divine wrath. A Malay ruler, no matter how 'Westernised', had to be *berdaulat* to be worthy of *disembah* (bowed to), at least in the hearts and minds of the Malay subjects. As long as this belief persisted, the nobat had to be duly maintained as it always had been for the rulers to have any political legitimacy, even when (perhaps especially when) they may not enjoy the absolute power they once had.

Although the policy of non-interference in matters of Malay custom and belief practiced by the British did not seem to have an impact on the nobat, indirectly, colonial political interference and actions had a profound effect on Malay court culture and its musical institution. Unlike the Dutch in Riau, where the nobat had to be performed by law to receive colonial Residents, there was no such specific order from the British. The forced abdication of the last Riau sultan by the Dutch also saw the nobat (made by the Dutch in Batavia) transferred to Terengganu after the demise of the sultanate. By the twentieth century, the Malay Peninsula and Brunei became the last safe havens for the nobat in the Malay world. The nobat was nonetheless engulfed in the colonial power interplay with the Malay sultans, becoming at times itself a political pawn. It was almost extinct in Selangor, occasionally borrowed from one sultanate to the other, thrust into the limelight by the media and ultimately used (for the first time) to install the newly created post of Yang Dipertuan Agong, the Head of State of Malaya. While looking at the historical development of the nobat during the British period, one must also not ignore early signs of Islamic revivalism shown in the destruction of some of the Selangor regalia in the late nineteenth century and followed decades later by an Islamic political party's objection to the use of the nobat during royal funerals.

The nobat institution had always been under the patronage of the sultan and its maintenance and survival solely depended on the ruler of the day. For generations the *orang kalur* or players of the nobat were duty-bound to follow the commands of the ruler without hesitation or question. It was part of their obligation as loyal subjects and keepers of royal tradition to execute any orders in keeping with the long-established master-subject relationship. This act of subservience was also born out of the fear of *tulah* based on the concept of *daulat*. Any major changes or development to the institution had to be approved by the ruler, members of the ruling family or palace management. While this control kept the nobat institution 'pure' from external influences, its total dependence on the institution of the sultanate meant that it was more vulnerable to extinction in a colonial state. The decrease in the Malay sultanates' political power under British rule and the precarious situation they were put into during the Malayan Union experiment (1946–1948) meant the nobat was also at risk of becoming extinct.

It can be argued that the rise of Malay nationalism prior to independence helped save the Malay monarchical system, which was seen as an important symbol of Malay power and identity. The close relationship between the Malay rulers and the United Malay Nationalist Organisation (UMNO), which spearheaded the nationalist movement, went back to its early formation at the Sultan of Johor's palace in Johor Bahru in 1946. UMNO's leaders saw that the newly independent *Tanah Melayu* (Malay Land) needed a centralised *kerajaan* where the united Malays could be governed under a single ruler, based upon the British constitutional monarchy system. Thus the post of Yang Dipertuan Agong was created and the nobat, long seen as a legitimising symbol, was repurposed as an absolutely essential pillar of the installation ceremony. This time the instruction came not from a sultan but from a politician (albeit of royal descent) who, in a rather precipitous rush towards independence, almost single-handedly altered the course of Malay royal history. It is doubtful that any other politician of non-royal pedigree or affiliation would have managed to convince the nine rulers to agree to a new post and with reinvented customs, which involved treading the line carefully between the desire for tradition and modern transformation. One can argue that this invention of tradition and the high-handedness in which certain traditional court practices were compromised can be seen as the beginning of the bureaucratization of Malay culture and identity, which decades later would engulf other art forms.

The Malay nobat went through many phases and cycles in its centuries-long development and served as an important agent in the process of Malay identity formation. Identity, argues Frith (1996, 109), is a 'process' rather than a fixed entity, and while mobility and circulation in the Indian Ocean helped spread the nobat and consolidate Malay identity, identity itself is mobile. While the ceremonies, repertoire and instruments of the nobat have somewhat stabilised and have been virtually unchanged for the last century, the process of identity creation continues. This process, which is largely 'authority-defined' in independent Malaysia (see A. B. Shamsul 1996, 477), began with the sultans and was taken over by leading politicians in the run-up to independence from the British. This was powerfully symbolised in the creation of the Yang Dipertuan Agong post and its new nobat ceremonies. Now, the very existence of the Malay sultanates (including the four nobat ensembles) in Malaysia depends on the patronage of the ruling political party. But any move towards dissolution of the institution would likely be politically disastrous for the ruling coalition since the Malays still look up to the sultans as symbols of pride and identity. Although technically the sultans remain the guardians of

Malay customs and leaders of Islam, it is the ruling political elites that actually hold the key to the successful continuation of Malay culture and identity, including the nobat institution.

It has been shown that sustained intra- and inter-cultural[3] encounters in the Malay world throughout the last millennium helped to develop and strengthen a sultanate's uniqueness in a highly connected and mobile region. Court literature was pivotal in providing a shared idea of history, ethnicity and culture, and this could be seen as an effort to secure, stabilise and ensure the continued existence of the Malay courts and their subjects. In discussing music and identity, Blacking's (1977, 7) observation on the continued repetition of outmoded and carefully rehearsed music has been used to explain a particular group's effort to maintain ethnic and historical identity (in Baily 1997, 46). Similarly, the nobat's largely unchanged, ritually repeated music can also be seen as part of a particular Malay sultanate's way of preserving its identity, even more necessarily in the growing multiethnic cosmopolitan society under British colonialism. Even as late as the early twentieth century, court manuals were still being written to define the nobat and its performance practices. Colonization did not rupture the nobat institution, but its indirect impact was noticeable.

The nobat continues to be mass mediated, especially during the installation of sultans and the Yang Dipertuan Agong, after independence. Its intriguing history and association with magic were still the main theme of reports and articles in the independence era. The exoticism attached to the nobat as espoused decades earlier by British scholarship has persisted in wider Malayan and later Malaysian discourse. This initial colonial curiosity about this mysterious powerful soundmark was embraced later by the local populace with the advent of radio and television, when the sight and sound of the nobat became accessible to millions of viewers. This British imperial legacy continued to this day but is now taken over by Malaysian writers, scholars and producers. However, the nobat still does not get enough attention for it to be generally considered a 'national art form' due to its 'closed' and 'elite' nature. Although I may argue that the nobat is the musical representation of the archetypal Malay art form due to its close association with the 'pillars of Malayness' discussed earlier, it is still not within the realms of popular or folk performing arts. Unlike *makyong*, wayang kulit and zapin, nobat does not function as a purely entertainment outfit (at least not at present), but as a signaling ensemble that for centuries, was widely related to authority and assertiveness. This, beside issues of accessibility, could be said to mask the nobat's mainstream appeal.

SIGNIFICANCE OF THIS RESEARCH

No significant study of the history of the Malay nobat has ever before been undertaken, either in Malay or English. By using the methods of historical ethnomusicology, this book has attempted to fill this gap by investigating the development of the nobat against the backdrop of increasing cross-cultural encounters in the early Malay world and wider Indian Ocean. It looks at indigenous court literature through the prism of ethnomusicology and does a comparative analysis with current remaining nobat ensembles. My previous study on the Perak nobat and field recordings of the Terengganu and Kedah ensembles greatly facilitated the musical analysis. For the first time, this resulted in the greater understanding of the music and repertoire of the Patani nobat as described in the *Hikayat Patani*.

This study also provides, for the first time, a cross-cultural study of the development of the Islamicate ceremonial/military ensemble across Eurasia and the Indian Ocean. It pools together both primary and secondary sources, including a number of iconographical works, in comparison with the Malay nobat, particularly in terms of functions and instrumentation. This enables us to view this ensemble from a wider visual perspective that covers the Islamicate world both geographically and chronologically.

My hope is that this work will contribute to the eventual acknowledgement of the Malay nobat as an important cultural heritage not only to the Malays but also the world. As the last remaining legacy of a major Islamicate musical tradition still performed within its original context, it would be fitting that this art form, like the Kelantanese *makyong* in 2005, be listed as one of UNESCO's 'World's Intangible Heritage of Humanity'.

SUGGESTIONS FOR FUTURE RESEARCH

This study is by no means a definitive work on the Malay nobat. In fact, it opens up windows for further research and exploration into the world of the nobat and its connection to the Islamicate world. No incontrovertible archaeological or documentary links have been established between the Malay nobat and similar ensembles found in South Asia and the Middle East. A closer look at the 'connected histories' of nobat ensembles across the Indian Ocean is needed, which would require access to resources in multiple languages such as Persian, Arabic and Turkish. Early literature on the political and trade connections between port cities in India and the Malay world could possibly provide details on the nature of the relationship. Within the Malay world, the early history of the nobat in Brunei, Riau and the east coast of Sumatera can

THE FUTURE

Malaysia is among a few countries left in the world that maintains its royal institution, constituting of nine sultans and the rotational post of Yang Dipertuan Agong. For centuries these *kesultanan* were viewed as divinely ordained guardians of Malay societies and a necessity for civilised existence. This 'God-given' power and authority, or 'shadow of God' from an Islamic perspective, resulted in the wielding of absolute power by the ruler. While this often led to abuse and oppression, the sultan is still revered as a symbol of Malay power and sovereignty—a *payung* or umbrella where the Malays seek guidance and refuge. The arrival of European colonisers sparked elements of fear, uncertainty and insecurity among the Malays, not only due to their overwhelming military and economic power but also cultural influence. The Malays worried particularly about the future of their *adat*, *raja*, *agama* and *bahasa*, the cultural foundations that define their very existence. This fear has continued to this day, not due to the physical presence of the colonisers but the legacy they left behind. With the *jawi* alphabet virtually no longer in use and English becoming more widely spoken among the younger generation, the declining use of *bahasa Melayu*—an important symbol of Malay identity—is of grave concern to the older generation.

Globalization and the relentless propagation of Western culture and values in the country are seen today as a new form of colonization. This includes what is viewed as the threat of Christianity,[4] and any form of Western influence[5] is viewed with suspicion. In response to this phenomenon, Malay-Muslims began to reassert their position and looked inwards towards their culture and religion as a form of defense mechanism. This led to the rising awareness and practice of Islam (including among the ruling elites), which became a threat to certain Malay *adat*. Traditional practices deemed un-Islamic are being slowly discarded including the use of the nobat in certain court rituals. Could the nobat institution that—ironically—came as part of the spread of Islam to the Malay world, eventually became incompatible with the practice of the religion?

Islamic revivalism in Malaysia has and will continue to affect the nobat institution. Certain rituals are no longer practiced or are performed quietly, away from the eyes of the public. Even the playing of the nobat to signal certain times of the Muslim prayers was stopped in Kedah as recently as 2013.

Contrary to popular belief, identity and tradition are not static but evolve through time. This evolution, adaptation and accommodation are crucial to ensure their viability and survival. But, like many traditional art forms, the speed of change that could probably outrun the ability of nobat to adapt itself, is the contending issue. On the other hand, looking at the current political dynamics in Malaysia, the constitutional monarchy system is still considered relevant and strong.[6] While this should ensure the continued survival of the nobat, some of its functions and related rituals may disappear over time. As an institution patronised by the courts, the nobat's survival or demise solely depends on the instruction or policies of the ruler or governing politicians. It is my hope that this study will help to stimulate public awareness of the nobat's importance as part of Malaysia's cultural treasure and the last living legacy of the Islamicate world.

NOTES

1. A. B. Shamsul argues that the three pillars were a politically driven ideology developed in the last century as a result of British colonization. This pillars, together with the Bumiputra (indigenous people) special rights were then incorporated into Malaya's constitution to safeguard the interest of the Malays in a growing multiethnic society. The practice of Islam (religion), Malay (language) and *adat* (customs) would later become the underlying factors to help define 'a Malay', according to the constitution.

2. According to an informer, the nobat of the Siak court was last performed to celebrate the birthday of Sultan Assaidis Syariff Kasim Sani, the twelfth Sultan of Siak in 1943.

3. Intra-cultural here means interactions between subculture of the larger Malay community and inter-cultural refers to encounters with non-Malay foreigners including Europeans.

4. Although proselytissation of Muslims by Christians or other religions in Malaysia today is an offence under Malaysian federal law, there is still fear among Malay-Muslims since Islam is considered as an essential part of being 'Malay'.

5. In the early twentieth century, Malays were reluctant to send their children to English mission schools fearing that they would become Christians. Today, organissations with links to or funded by the West, especially non-governmental organisations (NGOs) are often viewed as agents of Western interests or propaganda and of undermining Islam.

6. Sultans and the Yang Dipertuan Agong are still viewed with reverence as a symbol of Malay pride. They are also mediators in political disputes and seen as a unifying figure in a multiracial society.

Appendix

Transcription of 'Jong Beraleh' from the Perak Nobat

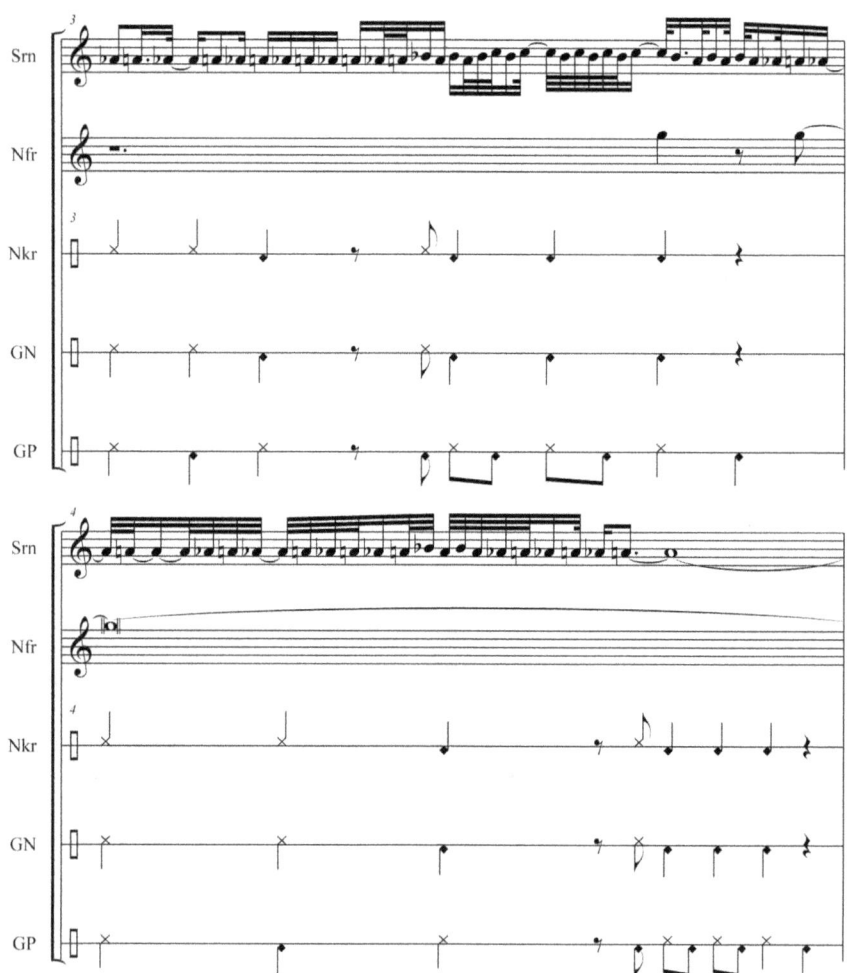

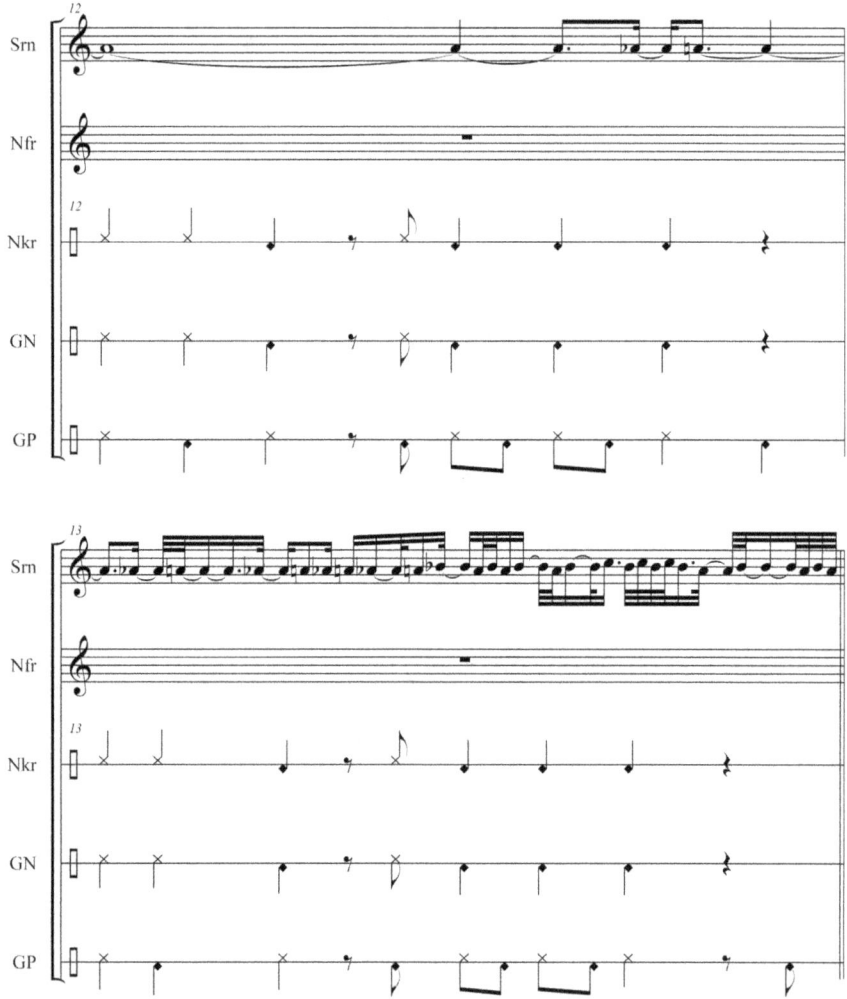

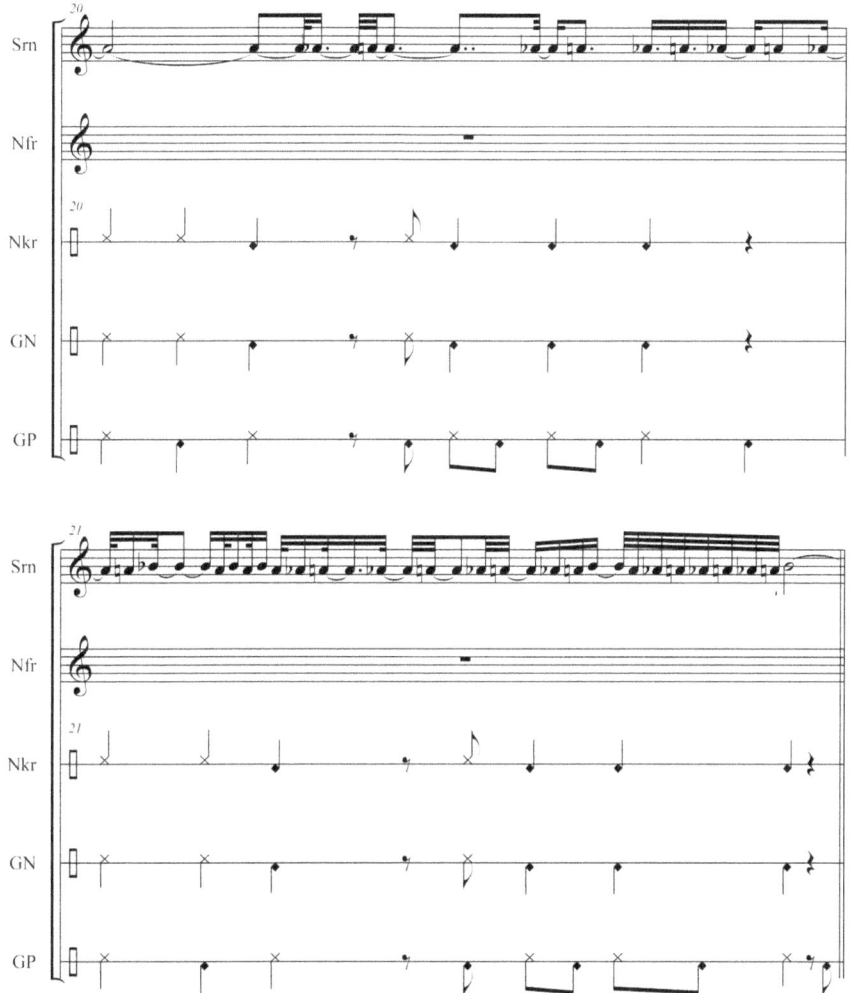

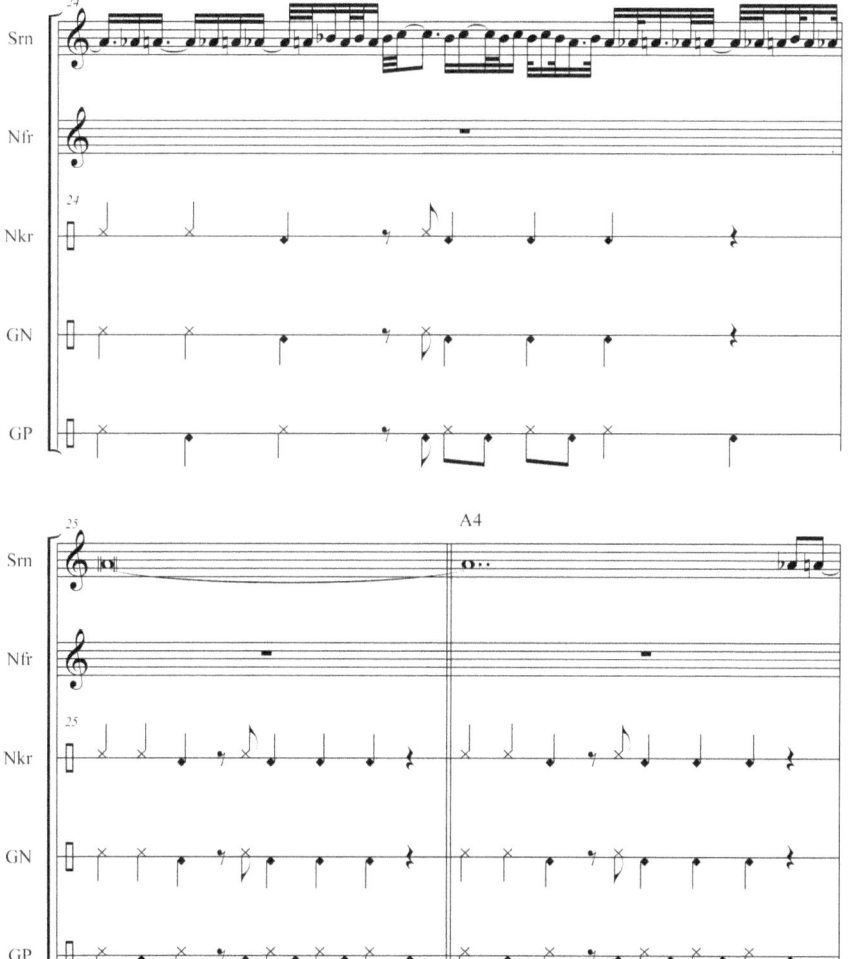

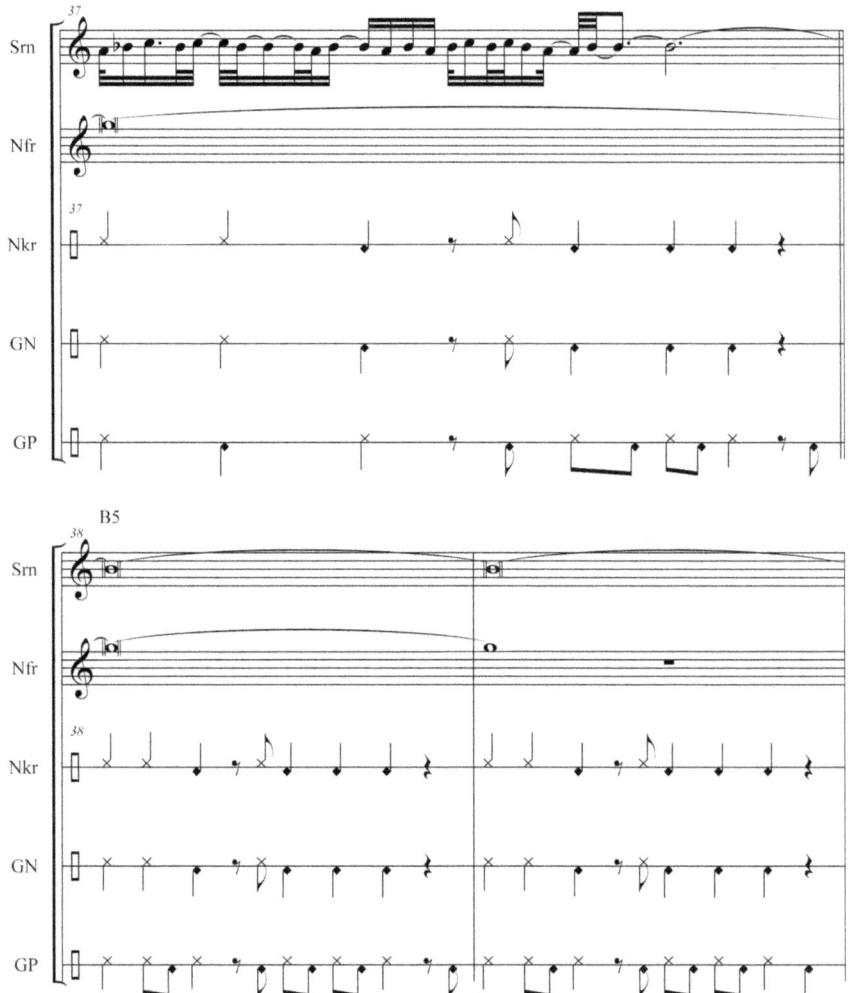

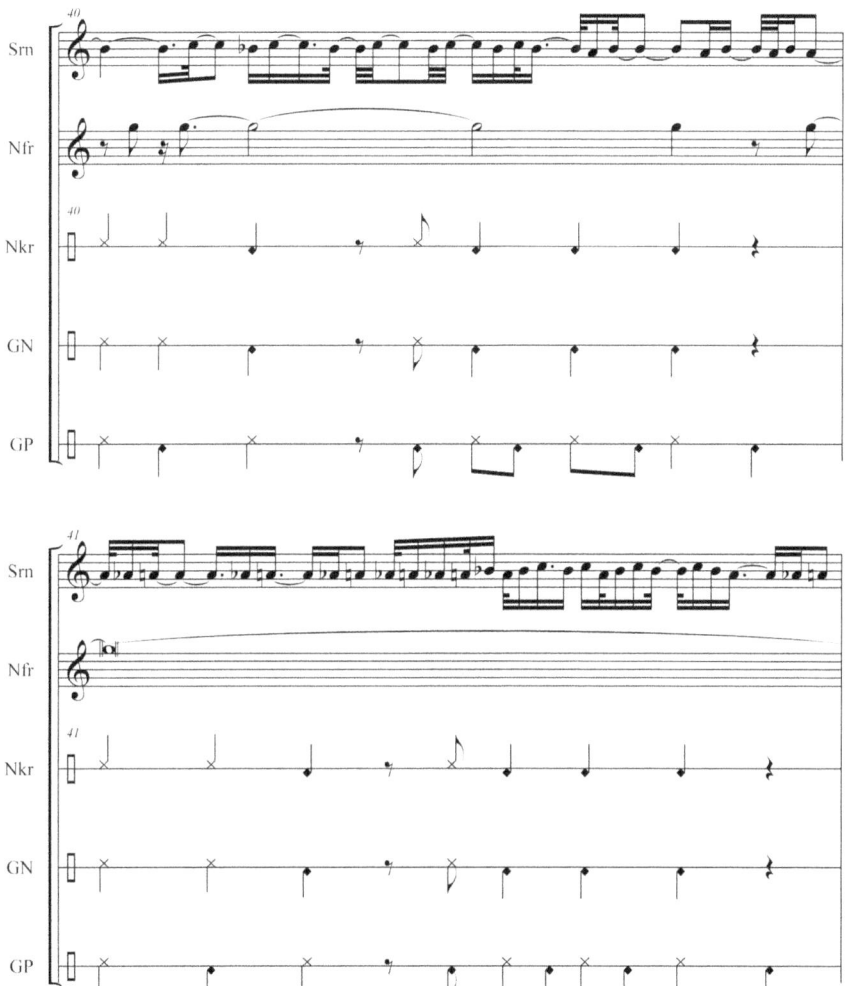

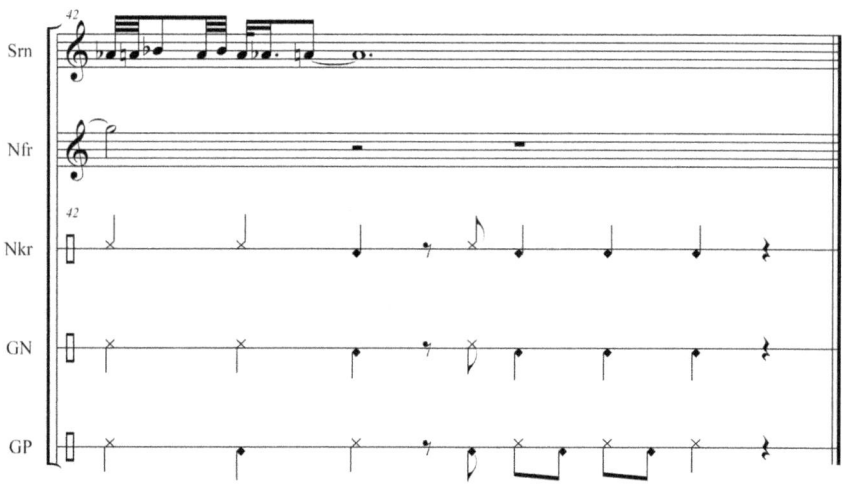

References

Abdul Rahman Tang Abdullah. 2008. 'Modernisation or Westernisation of Johor under Abu Bakar: A Historical Analysis'. *Intellectual Discourse* 16, no. 2: 209–31.

Abdul Samad Ahmad, ed. 1979. *Sulalatus Salatin (Sejarah Melayu)*. Kuala Lumpur: Dewan Bahasa dan Pustaka.

———. 1985. *Kerajaan Johor-Riau*. Kuala Lumpur: Dewan Bahasa dan Pustaka.

Abu'l Fazl ibn Mubarak. 1873. *Ain-i Akbari*, vol. 1. Translated by Blochmann. Calcutta: The Asiatic Society of Bengal.

Adib Vincent Tung. 1999. *Adat Pusaka Raja-Raja dan Orang Besar-Besar Negeri Perak Darul Ridzuan*. Ipoh: Compass Life Sdn. Bhd.

Affan Seljuq. 1976. 'Some Notes on the Origin and Development of Naubat'. *Journal of the Malaysian Branch of the Royal Asiatic Society (JMBRAS)* 49: 141–42.

Ahmad Fauzi Mohd Basri, eds. 1992. *Misa Melayu*. Kuala Lumpur: Dewan Bahasa dan Pustaka.

Alam, Muzaffar, and Sanjay Subrahmanyam. 2005. 'Southeast Asia as Seen from Mughal India: Tahir Muhammad's 'Immaculate Garden' (ca. 1600)'. *Archipel* 70: 209–37.

'Alam Shah Crowned Sultan of Selangor. Ancient Malay Ritual at Klang Ceremony'. 1939. *Straits Times* (January 27): 14.

al-Jazari, Ibn al-Razzaz. 1974. *The Book of Knowledge of Ingenious Mechanical Devices (Kitab fi ma'rifat al-hiyal al-handasiyya)*. Translated by Donald R. Hill. Dordrecht: D. Reidel Publishing.

al-Sabi, Hilal. 1977. *Rusum Dar al-Khilafah (The Rules and Regulations of the Abbasid Court)*. Translated with Introduction and Notes by Elie A. Salem. Beirut: Lebanese Commission for the Translation of Great Works.

Amirell, Stefan. 2011. 'The Blessings and Peril of Female Rule: New Perspective on the Reigning Queens of Patani, c. 1584–1718'. *Journal of Southeast Asian Studies* 42, no. 2: 303–23.

'Ancient State Drums to Beat in Astana'. 1939. *Straits Times* (March 2): 1.

Andaya, Barbara. 1979. *Perak, The Abode of Grace: A Study of Eighteenth-Century Malay State*. Kuala Lumpur: Oxford University Press.
———. 2011. 'Distant Drums and Thunderous Cannon: Sounding Authority in Traditional Malay Society'. *International Journal of Asia Pacific Studies (IJAPS)* 7, no. 2: 19–35.
———. 2012. 'Gates, Elephants, Cannon and Drums: Symbols and Sounds in the Creation of a Patani Identity'. In *The Ghosts of the Past in Southern Thailand: Essays on the History and Historiography of Patani*, edited by Patrick Jory, 31–52. Singapore: NUS Press, 2012.
Andaya, Barbara, and Leonard Andaya. 2001. *A History of Malaysia*. Hampshire: Palgrave.
Andaya, Leonard. 2001. 'Aceh's Contribution to Standards of Malayness'. *Archipel* 61: 29–68.
———. 2006. 'The Search for the 'Origins' of Melayu'. In *Contesting Malayness: Malay Identity Across Boundaries*, edited by Timothy Barnard, 56–75. Singapore: NUS Press, 2006.
———. 2008. *Leaves of the Same Tree: Trade and Ethnicity in the Straits of Melaka*. Honolulu: University of Hawai'i Press.
Anderson, Benedict. 1990. *Language of Power: Exploring Political Culture in Indonesia*. Ithaca: Cornell University Press.
al-Attas, Syed Naquib. 1969. *Preliminary Statement on a General Theory of the Islamization of the Malay-Indonesian Archipelago*. Kuala Lumpur: Dewan Bahasa dan Pustaka.
———. 1978. *Islam and Secularism*. Kuala Lumpur: Muslim Youth Movement of Malaysia (ABIM).
'A Regal Old Lady Bares a Sad Momento of Royal Pomp and Glory'. 1966. *The Straits Times* (March 20): 11.
Attali, Jacques. 2003. *Noise: The Political Economy of Music*. Minneapolis: University of Minnesota Press.
Ayalon, David. 2005. 'Studies on the Structure of the Mamluk Army'. In *Muslims, Mongols and Crusaders*, edited by Gerald Hawting, 42–120. Abingdon, Oxon: RoutledgeCurzon.
Aziz Deraman and Ramli Wan Mohamad. 1994. *Muzik dan Nyanyian Tradisi Melayu*. Kuala Lumpur: Fajar Bakti.
Azyumardi Azra. 2006. *Islam in the Indonesian World: An Account of Institutional Formation*. Bandung: Mizan Pustaka.
Baily, John. 1997. 'The Role of Music in the Creation of Afghan National Identity, 1923–1973'. In *Ethnicity, Identity and Music: The Musical Construction of Place*, edited by Martin Stokes, 45–60. Oxford: Berg.
———. 1980. 'A Description of the Naqqarakhana of Herat, Afghanistan'. *Asian Music* 11, no. 2: 1–10.
Barlow, Henry. 1995a. *Swettenham*. Kuala Lumpur: Southdene.
———. 1995b. 'Bibliography of Mubin Sheppard'. *Journal of the Malaysian Branch of the Royal Asiatic Society* 68, no. 2 (269): 59–66.

Barnard, Timothy. 2001. 'Texts, Raja Ismail and Violence: Siak and the Transformation of Malay Identity in the Eighteenth Century'. *Journal of Southeast Asian History* 32, no. 3: 331–42.

———, ed. 2006. *Contesting Malayness: Malay Identity Across Boundaries*. Singapore: NUS Publishing.

Benjamin, Geoffrey. 1987. 'Ethnohistorical Perspectives on Kelantan's Prehistory'. In *Kelantan Zaman Awal: Kajian Arkeologi dan Sejarah di Malaysia*. Kota Bharu: Muzium Negeri Kelantan: 108–53.

Bhabha, Homi. 2007. *The Location of Culture*. New York: Routledge.

Bhatia, Harbans Singh. 2001. *Rival Hindu Kingdoms and Sultans: Fusion of the Hindu and Muslim Civilizations*. New Delhi: Deep & Deep Publications.

Blacking, John. 1977. 'Some Problems of Theory and Method in the Study of Musical Change'. *Yearbook for Traditional Music* 9: 1–26.

Bougas, Wayne. 1986. 'Some Early Islamic Tombstones in Patani'. *Journal of the Malaysian Branch of Asiatic Society* 59, no. 1: 85–112.

———. 1994. *The Kingdom of Patani: Between Thai and Malay Mandala*. Bangi: UKM.

Braginsky, Vladimir. 2004. *The Heritage of Traditional Malay Literature: A Historical Survey of Genres, Writings and Literary Views*. Leiden: KITLV Press.

Brown, Charles. 1952. 'Sejarah Melayu: A Translation of Raffles MS 18'. *Journal of the Malaysian Branch of Asiatic Society* 25, parts 2 and 3.

Brown, Katherine. 2000. 'Reading Indian Music: The Interpretation of Seventeenth-Century European Travel-Writing in the (Re)construction of Indian Music History'. *British Journal of Ethnomusicology* 9, no. 2: 1–34.

———. 2006. 'If Music Be the Food of Love: Masculinity and Eroticism in the Mughal *Mehfil*'. In *Love in South Asia: A Cultural History*, edited by Francesca Orsini 61–83. Cambridge: University of Cambridge.

Butler, Judith. 1988. 'Performative Acts and Gender Constitution: An Essay in Phenomenology and Feminist Theory'. *Theatre Journal* 40, no. 4: 519–31.

Buyong Adil. 1971. *Sejarah Selangor*. Kuala Lumpur: Dewan Bahasa dan Pustaka.

Cohen, Dalia, and Ruth Katz. 2006. *Palestinian Arab Music: A Maqam Tradition in Practice*. Chicago: University of Chicago Press.

'Coronation of H. H. The Sultan of Johore'. 1886. *The Straits Times Weekly Issue* (August 5): 6.

Dasgupta, Arun Kumar. 1962. 'Aceh in Indonesian Trade and Politics: 1600–1641'. PhD dissertation. Ithaca, NY: Cornell University.

Davis, Ruth. 2004. *Ma'luf: Reflections on the Arab Andalusian Music of Tunisia*. Lanham, MD: Scarecrow Press.

D'Cruz, Marion. 1979. 'Joget Gamelan: A Study of its Contemporary Practice'. MA thesis. George Town, Malaysia: Universiti Sains Malaysia.

Deva, Chaitanya. 1975. 'The Double-reed Aerophone in India'. *Yearbook of the International Folk Music Council* 7: 77–84.

Devizes, Richard, and Geoffrey de Vinsauf, 1848. *Chronicles of the Crusades: Being Contemporary Narratives of the Crusade of Richard Coeur de Lion*. London: Henry G. Bohn.

Dick, Alastair. 1984. 'The Early History of the Shawm in India'. *The Galpin Society Journal* 37: 80–98.
Drewes, Gerardus. 1985. 'New Light on the Coming of Islam to Indonesia?' In *Readings on Islam in Southeast Asia*. Singapore: Institute of Southeast Asian Studies, 7–19.
Drewes, Gerardus, and Peter Voorhoeve. 1958. *Adat Atjeh: Reproduced in Facsimile form a Manuscript in the India Office Library*. 's-Gravenhage: Martinus Nijhoff.
Fadl Allah b. Ruzbihan. 1962. *Mihman-nama-i Bukhara*. Tehran: Bungāh-i Tarjumah va Nashr-i Kitāb.
Farhad, Hormoz. 2004. *The Dastgah Concept in Persian Music*. Cambridge: Cambridge University Press.
Farmer, George. 1912. *The Rise and Development of Military Music*. London: W. Reeves.
———, ed. 1937. *Turkish Instruments of Music in the Seventeenth Century: As Described in the Siyahat nama of Ewliya Chelebi*. Glasgow: The Civic Press.
———. 1949. 'Crusading Martial Music'. *Music & Letters* 30, no. 3: 243–49.
———. 1967 (1929). *A History of Arabian Music to the XIIIth Century*. London: Luzac & Co. Ltd.
———. 1987 (1913). 'Tabl-khana'. In *E. J. Brill's First Encyclopaedia of Islam, 1913–1936: Supplement*, edited by Martijn Theodoor Houtsma et al., vol. 9. Leiden: Brill.
al-Faruqi, Lois. 1981. *An Annotated Glossary of Arabic Musical Terms*. Westport and London: Greenwood Press.
———. 1985. 'The Suite in Islamic History and Culture'. *World of Music* 17, no. 3: 46–64, as quoted by Shiloah (1995): 131.
Firdausi, Abu'l Qasim. 1905. *Shahnama of Firdausi*. Translated by Arthur George Warner and Edmond Warner. London: Kegan Paul.
Flood, Finbarr. 2009. *Objects of Translation: Material Culture and Medieval 'Hindu-Muslim' Encounter*. Princeton, NJ: Princeton University Press.
Flora, Reis. 1983. 'Double-Reed Aerophones in India to AD 1400'. PhD dissertation. University of California, Los Angeles.
———. 1995. 'Styles of the Śahnāī in Recent Decades: From naubat to gāyakī ang'. *Yearbook for Traditional Music* 27: 52–75.
Foster, William. 1934. *The Voyage of Thomas Best to the East Indies, 1612–1614*. London: Hakluyt Society.
———. 1940. *The Voyages of Sir James Lancaster to Brazil and the East Indies, 1591–1603*. London: Hakluyt Society.
Frith, Simon. 1996. 'Music and Identity'. In *Questions of Cultural Identity*, edited by Stuart Hall and Paul du Gay, 108–27. London: Sage Publications Ltd.
'Full Regalia of Malay Court at Coronation: Princes and Chiefs Pay Homage to the Ruler'. 1939. *Straits Times* (January 27): 14.
'The Funeral'. 1895. *The Singapore Free Press and Merchantile Advertiser* (September 9): 3.
Ghulam-Sarwar, Yousof. 1976. 'The Kelantan Mak Yong Dance Theatre: A Study of Performance Structure'. PhD dissertation. Honolulu: University of Hawaii.

———, ed. 2004. *The Encyclopedia of Malaysia, Vol. 8, Performing Arts*. Singapore: Archipelago Press.
Gordon, Stewart, ed. 2003. *Robes of Honour: Khilat in Pre-Colonial and Colonial India*. New Delhi: Oxford University Press.
Groeneveldt, Willem. 1960. *Historical Notes on Indonesia and Malaya Compiled from Chinese Sources*. Djakarta: Bhratara, as quoted by Hadi (1992).
Gullick, John Michael. 1958. *Indigenous Political Systems of Western Malaya*. London: The Athlone Press.
Guo, Li. 1998. *Early Mamluk Syrian Historiography: Al-Yūnīnī's Dhayl Mir'āt al-zamān*. Leiden: Brill.
Guthrie, Shirley. 1995. *Arab Social Life in the Middle Ages: An Illustrated Study*. London: Saqi Books.
Hadi, Amirul. 1992. 'Aceh and the Portuguese: A Study of the Struggle of Islam in Southeast Asia'. MA thesis. Quebec: McGill University.
———. 2004. *Islam and State in Sumatra: A Study of Seventeenth-Century Aceh*. Leiden: Brill.
Hall, Daniel George. 1981. *A History of South-East Asia*. Fourth edition. London: MacMillan Press.
Hall, Kenneth. 1985. *Maritime Trade and State Development in Early Southeast Asia*. Honolulu: University of Hawaii Press.
Hanapi Mohd Ariff. 1984. *Peraturan-Peraturan Isti'adat Diraja Kedah*. Arkib Negara Cawangan. Kedah/Perlis.
Harper, Tim. 2001. *The End of Empire and the Making of Malaya*. Cambridge: Cambridge University Press.
Harrison, Brian. 1957. *South-East Asia—A Short History*. London: Macmillan.
Harun Mat Piah. 1982. 'Nobat Perak: Simbol Kebesaran Zaman Berzaman'. *Dewan Budaya* (July): 6–8.
Hesmondhalgh, David. 2013. *Why Music Matters*. West Sussex: Wiley-Blackwell.
'His Majesty the Yang di-Pertuan Agong'. 1957. *Straits Times* (June 21): 7.
Hobsbawm, Eric, and Terence Ranger. 1983. *The Invention of Tradition*. Cambridge: Cambridge University Press.
Ho, Meilu. 1991. *The Royal Nobat of Kedah, Malaysia*. MA Thesis, University of California, Los Angeles.
Houtsma, Martijn Theodoor et al., ed. 1993. *E. J. Brill's First Encyclopaedia of Islam: 1913–1936*. Leiden: E. J. Brill.
Ibn Battuta. 1929. *Travels in Asia and Africa 1325–1354*. Translated by Hamilton Gibb. London: Routledge.
Ibn Khaldun. 1958. *The Muqaddimah: An Introduction to History*. Translated by Franz Rosenthal. London: Routledge and Kegan Paul.
Ibrahim Syukri. 1985. *History of the Malay Kingdom of Patani*. Athens: Ohio University Press.
'Institution of Orders of Knighthood in Johore'. 1886. *Straits Times Weekly Issue* (August 12): 3.
Irving, David. 2010. *Colonial Counterpoint: Music in Early Manila*. New York: Oxford University Press.

Irwin, Robert. 1997. *Islamic Art*. London: Laurence King Publishing.
Ito, Takeshi. 1984. 'The World of the Adat Aceh: A Historical Study of the Sultanate of Aceh'. PhD dissertation. Canberra, Australia: Australian National University.
Iza Hussin. 2007. 'The Pursuit of the Perak Regalia: Islam, Law and Politics of Authority in the Colonial State'. *Law & Enquiry* 32, no. 3 (Summer): 759–88.
Jairazbhoy, Nazir. 1970. 'A Preliminary Survey of the Oboe in India'. *Ethnomusicology* 14, no. 3: 375–88.
———. 1980. 'The South Asian Double-Reed Aerophone Reconsidered'. *Ethnomusicology* 24, no. 1: 147–56.
Jelani Harun. 2008. 'Nobat Sultan Terengganu: Suatu Kajian Sumber Rekod Pejabat Sultan Terengganu 1910–1946'. Paper presented at the 'Majlis Wacana Warisan, Khazanah Sepanjang Zaman: Rekod Pejabat Sultan Terengganu 1910–1946'.
Johns, Anthony. 1957. 'Malay Sufism: As Illustrated in an Anonymous Collection of Seventeenth-Century Tracts'. *Journal of the Malayan Branch of the Royal Asiatic Society* 30, no. 2 (178) (August): 3–99, 101–11.
———. 1961. 'Sufism as a Category in Indonesian Literature and History'. *Journal of Southeast Asian History* 2, no. 2: 10–23.
Joinville, Jean de, and Geoffroy de Villehardouin. 2008. *Chronicles of the Crusades*. London: Penguin Classics.
Jones, Russel, ed. 1997. *Hikayat Raja-Raja Pasai*. Shah Alam: Fajar Bakti.
Kartomi, Margaret. 1990. 'Music in Nineteenth Century Java: A Precursor to the Twentieth Century'. *Journal of Southeast Asian Studies* 21, no. 1 (March): 1–34.
———. 1997. 'The Royal Nobat Ensemble of Indragiri in Riau, Sumatra, in Colonial and Post-Colonial Times'. *The Galpin Society Journal* 50 (March): 3–15.
———. 2012. *Musical Journeys in Sumatra*. Champaign, Illinois: University of Illinois Press.
Krishnaswamy, Subrahmanyam. 1965. *Musical Instruments of India*. New Delhi: Ministry of Information and Broadcasting, Publications Division.
Ku Zam Zam Ku Idris. 1978. 'Muzik Tradisional Melayu di Kedah Utara: Ensembel-Ensembel Wayang Kulit, Mek Mulung dan Gendang Keling dengan Tumpuan kepada Alat-Alat, Pemuzik-Pemuzik dan Fungsi'. MA thesis. Kuala Lumpur, Malaysia: Universiti Malaya.
———. 1993. 'Nobat: Music in the Service of the King—the Symbol of Power and Status in Traditional Malay Society'. *Tinta Kenangan: Bingkisan Untuk Profesor Datuk Dr. Haji Mohd Taib Osman Sempena Persaraannya dan Perlantikannya Sebagai Naib Canselor Universiti Malaya*, edited by Nik Safiah Karim, 175–93. Kuala Lumpur: Jabatan Pengajian Mealyu, Universiti Malaya.
———. 1994. 'Alat-Alat Muzik Nobat: Satu Analisis tentang Simbolisme dan Daulat dalam Kesultanan Melayu'. *Tirai Panggung* 2: 1–10.
Laffan, Michael. 2011. *The Makings of Indonesian Islam: Orientalism and the Narration of a Sufi Past*. Princeton, NJ: Princeton University Press.
Lambton, Ann Katharine. 1987. 'Nakkarakhana'. In *E. J. Brill's First Encyclopaedia of Islam, 1913–1936: Supplement*, vol. 9, edited by Martijn Theodoor Houtsma et al. Leiden: Brill.

Lian Kwen Fee. 2001. 'The Construction of Malay Identity Across Nations: Malaysia, Singapore and Indonesia'. *Bijdragen tot de Taal-, Land- en Volkenkunde* 157, no. 4: 861–79.

Lindsay, James. 2005. *Daily Life in the Medieval Islamic World*. Westport: Greenwood Press.

Linehan, William. 1951. 'The Nobat and the Orang Kalau of Perak'. *Journal of the Malaysian Branch of the Royal Asiatic Society* (*JMBRAS*) 24, no. 3: 60–68.

'Lustration And Coronation Ceremonies Described'. 1939. *Straits Times* (January 25): 1.

Madina, Muhammad. 1997 (1973). *Arabic-English Dictionary of the Modern Literary Language*. Kuala Lumpur: Hizbi.

'Malaya's King Installed: Ceremony Was Brilliant Blend of the Old and the New'. 1957. *Times* (September 3): 1.

Malay Concordance Project, Australian National University. 2021. 'Adat Raja Melayu', 'Hikayat Amir Hamzah', 'Hikayat Hang Tuah', 'Hikayat Patani', 'Hikayat Raja Pasai', 'Hikayat Siak', 'Misa Melayu', and 'Sejarah Melayu.' MCP Simple Search. Accessed October 8. http://mcp.anu.edu.au/Q/standard.html.

Matheson, Virginia. 1972. 'Mahmud, Sultan of Riau and Lingga (1823–1864)'. *Indonesia* 13: 119–46.

———. 1979. 'Concepts of Malay Ethos in Indigenous Malay Writings'. *Journal of Southeast Asian History* 10, no. 2: 351–71.

———. 1989. 'Pulau Penyengat: Nineteenth Century Islamic Centre of Riau'. *Archipel* 37, no. 2: 153–72.

Matusky, Patricia. 1993. *Malaysian Shadow Play and Music: Continuity of an Oral Tradition*. Kuala Lumpur: Oxford University Press,

Matusky, Patricia, and Tan Sooi Beng. 2004. *The Music of Malaysia, The Classical Folk and Syncretic Traditions*. Hampshire: Ashgate Publishing.

Maxwell, William. 1881. 'An Account of the Malay 'Chiri', a Sanskrit Formula'. *Journal of the Royal Asiatic Society of Great Britain and Ireland, New Series* 13, no. 1 (January): 80–101.

———. 1882. 'A History of Perak form Native Sources'. *Journal of the Malaysian Branch of the Royal Asiatic Society* (*JSBRAS*) 9 (June): 85–108.

Milner, Anthony. 1981. 'Islam and the Malay Kingship'. *Journal of the Royal Asiatic Society of Great Britain and Ireland* 1: 46–70.

———. 1982. *Kerajaan: Malay Political Culture on the Eve of Colonial Rule*. Arizona: University of Arizona Press.

———. 2002. *The Invention of Politics in Colonial Malaya*. Cambridge: Cambridge University Press.

———. 2008. *The Malays*. West Sussex: Wiley-Blackwell.

Mohd Anis Md Nor. 1993. *Zapin: Folk Dance of the Malay World*. Singapore: Oxford University Press.

Mohd Ghouse Nasuruddin. 1992. *The Malay Traditional Music*. Kuala Lumpur: Dewan Bahasa dan Pustaka.

Mohd Hassan Abdullah. 2005. 'Kompang: An Organological and Ethnomusicological Study of a Malay Frame Drum'. PhD dissertation. Newcastle upon Tyne: University of Newcastle upon Tyne.

Mohd Taib Osman. 1989. *Malay Folk Beliefs, An Integration of Disparate Elements*. Kuala Lumpur: Dewan Bahasa dan Pustaka.

Monelle, Raymond. 2006. *The Musical Topic: Hunt, Military and Pastoral*. Bloomington: Indiana University Press.

Moreland, William, ed. 2002. *Peter Floris: His Voyage to the East Indies 1611–1615*. Bangkok: White Lotus.

Muhammad Haji Salleh. 2011. *The Epic of Hang Tuah*. Kuala Lumpur: Institut Terjemahan Negara Malaysia Berhad.

Nettl, Bruno. 1992. 'Historical Aspects of Ethnomusicology'. In *Ethnomusicology: History, Definition and Scope*, edited by Kay Kaufman Shelemay, 40–54. New York: Garland Publishing.

Nicolas, Arsenio. 1994. *Alat-Alat Muzik Melayu dan Orang Asli*. Bangi: Universiti Kebangsaan Malaysia.

———. 2011. 'Early Musical Exchange between India and Southeast Asia'. In *Early Interactions between South and Southeast Asia*, edited by Pierre-Yves Manguin et al., 347–69. Singapore: ISEAS.

Nicolle, David, and Angus McBride, 2006. *Men at Arms: The Mamluks 1250–1517*. Oxford: Osprey Publishing.

Numani, Shibli. 2004. *Makers of Islamic Civilization: Umar*. New Delhi: I. B. Tauris.

Puaksom, Davisakd. 2009. 'Of a Lesser Brilliance: Patani Historiography in Contention'. In *Thai South and Malay North: Ethnic Interactions on a Plural Peninsula*, edited by Michael Montesano and Patrick Jory, 71–90. Singapore: NUS Press.

Racy, Ali Jihad. 2004. *Making Music in the Arab World: The Culture and Artistry of Tarab*. Cambridge Middle East Studies. Cambridge: Cambridge University Press.

Rahimah Abdul Aziz. 1997. *Pembaratan Pemerintahan Johor, 1800–1945: Suatu Analisis Sosiologi Sejarah*. Kuala Lumpur: Dewan Bahasa Pustaka.

Raja Badri Shah Tunku Nong Jiwa and Mubin Sheppard. 1962. 'The Kedah and Perak Nobat', *Malaya in History* 7, no. 2: 7–11.

Raja Bendahara et al. 1935. *Adat Lembaga Orang-Orang Melayu Di Dalam Negeri Perak Darul Ridzuan*, Taiping.

Raja Chulan. 1968. *Misa Melayu*. Kuala Lumpur: Pustaka Antara.

Raja Iskandar Bin Raja Halid. 2010. 'The Orang Kalur: Musicians of the Royal Nobat of Perak'. In *Music: Local Culture in Global Mind*, edited by Gina Jähnichen and Julia Chieng. Serdang: Universiti Putra Malaysia Press.

———. 2018. *The Royal Nobat of Perak*. Kota Bharu: UMK Press.

Reid, Anthony. 1993. *Southeast Asia in the Modern Era*. New York: Cornell University Press.

———. 2001. 'Understanding Melayu (Malay) as a Source of Diverse Modern Identities'. *Journal of Southeast Asian Studies* 32, no. 3 (October): 295–313.

'Retirement of Mr. E. E. Galistan. Chief Marine Engineer. A Keen Sportsman and Volunteer'. 1930. *Straits Times* (April 8): 19.

Ricklefs, Merle. 2001. *The Modern History of Indonesia Since C. 1200*. Stanford, CT: Stanford University Press.
'Royal Wedding at Kuala Kangsar'. 1910. *Straits Times* (June 1): 6.
Sadie, Stanley, ed. 1984. *The New Grove Dictionary of Musical Instruments*. New York: Macmillan Press.
Sambamoorthy, P. 1967. *The Flute*. Madras: Indian Music Publishing House.
Said, Edward. 2003. *Orientalism*. London: Penguin Books.
Sarkissian, Margaret. 2000. *D'Albuquerque's Children: Performing Tradition in Malaysia's Portuguese Settlement*. Chicago: University of Chicago Press.
Sawa, George. 1989. *Music Performance Practice in the Early Abbasid Era: 132–320 AH/750–932 AD*. Toronto: Pontifical Institute of Mediaeval Studies.
Sayyid Qudratullah Fatimi. 1963. *Islam Comes to Malaysia*. Singapore: Malaysian Sociological Research Institute.
Schafer, R. Murray. 1994. *The Soundscape: Our Sonic Environment and the Tuning of the World*. Rochester, VT: Destiny Books.
Shakuntala, K. V. 1968. 'Martial Musical Instruments of Ancient India'. *Sangeet Natak* 10: 5–11.
Shamsul, Amri Baharuddin. 1996a. 'Debating About Identity in Malaysia: A Discourse Analysis'. *Southeast Asian Studies* 34, no. 3: 476–99.
———. 1996b'The Construction and Transformation of a Social Identity: Malayness and Bumiputeraness Re-examined'. *Journal of Asian and African Studies* 52: 15–33.
———. 2001. 'A History of an Identity, an Identity of a History: The Idea and Practice of 'Malayness' in Malaysia Reconsidered'. *Journal of Southeast Asian Studies* 32, no. 3 (October): 355–66.
Sharifuddin, P. M., and Abdul Latif Haji Ibrahim. 1977. 'The Royal Nobat of Brunei'. *The Brunei Museum Journal* 4, no.1: 7–20.
Sheppard, Mubin. 1962. 'The Kedah and Perak Nobat'. *Malaysia in History* 7, no. 2: 7–11.
———. 1979. *Taman Budiman: Memoirs of an Unorthodox Civil Servant*. Kuala Lumpur: Heinemann Educational Books (Asia) Ltd.
———. 1972. *Taman Indera, a Royal Pleasure Ground; Malay Decorative Arts and Pastimes*. Kuala Lumpur: Oxford University Press.
———. 1983. *Taman Saujana: Dance, Drama, Music, and Magic in Malaya, Long and Not-So-Long Ago*. Kuala Lumpur: International Book Service.
———. 1989. 'History of the Malay Nobat'. *New Straits Times* (September 18).
Shiloah, Amnon. 1995. *Music in the World of Islam: A Socio-Cultural Study*. Detroit, MI: Wayne State University Press.
Shome, Anthony. 2002. *Malay Political Leadership*. London: RoutledgeCurzon.
Siti Hawa Hj, Salleh, ed. 1992. *Hikayat Patani*. Kuala Lumpur: Dewan Bahasa dan Pustaka.
Skeat, William. 2004 (1900). *Malay Magic: An Introduction to the Folklore and Popular Religion of the Malay Peninsular*. Kuala Lumpur: JMBRAS.
Spiller, Henry. 2004. *Gamelan: The Traditional Sounds of Indonesia*. Santa Barbara, CA: ABC-CLIO.

Subrahmanyam, Sanjay. 1997. 'Connected Histories: Notes Towards a Reconfiguration of Early Modern Eurasia'. *Modern Asian Studies* 31, no. 3 (July): 735–62.
———. 2005. *Explorations in Connected History: From Tagus to the Ganges*. New Delhi: Oxford University Press.
Sumarsam. 1995. *Gamelan: Cultural Interaction and Musical Development in Central Java*. Chicago: University of Chicago Press.
Stokes, Martin, ed. 1997. *Ethnicity, Identity and Music: The Musical Construction of Place*. Oxford: Berg.
'Sultan of Selangor: The Installation Ceremony'. 1903. *Straits Times* (November): 6.
Swain, Joseph. 2013. *Historical Dictionary of Baroque Music*. Lanham, MD: Scarecrow Press.
Swettenham, Frank. 1878. 'A Malay Nautch'. *Journal of the Malaysian Branch of the Royal Asiatic Society* (*JSBRAS*) 2 (December): 163–67.
———. 1895. *Malay Sketches*. London: John Lane.
Syed Alwi Sheikh al-Hadi. 1986 (1960). *Adat Resam dan Adat Istiadat Melayu*. Kuala Lumpur: Dewan Bahasa dan Pustaka.
Sykes, Percy. 1909. 'Instruments in Khorasan, with Special Reference to the Gypsies'. *Man* 9: 161–64.
Tan Sooi Beng. 1993. *Bangsawan: A Social and Stylistic History of Popular Malay Opera*. Singapore: Oxford University Press.
———. 2005. 'From Folk to National Popular Music: Recreating Ronggeng in Malaysia'. *Journal of Musicological Research* 24: 287–307.
Tay, Eddie. 2011. *Colony, Nation, and Globalisation: Not at Home in Singaporean and Malaysian Literature*. Hong Kong: Hong Kong University Press.
Teeuw, Andries and David Wyatt. 1970. *Hikayat Patani: The Story of Patani*. The Hague: Martinus Nijhoff.
Temple, Richard Carnac, ed. 1919. *The Travels of Peter Mundy in Europe and Asia: 1608–1667*, vol. 3, parts 1 and 2. London: Haklyut Society.
Teuku Iskandar, ed. 1986. *Kamus Dewan*. Kuala Lumpur: Dewan Bahasa dan Pustaka.
Tingey, Carol. 1994. *Auspicious Music in a Changing Society: The Damai Musicians of Nepal*. New Delhi: Heritage Publishers.
Touma, Habib. 1996. *The Music of the Arabs*. Portland: Amadeus Press.
'Trengganu Affairs. Definite But Slow Advance in 1917'. 1918. *Straits Times* (October 29): 2.
'Trengganu Sees Old and New'. 1949. *Straits Times* (June 4): 4.
Trivedi, Madhu. 2010. *The Making of the Awadh Culture*. New Delhi: Primus Books.
Trocki, Carl. 2007. *Prince of Pirates: The Temenggong and the Development of Johor and Singapore, 1784–1885*. Singapore: NUS Press.
Tunku Abdul Rahman. 1978. *Viewpoints*. Kuala Lumpur: Heinemann Educational Books.
———. 1983. *Lest We Forget: Further Candid Reminiscences*. Kuala Lumpur: Eastern Universities Press.
Turino, Thomas. 2008. *Music as Social Life: The Politics of Participation*. Chicago: University of Chicago Press.

Van Leur, Jacob. 1955. 'Indonesian Trade and Society: Essays in Asian Social and Economic History'. *Selected Studies on Indonesia*, edited by Willem Frederik Wertheim. The Hague: W. van Hoeve Ltd., 147–156.
Wade, Bonnie. 1986. 'Music as Symbol of Power and Status: The Courts of Mughal India'. In *Explorations in Ethnomusicology: Essays in Honor of David P. McAllester*, edited by Charlotte Johnson Frisbie, 97–109. Detroit Monographs in Ethnomusicology, no. 9. Detroit: Information Co-ordinators.
———. 1998. *Imaging Sound: An Ethnomusicological Study of Music, Art and Culture in Mughal India*. Chicago: University of Chicago Press.
Wan Mohd Amin. 1966. *Pesaka Selangor*. Kuala Lumpur: Dewan Bahasa dan Pustaka.
Warner, Arthur, and Edmond Warner, trans. 1905. *The Shahnama of Firdausi*. London: K. Paul Trench, Trubner Company.
Waterson, Roxana. 1990. *Living House: An Anthropology of Architecture in South-East Asia*. Singapore: Oxford University Press.
Welch, David, and Judith McNeill. 1989. 'Archaeological Investigations of Pattani History'. *Journal of Southeast Asian Studies* 20, no. 1: 27–41.
Wheatley, Paul. 1961. *The Golden Kheronese: Studies in the Historical Geography of the Malay Peninsula Before AD 1500*. Kuala Lumpur: University of Malaya Press.
Wilkinson, Richard. 1901. *A Malay-English Dictionary: Part I (Alif to Za.)*. Singapore: Kelly and Walsh Limited.
———. 1932. 'The Nobat in Some Malay Studies'. *Journal of the Malaysian Branch of the Royal Asiatic Society (JMBRAS)* 10, no. 1 (113) (January): 79–86.
Wink, André. 1996. *Al-Hind: The Making of the Indo-Islamic World, Vol. 1, Early Medieval India and the Expansion of Islam, Seventh–Eleventh Centuries*. Leiden: Brill.
Winstedt, Richard. 1929. 'The Perak Royal Musical Instruments'. *Journal of the Malaysian Branch of the Royal Asiatic Society (JMBRAS)* 7, no. 3 (October): 451–53.
———. 1935. 'A History of Malaya'. *Journal of the Malaysian Branch of the Royal Asiatic Society (JMBRAS)* 13, no. 1 (121) (March): iii–270.
———. 1945. 'Kingship and Enthronement in Malaya'. *Journal of the Royal Asiatic Society of Great Britain and Ireland* 2 (October): 134–45.
———. 1993 (1925) *The Malay Magician: Being Shaman, Saiva and Sufi*. Kuala Lumpur: Oxford University Press.
Winstedt, Richard, and Richard Wilkinson. 1934. 'A History of Perak'. *Journal of the Malaysian Branch of the Royal Asiatic Society (JMBRAS)* 12, no. 1 (118) (June): 1–180.
Wright, Owen. 1987. 'Nawba'. In *E. J. Brill's First Encyclopaedia of Islam, 1913–1936: Supplement*, edited by Martijn Theodoor Houtsma et al., vol. 9. Leiden: Brill.

Glossary

(A – Arabic, M – Malay, P – Persian, S – Sanskrit)

adat (A, M)	Malay customs
'alah (A)	outfit or symbol of a caliph's power
alam (A, M)	the world
'alam (A)	banners and flags used by Muslim armies
alat kerajaan (M)	regalia of the state
al-mulk (A)	kingship
al-Rashidun (A)	the first four righteous caliphs of Islam—namely, Abu Bakar, Umar, Ali and Uthman
anak, anakanda (M)	a child
asr (A)	Muslim late afternoon prayer
ayahanda (M)	father
bahasa (M)	language
bakal (M)	future; *bakal* sultan is future sultan
baju Melayu (M)	traditional Malay attire for men
balai (M)	a hall, building; also pavilion where the nobat is kept
balairong seri (M)	audience hall of the palace
baluh (M)	main body of the *serunai*
batang (M)	long, straight object
beduk (M)	long, one-sided wooden drum used in mosques to call for prayer
bendahara (M)	post similar to the prime minister in a Malay sultanate

berangkat (M)	to depart
berdaulat (M)	a sultan bestowed with divine essence
berjamu (M)	ritualistic ceremony to appease the spirits
berkabung (M)	mourning, a mourning period of one hundred days is observed in Perak when a sultan passes away
berpalu (M)	Perak nobat pieces which are played randomly
bersaf-saf (M, A)	rows of praying men or women, as in a Muslim congregation prayer
caping (M)	lip disc of the *serunai*
ceropong (M)	bell-shaped lower end of the *serunai*
ciri (S)	proclamations read by the palace chief herald in Sanskrit
dargah (P)	a Sufi shrine
daulat (M, A)	divine essence bestowed upon the sultan
derhaka (M)	a rebellious or treacherous act against the sultan, an act believed could incur divine intervention
devaraja (S)	Hindu concept of king as divine universal ruler
dīn (A)	religion
dinobatkan (M)	drummed or installed as sultan
disembah (M)	bowed to, as a form of respect to a sultan
duff (A)	single-sided drum or tambourine used in Muslim societies
'Eid al-adha (A)	Muslim religious celebration of sacrifice
'Eid al-fitr (A)	Muslim religious celebration at the end of Ramadan
fajr (A)	dawn, Muslim morning prayer
gendang (M)	cylindrical, double-headed drum hit with the hands or stick
gong (M)	circular, knobbed bronze or brass percussion instrument
guruh (M)	thunder; term used to describe a playing technique of the nobat drums
hari (M)	day
hijaz (A)	the Arab Peninsula
hikayat (M)	story or tale

hulubalang (M)	a military leader or noble
ibu (M)	a mother
iftar (A)	breaking of fast, especially during Ramadan
istiadat (M)	ceremony, usually relating to formal royal ceremonies
isya' (A)	Muslim evening prayer
jahiliah (A)	pre-Islamic period of ignorance in Islamic historiography
jerit (M)	scream, term used in *serunai* playing in the Perak nobat
jerun (M)	type of wood for making gendang
Jumaat (M, A)	Friday
kahwin (M)	to marry
karna, karnay, karrenay (P)	long trumpet used in royal processions
keling (M)	a term used by Malays to denote an Indian
kemangkatan (M)	passing of a royal ruler
kerajaan (M)	royal state or government
keris (M)	traditional Malay dagger
kepala (M)	head
kesultanan (M)	sultanate
kopak-kopak (M)	a pair of small, handheld cymbals made of copper attached to a string
kota (M)	fortified palace, fort, city
kuffar (A)	infidels; term used by Muslims to describe non-believers
kus or kusat (P)	large, mounted kettledrum
lagu (M)	a song or musical piece
lari (M)	runs away, run-off
lubang (M)	a hole, as in the hole of the *serunai*
maghrib (A)	evening or sundown, a time for evening prayer
mahaguru (S)	great teacher
majlis (M, A)	a gathering
mak yong (M)	traditional Malay dance drama found in Kelantan, Terengganu and South Thailand
mali (M)	a conical silver tube that holds the reed of the *serunai*

malik (A)	king, ruler, one of the ninety-nine names of Allah in Islam
malu (M)	ashamed, in the context of Malay culture, to bring dishonor to the name of a sultan
maqamat (A)	assembly, new literary genre of the thirteenth century
maratib (A)	rank, degree, used to describe the insignia of royalty
masjid (M, A)	a mosque
mehter (P)	Ottoman military band
memulih (M)	to revive, term used as part of a ritual to 'awaken' the court regalia
mengadap (M)	facing or having an audience with a sultan
menjunjung duli (M)	installation of heirs and chiefs, and pledge of allegiance ceremony
menjunjung kasih (M)	thank you, used within royal context
menyelang (M)	intermittent; also used to describe the interlocking playing of the Perak nobat drums
menyembah (M)	to salute or bow, as a form of respect to a sultan
merawan (M)	a type of hard wood
merayu (M)	to plead, a term used to describe the playing of the *serunai* in the Perak nobat ensemble
merdu (M)	melodious
merenjis (M)	to sprinkle, usually scented water during a Malay marriage ceremony
mizmar (A)	double-reed wind instrument played in Arab music, similar to the Turkish *zurna*
nafiri or *nafir* (A, P)	long conical trumpet played in a *nobat* ensemble
nama (M)	name
nangka (M)	jackfruit
naqqara (A, P)	kettledrum played in a military/ceremonial band
naqqarakhana (P)	drum house or military/ceremonial band of the Afghans, Persians and Mughals
nauba (A)	term used to denote military/ceremonial band or musical sequence in North Africa, Andalusia, and during the Ummayad caliphate

naubat (A, P)	royal military/ceremonial band of the Mughal courts
nenek moyang (M)	ancestors
nengkara (M)	single-headed kettle drum of the nobat ensemble
nikah (M)	marriage, solemnization
nobat (M)	royal ceremonial ensemble in Malay courts
nugeraha, anugerah (M)	gifts; can be in the form of titles bestowed by sultans
orang kalur (M)	hereditary musicians of the Perak, Kedah and Selangor nobat
pantang larang (M)	taboos
payung (M)	umbrella
pedang kerajaan (M)	state sword; part of the regalia of the sultan
pegawai (M)	officer
pemakaman (M)	burial ceremony
penghulu (M)	village headman
perang (M)	war
peterakna (M)	a platform on the top of the structure where the royal ceremonial lustrations and bath are conducted
petik (M)	to pluck
pipit (M)	reed of the *serunai*
pucuk rebung (M)	bamboo shoots
puja pantai (M)	a ritual where spirits of the sea are appeased before fishermen go out to sea
qiamah (A)	the end of time
ragam (M)	song, rhythm also used to describe songs of the nobat
Ramadan (A)	month of fasting for Muslims
saka (M)	ancestral or guardian spirits
salah, solah (A)	Muslim prayer
saqah (A)	rear guard
sastera (M)	literature
sawlajan (A)	drumsticks
sejarah (M)	history
semangat (M)	spirit or inner strength
sembunyi (M)	threadfin fish
serambi (M)	veranda

serunai (M)	quadruple-reed shawm with seven holes played in traditional Malay music including nobat, shadow puppet and *silat* ensembles
shahnai (P)	double-reed shawm or oboe
sharbush (A)	caps worn by Mamluk musicians
silat (M)	Malay traditional martial art
singgahsana (M)	royal *dais* where the Sultan sits usually on the east side of the throne room
subuh (M, A)	early morning, time for first Muslim prayer of the day
surau (M)	a small mosque
surnay (P)	a double-reed woodwind instrument, oboe or shawm also known as *zurna*, played in folk music in parts of Europe, Central Asia and North Africa
susur galur (M)	lineage
Syaaban (A)	eighth month of the Muslim calendar
Syawal (A)	tenth month of the Muslim calendar
tabal (M)	to install a sultan, derived from the word *tabl*
tabl (A)	drum, or a type of drum, used in Indian classical music
tablkhana (A)	drum house or military/ceremonial band of the Abbasid, Fatimid caliphates
tabuh (M)	large signalling drum, usually found in mosques and madrasah
tanah (M)	land
tariqa or *tarikat* (A, P)	a school or Sufi order
tengkolok (M)	traditional Malay headgear
tepung tawar (M)	to bless, usually by sprinkling rice or scented water in a ceremony
tetap (M)	fixed or constant
tingkah (M)	alternate, term used in describing interlocking playing of drums
tongkat (M)	walking stick
tulah (M)	divine curse incurred upon those who have committed an act of derhaka
tulisan (M)	writing
turun-naik (M)	down and up

ummah or *umma* (A)	a supranational community or brotherhood in Islam
wajib (M, A)	compulsory or obligatory act in Islam
waris negeri (M)	successors to the royal throne
wayang kulit (M)	Malay shadow theatre
Yang Dipertuan Agong (M)	supreme ruler, a unique rotational royal post in Malaysia
Yang Amat Mulia (M)	the most honourable (royal address)
Yang Mulia (M)	the honourable (royal address)
Zulhijjah (A)	the twelfth month of the Muslim calendar

Index

Page references for figures are italicized

Abbasid(s), 2; 14, 17, 20; Caliphate, 11, 18; dynasty, court, caliphs, 16; -Seljuk, 19, 21
Abdullah bin Abdul Kadir, 92; Munshi, 92
Abdullah Mukarram Shah, Sultan, 152
Abdullah, Sultan, 155, 179
Abdul Aziz, Encik, xviii; *Toh Setia Guna*, 69
Abdul Aziz, Sultan, 167–68
Abdulcelil Levni, 31
Abdul Jalil Shah, Sultan, 104
Abdul Ghafur Mohaidin Shah, Sultan, 104
Abdul Rahman Muadzam Shah II, Sultan, 48
Abdul Rahman, Sultan, 49, 50, 85, 161
Abdul Samad, Sultan, 53, 162, 175
Aceh(nese), 8, *47*, 51, 84n2, 90–94, 102–108, 111; 121, 127–40, 146, 149nn5–7, 150n15, 183, 210–11; Grand Mufti of, 150; immigrants, 94; Johor and, 119; Kingdom of, 124; music, 149; Power, 82; religious event in, 145; the rise of, 121; Sultanate, Kings of, 130, 152, 214; weakening of, 148

Abu Bakar, Caliph, 15, 221
Abu Bakar, Sultan, 48, 153–161, 209
Abu Muhammad al-Qasim ibn Ali al-Hariri, 27
Abu l-Hassan 'Ali ibn Nafi', 17. *See also* Ziryab
adat (customs)*,* 6–7, 94–98, 132–39, 190n1; *istiadat,* 6–7, 49, 72, 82, 92–98, 100–108; Malay, 152; Malay court, 125; manuals of, 124; and *pantang larang* (taboos), 84; *Penghulu,* 162; in Perak, 149; royal, 164; *pertabalan,* 65, 106
Adat Aceh, vii, xiii, 85n11, 88, 102–109, 111, 123, *147,* 149n1, 82, 214
Adat Lembaga Orang-Orang Melayu Di Dalam Negeri Perak Darul Ridzuan, 69, 73, 85
Adat Pusaka Raja-Raja dan Orang Besar-Besar Negeri Perak Darul Ridzuan, 85n10. *See also* Adib Vincent Tung
Adat Raja-Raja Melayu, xiii, 111, 133
adhan, 130
Adib Vincent Tung, 85, 209
aerophones, 53, 110, 212

229

230 Index

Africa, 14, 213–17; North, 2–3, 17, 43, 81, 226
Ahmad Fauzi, 52
Ahmad Shah Qajar, 35
Ahmad, Sultan (Terengganu), 161
al-Attas, Syed Naquib, 94, 210
Alaudin Ri'ayat Shah, Sultan, 127–128
Alaudin Sulaiman Shah, Sultan, 67
Ali ibn Abi Talib, Caliph, 15
Andaya, B., 1–6, 45, 52, 71, 89, 98, 105, 152, 175–79, 210
Andaya, L., 121–28, 148, 152–53
animist, 44, 99; anismistic, 44, 68
Arab(s) / Arabic / Arabian, xvii; 2–8, 12, 14–18, 20, 26, 58, 64, 71, 81–87, 149, 150, 188, 213–18, 215–21; of the hijaz, 13; horses, 129; *jahilliah*, 13; loanword, 131; Music, 211–12, 224; Peninsula, 223; -speaking world, 27; turban, 29
'Arak-Arak,' 70, 111; 'Arak-Arakan,' 70, 112–14; 'Atandis,' x, 76–77
Asr, 21
Ataillah Mohammed Shah, Sultan, 47
al-Aziz Nizar, 24
Azlan Shah, Sultan, 85, 176

Balai Besar, xi
Balai, 66, 92, 102–103, 221; *Besar*, 172; *gendang*, 103; *keujruen*, 133; *Nobat*, 9, 69, 81, 102; *pedang*, 133, 146
Balairong, 96; *Seri*, 44, 65, 171
bangsi, 51, 149
Batavia, 54, 185
beduk, 63, 83, 102–103, 122, 222
Bendahara, 92–97, 103–109; 160, 222; Datuk Cerak Kin, 92, 109; Kayu Kelat, 98; of Pahang, 156; Raja, 52, 73, 154, 216
'Berangkat,' 133, 222; 'Gendang,' 70, 132–38, 144–46, 164; 'Genderang,' 132–37, 145–47; 'Raja,' 70–71, 111–14; 'Syah Alam,' 138
berdaulat, 63; 185; *raja*, 84, 184–85
berjamu, 99, 222

berkabung, 66, 222
berkhatan, 68
berpalu (*lagu*), 113, 222
Birch, J. W. W., 154–158, 184
Brahmin, 71, 157
British, vii, xi, xvii, xix; 104, 123; colonial policy, 6, 152; colonial/scholar administrators, 8, 151–156; -controlled Johor, 48; the courts' sustained encounter, 7; East India Company, 34; imperial plans, 151; intervention, 3, 153–74; Pathé (News), xi, 168, 172; power over Malay ruling elites, 157; power struggle with the Dutch/rivalry 51, 153; resident, 49, 154; traveler, 140
Beruas, 97, 105, 125; king of, 46
bronze, 60, 181, 223
Brunei, x, 3, 11, 43; *62, 70; 84*, 90, 121–27; 175, 188, 217; courts, 147; Kingdom of, 44; the last save havens for the nobat, 185; musicians, 72; nobat, 53–55, 60
Buddhist, 51, 82; courts and temples, 91; Hindu-, 2, 6, 8, 43–45, 68, 82, 100, 119, 132, 14
Bugis: from Celebes, 48; migration of, 94; origins, 160; prince by the name of Raja Lumu, 52   52
Bumiputra, 190n1
Bujang Ilir, 70
Bujang Alulu Dalul, 112
Buyong Adil, 164, 211

Cau Seri Bangsa, 46, 95
caping, x, 57, 222
Central Asia(n), 3, 6, 14, 18, 20, 26, 82, 81, 226
ceremony, 17, 24, 27, 429; 63; 85n8, 113, 144, 223–27; bathing, 71, 160; birth, 68; burial, 67; Eid al-Fitr, 139; fasting month/Ramadan, 131–32; installation, 44, 64–65, 96–99, 108, 133, 165–67, 170–71, 86,

209, 215–18, 225; *Istiadat Meletak Kerja*, 134; lying-in-state, 48–49, 161; *menjunjung duli*, 97, 133, 168, 224; mourning, 66; oath-taking, 91; royal procession to the masjid, 135–38, 146; sacrificial, 145n5; Siamese court, 100; of Syah Alam's slaughtering of the animals, 140

ceropong, 57, 222

China, 14, *70*, 71, 229; missions to, 90; musicians to, 91

Chinese, 170; citizenship, 168; history, 91; immigrants, 179n2; intellectual traditions, 18; secret societies, 154; Sources, 213; Spirit, 71

chronicles, xix, 6–7; court, 87, 93; Malay, 103; Nakhon, 91

ciri, 66, 222

chora mandakini, 51–52

cymbals, 30–36, 40, 135–37, 147, 81; clashing of, 72; a pair of small, 20, 53, 61, 223

Daeng Kemboja, 52

Dang Gidang, *70*

Dang Gendang, x, *77*

daulat, 4–7, 42–44, 63–69, 82, 90–98, 214, 222; bestower of, 83; is seen as the fluid central power, 101; Malay concept of, 84; Malay rulers bestowed with, 121; *raja berdaulat*, 84, 185; the ruler's majesty and, 120; a sultan's, 182; Sultan Manzur's, 99; *Tuanku*, 100, 105

Delhi: Sultan of, 127; Sultanate, 25–26, 105

derhaka, 222–27; act of, 43, 84, 185; a person who goes against the ruler, 101

drum(s), 20, 37, 40, 139, 209–10; are also known as *gendang melalu*, 73; and flags in a royal outfit, 34; are struck seven times in seven tunes, 131; barrel, 55; beating of, 15–18, 27; *beduk*, 63, 103; blow the trumpets together with the, 117; capture of the, 25; customs of bestowing, 125; *damamah*, 32; dampening or muting of the, 116; deep-sounding, 72; different strokes of the, 78; ensemble of conch and, 26; full installation, 46; head of the royal, 132; implications of the, 106; importance of the, 64; in royal processions, 91; interlocking, 81, 224–27; *kus*, 31; large ensemble playing big, 62; mounted, 24; *naqqara*, xvii, 21, 30; noise of the, 136; official in charge of the, 135–37, 146; of Terengganu, 54, 175; of the nobat, 66, 162; patterns or styles, 111; rhythms played by the, 83; right hand respectively on all three, 74; royal, 51, 89, 98–99, 114, 157; silver, 56, 144, 167; skins, 163; state, 110; symbols of sovereign power, 81; synchronized with the, 80; syncopation of the two, 76; technique(s), 88, 223; tremendous aural effect of the, 36; *tubul*, 105; two large, 48–49; were then beaten, 134, 140; with many trumpets, 129

dynamic(s): changing political and cultural, 6; current political, 190; form, intensity, melody and, 63; of Malay politics, 124; political and social, 7; religious, 8; socioeconomic and political, 5; tempo and, 78

dynasty: Artuqid, 19; Abbasid, 16; Hulu, 92, 109; Marinid, 30; Qajar, 34–35; Umayyad, 15

East: side of the *balairong seri*, 44, 65; *Mashriq*, or the Arab, 17; Muslim influence also spread towards the, 25

East India Company, 152

Egypt(ian), 17, 22; copy of al-Jazari's books, 20; Crusaders in, 24; Mamluk army in Mansurah, 36; scholar, 128

'Eid: al-Adha, 41, 69, 103, 131–38, 140–145, 222; *al-Fitr,* 27, 41, 69, 102, 131–39, 141, 222; celebrations, 12, 24, 29, 148; festivals, 25; prayers, 149n10

fakir(s), 93, 119
Farmer, H. G., 11–17, 20–24, 30–36, 105, 212
al-Faruqi, L., 13, 16, 212
Fatimid, 2, 24, 27, 43, 227
Fazl, Abu'l, xi, 32–40, 110, 136, 143, 144, 209
Federation of Malaya, 168–70, 183
Firdausi, Abu'l Qasim, ix, 24, 25, 37–39, 212–19. *See also* Shahnama of Firdausi
Flute(s), 51, 149, 217
form (musical), 63
folk, 187, 211–18 226
functions, 63, 113; ceremonial, 13; court(ly), 5, 83; how the ensemble, 7; and instrumentation, 188; in the religious ceremonies of the Acehnese sultanate, 8; royal, 3; symbolic and spiritual, 6; the *tablkhana's* major, 24

gambang, 110
gamelan, 78, 174, 218; joget, 184, 211
gendang, x, 30, 45, 54, 65–67, 70, 78, 82, 85n13, 99–117, 129, 136, 143, 162–63, 214, 223; *anak,* 49, 55, *62, 70,* 73, 76; *balai,* 102–103; *berangkat,* 132–38, 144–47, 164; *besar,* 50, 120; double-headed, 181; *kecil,* 55, *62; ibu,* 49, 55, *62,* 73, 76; *melalu,* 55, 73–74; *membentung, 112;* nobat, 52, *56, 62,* 73–77, 105; *peningkah,* 55, *56, 62,* 74–77; *perang,* 113–115; *tabal,* 73
Gendang Berangkat, *70*
Gendang Perang, *70,* 113
genderang, 54, 64, 96–98, 109, 131–39, 140–49

gong(s), x, 25, 26, 37, 53, 60, *62,* 67, 73, 83–85, 109–10, 136–47, 181, 223
government, 8, 35, 97, 167, 223; British, 165; of Her Majesty the Queen, 159; Malay, 89

Harun al-Rashid, 16
Harun Mat Piah, 4, 213
Hikayat Aceh, 104
Hikayat Amir Hamzah, 109, 134, 215
Hikayat Hang Tuah, 70, 103, 111, 125, 136, 215
Hikayat Patani, 50, 68–69, 70–76, 81–88, 92, *112,* 121, 130, 182–88, 215
Hikayat Raja-Raja Pasai, xiii, 8, 45, 53–54, 64–69, 93–98, 110–19, 133, 214–15
Hikayat Siak, 103, 215
Hinduism, 6, 26, 66, 71–72, 91, 182, 211–12, 222; -Buddhist, 2, 6, 8, 26, 43–45, 68, 82, 91, 100, 119, 132, 149n3
Hobsbawm, Eric and Terence, Ranger, 12, 213
horns, 17, 27, 36, 63, 83, 135–36, 143
de Houtman, Cornelis, 128, 134

Ibn Battuta, 105
India(n), ix, xvii, 5, 14, 18, 26, 32, *33,* 34, 42, 45, 47, 54, 57, 63, 68, 93, 105, 127, 170, 211–17, 223; Bells, 37, 40; Mughal, 103, 209, 219; Ocean, xviii, 2–9, 82, 90, 95, 125, 130, 182–188
Indonesian, 94, 183, 210–19
invented tradition, 12, 186
Idris Shah I, Sultan, 53, 158, 163–64, 178
Idris Iskandar Shah II, Sultan, xx, 172
Iran, ix, 14, 17–18, 32, 35, 37, 42, 47, 54, 57, 175
Iskandar Muda, Sultan, x, 51, 129, *142,* 150n15

Iskandariah Palace, xviii, 65, 168
Iskandar Zulkarnain, 85n12, 134; Nobat, 70, 111
Islam(ic), xvii, 2–9, 12–19, 40–45, 67–68, 71, 82, 87, 92–95, 125–28, 132–35, 146–48, 153, 173, 177, 181, 183–89, 210–17, 221, 224, 227, 229; coming of, 4, 100, 181, 212; cradle of, 94, 124; five pillars of, 131, 149n4; pre-, 24, 26, 90, 223; most revered figures in, 134
Islamicate, 1–2, 11, 13, 742–45, 54, 63, 95, 136, 181–82, 188, 190
istiadat, 6–7, 64; *menjunjung duli,* 65; *pertabalan,* 53, 63–65. See also *adat istiadat*

Japanese, 167, 169
Jawi, 81, 87, 92, 115–16, 119, 130, 183, 189
al-Jazari, ibn al-Razzaz, ix, 13, 18–19, 20–21, *22–23,* 30, 32, 209
al-Jazari, Shams al-Din, 425
al-Jazira, 19
Johor, 48, 51–52, 90, 97, 103, 119, 126–27, 148, 153, 158, 160–61, 167–69, 186; the prince of, 108; -Riau, 49, 70, 75, 85n11, 159; Yang Dipertuan of, 104–106; Yang Dipertuan Muda of, 107, 120
'Jong Beraleh,' x, *70, 74,* 191

Kampar (Sumatera), 46, 48, 84, 125–26
Kedah, x, xix; court, 3; nobat, xi, 9n3; *orang kalur* of, xx; Raja of, 43
kettledrums, 15, 17, 20–21, 24–26, 29–37, 40, 45, 48, 54, 94, 135–36, 223
Kingdom(s), 2, 48, 82, 91–92, 105, 110, 126, 128, 143, 146, 211, 213; of Aceh, 124; of Brunei, 44; Islamic/Muslim, 127, 130; Malay, 94
kingship, 2, 14, 18, 52, 90, 100, 169, 181, 215, 219, 221

kopak-kopak, x, 52, 61, *62,* 73, 83, 109–10, 223
Kuala Kangsar, 168, 173, 217
Kuala Lumpur, xix, 45, 85, 92, 94, 161, 169–70, 177, 209–219
Kuala Terengganu, 162, 173
Ku Zam Zam, 4, 47, 70, 214

lagu, 69–70, 73–74, 76–79, 83, 111, 132, 139
'Lagu Arak-Arak,' 70. *See also* 'Arak-Arakan'
lagu tetap, 113–14
lagu berpalu, 113, 222
legitimized, 12
Linehan, William, 70–71, 156, 225
loyalty, 65, 84, 91, 98

Magic(al), 61, 80–91, 106, 108, 136, 177, 184, 187, 217, 219; Malay, 156–57, 217
mahaguru, x, 61, *62,* 224
Maharaja Derbar Raja, 47
Mahmud Shah (Syah), Sultan (Melaka), 48, 95, 97
Mahmud Shah, Sultan (Perak), 52, 71
makyong, 55, 114, 116, 120, 174, 187, 188, 212
Malayness, 5, 123, 127, 152–53, 183–84, 187, 210–11, 217
Malay Annals, 45. See also *Sejarah Melayu*
Malaya(n), xiii, 6, 8, 130, 171–77, 187, 190n1, 213–19; British, 151; Federation of, 169–70, 183; Head of State of, 185; Union, 167–68, 186
Malaysia(n), x, xviii, xx, 29, 67, *84, 88,* 91, 94, 102, 149n6, 151–153, 156, 169, 177–79, 186–90, 209–11, 213–219, 227; Arkib Negara (National Archives), xiii, xix, *50, 60,* 165, *166, 171,* 173, *176;* courts (of), 3, 11, 147; Islamic Party (PAS), 67; Peninsular, 43–44, 176

234   *Index*

Malik al-Saleh, Sultan, 8n2, 93
Malik al-Zahir, Sultan, 127
man (nobat song or form), 70
Maqamat (al-Hariri), ix, 20, 27, *28,* 30, 224
marriage, 32, 45, 49, 52, 64, 67–68, 71, 94, 104–107, 134, 224–25
Matusky, P., 57, 73, 78, 215
Maxwell, W. E., 51, 156, 215
Mecca, 4, 13, 45, 64, 94, 127–28, 149n4
Meilu Ho, 73, 76, 85, 105, 113, 116–18, 151n2, 213
Melaka, xv, 4, 8, 43, 45–46, 48–49, 51–52, 54, 61, 65, 68, 72, 184, 90, 94–100, 103, 105, 110–11, 119–30, 132–34, 148–49, 152, 161, 167, 176, 182–183, 183, 210
melody, 49, 63, 73–74, 78–80, 82–83, 111–14, 117, 137
membranophones, 53
menteri, 46, 95–96, 106–107, 133
Merah Silu, 93
Miksik, John, xi, 175–76, 179n6
Milner, Anthony, 1–6, 89, 94, 108, 123, 183, 215
mimicry, 12–13, 15, 153, 178
Misa Melayu, xiii, 52–53, 60, 65–67, 69, 85, 88, 97, 101, 109, 111, 136, 149, 209, 215–16
Mohd Anis Md Nor, 3, 215
Mohd Ghouse Nasuruddin, 3, 215
Mosque(s), 19, 27, 29, 63, 68–69, 83, 92, 102–103, 130, 135, 138–49, 222, 224, 226–27
mufti, 66, 150n15
Mughal(s), ix, 2, 11, 18, 25, 32–34, 42–43, 103, 110, 128, 136, 143, 148, 209, 219, 225
music(al) / musicians, ii, xvii, xviii, xi, xix, xx, 1–7, 11, 13–18, 20–21, 24–37, 40–41, 48–49, 51, 61–63, 71–73, 76–84, 88, 91, 106, 109–11, 114, 116–21, 124, 127, 129, 131, 134–39, 142–49, 156, 160–62, 174, 181–89, 210–19, 223–29

Muslim, xvii, 2–5, 9n3
Muzaffar Shah, Sultan (Perak), 48, 51
Muzaffar Shah III, Sultan (Perak), 66

nafir / *nafiri,* ix, x, 20–21, 25, 28–34, 43, 45, 50–54, 59, 62, 66–67, 69, 72–75, 78, 82, 85, 94–95, 99–1000, 109–110, 113–114, 116–19, 129, 131, 136–37, 139, 143, 147, 155, 162–63, 174, 181, 225
naqqara, ix, xvii, 17, 20–21, *28,* 29–30, 32, 34, 37, 40, 54, 225
naqqarakhana, ix, xvii, 2, 11–13, 17, 26–27, 30, 32, 34–35, 40–42, 45, 62, 95, 103, 210, 225
nauba / *naubat* / *nuba,* iv, xi, xvii, 2–3, 11–21, 25–26, 30–34, 40–47, 62, 68, 95, 103, 140, 173, *174,* 181, 209, 212, 225
nengkara, 30, 45, 54–55, *62,* 73–74, 76–79, 81–83, 121, 129, 136–37, 143–44, 147, 181, 225
Nettl, Bruno, 182, 216
Nicolas, Arsenio, 91, 147, 149, 216
'Nobat Khamis,' 70
'Nobat Subuh,' *70,* 71, 83, 101–102, 111, *112,* 113–14
'Nobat Tabal,' 44, *70,* 71

orang kalur, xx, 53, 71–72, 81–82, 156, 163, 174, 185, 189, 216, 225
orang muntah lembu, 72, 156

Palace(s), xviii, 2, 7, 16–17, 21, 24, 26, 31–32, 37, 49, 63, 66, 92, 96–97, 100–103, 107, 111, 127, 129, 131–32, 134, 137–38, 140–41, 145–46, 149n7, 161, 167, 170, 181, 185, 221–23; Artuklu, 19; Iskandariah, 65, 168, 171; Johor, 186; Jugra Istana (Selangor), 175; Kedah, xix; National (Istana Negara), 45; Patani, 91; Perak, 44, 157; Terengganu, 50, 162, 165, 174
pantang larang, xviii, 63, 84, 225. *See also* taboos

Parameswara, 45, 126
Pasai, 9, 51, 93–95, 98–99, 126–28, 134, 150n14–15
Pawang Diraja, 69
pentasyllabic, *115*
Penyengat, 48, 85, 215
Perak, xi, xix, 44, 48, 51, 54–55, 57, 60, *62*, 65–68, 74, 76, 78, 81–83, 85n10, 90, 94, 97–98, 102, 111, 150, 156, 162–63, 147–48, 149n8, 153–57, 164–67, 171–72, 175, 183, 191, 209, 219, 210, 214, 222; nobat, x, xviii, 3, 52, *56, 59,* 69–70, 73, *77,* 79–80, 99, 113–18, 121, 173, 188–89, 223–24, 213, 216–17, 229; *orang kalur,* xx, 53, 72, 215, 225; Sultan Abdul Aziz of, 168; Sultan Azlan Shah of, 176; Sultan Idris of, 158, 163, 178; Sultan Mahmud Shah of, 71
Persian, xvii, 2, 7, 12–17, 24, 26, 30, 32, 40, 43, 149n2, 188, 212, 221, 225; Indo-, 87; Romance, 109
pertabalan, 2, 53, 63–65, 97–98, 106, 108, 133
pipes, 25, 36, 51
Portuguese, 8, 48 123, 125–28, 176, 182, 213, 217
Prime Minister, 42, 52, 94, 103, 122n5, 168, 222
power, political, 24; agents of change, 2, concede all, 167; and economic, 148; growing economic and, 83; Sultan's economic and, 153
power, symbol of (the speaker's), 7, 24, 34, 135
Power(ful), ii, iii, xvii, xviii, 210, 214, 219; Aceh as a new regional, 125; and advanced civilizations of the time, 13; and the sacred, 12; as bestower of *daulat,* 183; aural display of royal, 168; aural symbol of Muslim, 41; befitting of the newfound, 15; bestowed with supernatural, 98; began to assert his, 52; British officials had over Malay ruling elites, 157; competing European, 156; and consolidating Johor's influence over Patani, 107; display of, 32; elevate their status and consolidate their, 87; emanating from the source of, 111; and the establishment of *kerajaan,* 99; governed by the concept of *daulat* (divine ruling), 84, 90; gradual erosion of the rulers, 154 ; iconic signs, 11; important reminder of his, 130; in installing whoever he pleased, 108; interplay affect Malay royal customs, 152; interplay with the Malay sultans, 185; issue of royal, 179, 184; Javanese concept of, 121n3; kingdom in the Malay world, 48; lay with the district chiefs, 89; Malay community, 123; Malay notion of divine royal, 6; Malay sultanate which was growing in, 126; mark of their seniority and, 25; Melaka's growing, 95; of a sultan 78; of the instruments as part of the court regalia, 69; *orangkaya* of Patani, 104; regal concerns with genealogy of, 4; rise of Melaka as a regional, 45; shows the physical, 37; soundmark, 187; sound represented Ottoman military, 30; Sultan Manzur Shah's divine, 100; Temenggong Ibrahim was given, 159; to be reckon with in the region, 119; -usurping Yang Dipertuan Muda of Johor, 120; vacuum left by the fall of Melaka, 105; value placed on these instruments of, 110
power and sovereignty/authority/ dominance/wealth/governance/ identity, 1, 8, 17–19, 43, 82, 101, 170, 181–82, 186, 189
power in Western Asia and Europe, 14
power struggles: between the British and the Dutch, 51; during the Kelantan dynasty, 109
Prophet Ibrahim / Abraham, 133–34, 138, 166

Prophet Muhammad: birth of the, 13; call prayer from the time of the, 68; companions of the, 12; death of, 15; family of the, 4; miraculously converted after meeting, 93; prophecy about the coming of the messiah, 29; sayings / *sunnah* of the, 132, 135, 149; uncle of, 134
Puteri Mandi Mayang (Lenggang), *70–71*

Queen, 102–104, 106–107, 209; of Bentan, 45; Elizabeth (of England), 128, 152; Ijau (of Patani), 98; of Patani, 105; Victoria, 159

Ragam, 73, 76, 83, 89, 96, 101–102, 106, 109, 111, *112*, 113–19, 121, 131–33, 226; 'Adani,' *147*; 'Biram Medeli,' 140, 145, *147*; 'Kembali Dari Masjid,' *147*; 'Kuda (Berlari),' *70*, 139, 141, 145, *147*; 'Mahligai,' *147*; 'Sani,' *147*; 'Siwajan,' 136–37, 141, 144, 146, *147*
Ramadan, 25, 27, 29, 69, 103, 131–35, 149n4, 222, 226
Raja Chulan, 52, 216
Raja Iskandar Raja Halid, ii, iii, 4, *33, 44, 55–62, 63, 74–79, 80*, 113, 121, 149, 216, 229,
Raja Lumu, 52, 71
Raja Muda: of Perak, 97; Raja Abdullah (Perak), 154; Raja Iskandar (Perak), 66–67; of Selangor, 158, 164–65, 176
Regalia: Aceh, 133; appropriate Friday, 146; as symbols of his power and authority, 170; destroyed, 162; guardian *jinns* of the state and their, 99; importance of the, 52; installed with full, 161; making of the, 171; of Malay Court at Coronation, 212; Melaka, 126; ruler and the, 101; Patani, 109; Perak, 154, *155*, 214; Selangaor, 175, 185; significance of the, 156; state/court/royal, xi, xviii, 1–2, 6, 43, 53–54, 61, 68–69, 82, 88–89, 110, 120, 133, 138, 152, 157, 163, 182, 184, 221, 224; Terengganu, 49
Reid, Anthony, 4, 94, 123–24, 117, 216
repertoire, xix, 7, 45, 48, 50, 52–53, 69–70, 79, 83, 88, 91, 111, 113, 120, 148, 182, 186; Kedah nobat, 72, 81; Patani nobat, 188; Perak nobat, 72–76, 148; Selangor nobat, 73, 148; Terengganu, 72
Riau, x, 121, 154; archipelago of Indonesia, 3; courts, 132; Dutch Resident of, 54, 178; ensemble was brought from, 161; Johor-, 48–49, 52, 70, 75, 85n11, 209; Kandis Museum, 56, *60*; -Lingga, xi, 43, 49, 53, 109, 111, 159–60, 175, 179n4; Muslim scholars in, 153; nineteenth-century, 116, 133; nobat, 112, 176, 188, 214; sultan/sultanate, 174, 185, 215
ritual(s) / ritually, 91, 145n6, 157, 165, 183, 190, 209, 222; court, 14, 132, 189; marked by a certain *istiadat* or, 64; nobat as a, 44; sacrifice/ sacrificial, 139–40; performed by the state (court) shaman, 63, 69; propitiation, 99; religious (and healing), 12, 68; remains an important part of the Sultan's installation, 65; repeated music, 187; supernatural elaborate, 184; Zoroastrian, 41

Sadie, S., 26, 217
Said, Edward, 178, 217
saka, 63, 226
Sanskrit, 26, 66, 215, 221, 222
Sassanid(s), 14, 16, 18
Sawa, George, 16, 45, 217
Sejarah Melayu, ix, xiii, 43–46, *47*, 54, 65, 70, 72, 95, 103–104, 110–111, 119–20, 125–26, 130, 148, 209, 215. *See also* Malay Annals

serunai, x, 45, 54, 57, *62*, 66–67, 72–74, 76, 78–79, 80–83, 99, 109, 110–119, 121, 129, 136–39, 143, 81, 221–26

Selangor, xi, xix, 3, 44, 49, 52–55, 62, 67, 70–71, 73–74, 82–83, 113, 133, 147, 158, 161–67, 175, 179, 183, 185, 209, 211, 218–19, 225

shawm(s), 26, 36, 45, 143, 212; double-reed, 30; played on horseback, 32; quadruple-reed, 57, 226

sahnai/shehnai, xvii, 26, 212

Shamsul, Amri Baharuddin, 5, 12, 123–24, 152, 156, 179, 183, 186, 190n1, 217

Sheikh Abdul Ghani, 53, 162

Sheikh Abu al-Khair, 128

Sheikh Ismail, 45

Sheikh Muhammad Yamani, 128

Sheikh Said, 93–94

Shekh Syamsuddin al Sumatra'i (Sumatrani), 139, 150

Sheppard, Mubin, xi, 3–4, 45, 49, 54, 71, 85, 88–89, 106, 162, 172–79, 210, 216–17

Shiloah, Amnon, 13, 17, 24, 45, 212, 217

Singapore, xv, xix, 45, 48–50, 72, 92, 152, 158–59, 161, 169, 174, 210, 212–13, 215–19, 229

Siva, Lord, 72

signaling, 71, 187

Skeat, W.W., xi, 92, 156–58, 162, *163,* 175–77, 179n7, 217

South Asia(n), xvii, 4–5, 20, 26, 30, 42, 62, 64, 82, 87, 128, 181, 214, 216; nobat/nauba, 3, 6, 45, 72, 188; traditions, 11

Southeast Asia(n), 44–45, 53, 181, 184, 209, 211–13; characteristics of, 128; coming of Islam in, 100; courts and temples of, 91; European inquiry and scholarship of, 123; Europeans reach the shores of Melaka and, 125; from the Near East to, 3; greetings and salutations in, 68; and its people, 87;

mainland and island, 90; music, 73, 76–77, 88; nobat institution, 3

sovereignty, ii, iii; Aceh saw this as a threat to its, 51; acknowledgement of, 95; Malay notion of, 5; power and, 1, 6–8, 43, 82, 148, 182, 189; ruler's status and, 2; surrender their full, 167; symbol of (his), 35, 89, 108; to fully claim, 52; undermine its, 119

Stokes, Martin, xx, 1–2, 11, 210, 218

Subrahmanyam, Sanjay, 1, 5, 41, 127, 209, 218

subuh (prayer), 68, 226; Nobat, 70–71, 83, 101–102, 111, *112,* 113–14

Sulalatus Salatin, 85, 209. See also *Sejarah Melayu*

Sumatera, x, xv, 8, 48, 51, *60,* 90, 126; east coast of, 84n1, 188; Indragiri nobat of, 72; north, 149; religious scholar from, 53, 162; southeast, 161

Syaaban, 69, 131–32, 226

Syed Alwi, 43, 109, 111–12, 116, 218

Syed Naquib al-Attas. *See* al-Attas

Symbol(s)/symbolism/symbolic/symbolize(s): a caliph's power and authority, 17, 221; befitting of newfound power, 15; British colonial superiority, 184; gesture acknowledging the religious, 135; justly manifested through proper symbols, 41; political power, 12; power-, xvii; power and sovereignty, 1, 7–8, 43, 82, 108, 182, 189; regional sultanates maintain the nobat's, 128; royal(ty) (status, authority), 14, 27, 40, 44; and Sounds in the Creation of a Patani Identity, 210; slaughter, the ruler's sacrificial act, 139; and spiritual functions intact, 6

symbol of: a ruler's dominion, 95; of a Sultan's *daulat,* 84; of authority/greatness, 37, 89, 119, 125; of ethnic identity, 183; of his sovereignty

/ sovereign power, 35, 181; of kingship, 52; of Malay pride, 190n6; of military pride, 34; of modernity and success, 153; of power (and agents of political change), 2, 13, 24, 42; of power and wealth/authority/ identity/status, 19, 170, 186, 214, 219; of prestige and influence, 156 Sultan Manzur's *daulat*, 99; the end of an era, a culmination of British colonial scholarship, 177; the nobat seen as a, 164; the sacred nature of the *orang kalur*, 72; the *tablkhana* became and important, 25; written in the Jawi alphabet, 116

Sufi(sm), 128, 150n14, 214, 219; -based Islam, 6; the ensemble's history and connection to, 20; *fakir* (ascetic), 93, 135; influence, gradual cultural transformation, 7; shrines, 3, 19, 68, 222; *tariqas,* 5, 227; traveler, 127

Sultanate(s), 6, 18, 67, 96, 107, 119, 148, 162, 167, 172, 182, 185, 187, 214, 222–23; Acehnese, 8, 51, 130–31, 152; Delhi, 25–26; emergence of new, 123; Malay, 5, 7–8, 44, 48, 50, 52, 65, 82, 84, 89, 106, 110, 120, 124–26, 129–30, 153, 175, 182, 186; Melaka, 45, 68, 94, 99, 100, 122n5, 125, 127, 133–34; Muslim, 3–4, 95; Patani, 88, 90, 92, 105, 110, 121; Riau-Lingga, 43, 109, 161, 174; Turkmen, 19

Swettenham, Frank, 151–52, 156–58, 177, 179, 210, 218

tabal, 43, 64; *Adat,* 65; *ditabalkan,* 52, 94; *genderang / gendang,* 54, 73; Nobat, 44, *70,* 71. See also *pertabalan*
tabla, 64. See also *tablakhana*
Tanjung Patani, 90
Tanjung Pinang, 176
taboos, xviii, 63, 82, 84, 225. See also *pantang larang*

tempo, 17, 74, 78, 81, 83, 85n13
Tengku Abdul Rahman, 154
Tengku Embong Fatimah, 49–50
Tengku Hamidah, 154
Tengku Kelana Jaya, 164–67
Tengku Mohammed Jewa, 47
Tengku Musa Eddin, 164
Terengganu, x, xi, xv, 3, 44, 49–50, 53, 56–57, *59, 62,* 70, 72–75, 78, *88,* 91, 162, 170, 178, 183, 185, 188, 214, 224; Batu Bersurat, 82, 87; Istana Kolam, 174; Kuala, 173; nobat, ix, x, xix, 54, *55,* 61, 69, 80, 82, 89, 111, 133, 161, 175; -Riau nobat, 176; Sultan of, xi, 165–67
timekeeper, 2, 13, 16, 18–19, 32, 82, 101, 181
Toh Seri Nara Diraja, 66, 156
Toh Setia Guna, 69
Trumpet(s), 17, 24, 33, 36, 40, 59, 94, 103–104, 110, 113, 129, 134, 143, 157–58, 162, 164, 181, 223, 225;blowing of, 15, 27, 113, 117–18; *karrenay/karnay,* 25, 30, 32, 223; *nafir/nafiri/anfar,* 20–21, 29, 31, 34, 45, 105, 225
tulah, 63, 84, 101, 185, 227
Tuanku Abdul Rahman, 45
Tuanku Bahiyah, 67, 169
Tunku Abdul Rahman, 67, 168–73, Tunisia, 17

ulama, 128
ummah, 11, 227
Umayyad, 2, 14–16, 29, 34, 43
Unison: play(ed) in, 74–77
United Malay Nationalist Organization (UMNO), xiii, 167, 186
United States, 92, 229
unity, 6, 89

Wade, Bonnie, 5, 13, 18, 30, 219
Wan Mohd Amin, 53, 162–64, 219

wayang kulit, 55, 78, 91, 114, 187, 214, 227
wajib, 146, 227
wedding(s), 67, 133, 162, 217
Wilkinson, R. J., xi, 3–4, 45, 149, 150, 155, 158, 177, 219
Winstedt, R. O., xi, 44, 51, 132, 155, 157, 167, 177, 219
worship(ping), 93, 132

Yamtuan Muda, 48, 52, 179n3
Yang Dipertuan Agong, xi, xvii, 7, 44–45, 169, 170–71, 173, 178, 185–89, 208n6, 213, 227
Yusuf of Perak, Sultan, 168

Zainal Abidin III, Sultan, 49, 162
zapin, 187, 215
Zoroastrianism, 14, 41

About the Author

Raja Iskandar Bin Raja Halid is an ethnomusicologist and senior lecturer in the Department of Heritage, Faculty of Creative Technology and Heritage at Universiti Malaysia Kelantan, Malaysia. He holds a bachelor's in music degree from the National Academy of Arts, Culture and Heritage (ASWARA), a bachelor's in applied arts (music technology) and master of arts (ethnomusicology) from Universiti Malaysia Sarawak (UNIMAS), and a PhD in music research (ethnomusicology) from King's College London.

In 2011, Raja Iskandar was appointed visiting fellow at King's College London under the "Musical Transitions to European Colonialism in the Eastern Indian Ocean" project, funded by the European Research Council (ERC). He has published several articles on the Malay nobat and has presented papers at conferences in the United States, United Kingdom, Turkey, Singapore, China, Australia, the Philippines, Thailand, Malaysia and Indonesia.

Raja Iskandar is the author of the book *The Royal Nobat of Perak* (2018). His research interests lie in the areas of Malay court music, identity, colonialism, Islam and popular culture.

www.ingramcontent.com/pod-product-compliance
Lightning Source LLC
Chambersburg PA
CBHW062133300426
44115CB00012BA/1902